INDIA'S TRADE POLICY

Other Books by the Author

India's Tryst With Destiny
India Unlimited: Reclaiming the Lost Glory
My Father: The Extraordinary Life of an Ordinary Man
An Economist's Quest For Reforms: The Vajpayee and Singh Years

INDIA'S TRADE POLICY

The 1990s and Beyond

ARVIND PANAGARIYA

HARPER
BUSINESS

An Imprint of HarperCollins *Publishers*

First published in India by Harper Business 2024
An imprint of HarperCollins *Publishers*
4th Floor, Tower A, Building No. 10, Phase II, DLF Cyber City,
Gurugram, Haryana – 122002
www.harpercollins.co.in

2 4 6 8 10 9 7 5 3 1

Copyright © Arvind Panagariya 2024

P-ISBN: 978-93-5489-933-1
E-ISBN: 978-93-5489-959-1

The views and opinions expressed in this book are the author's own and the facts are as reported by him, and the publishers are not in any way liable for the same.

Arvind Panagariya asserts the moral right to be identified as the author of this work.

All rights reserved. No part of this publication may be reproduced, stored in a retrieval system, or transmitted, in any form or by any means, electronic, mechanical, photocopying, recording or otherwise, without the prior permission of the publishers.

Typeset in 11.5/15.4 Adobe Garamond at
Manipal Technologies Limited, Manipal

Printed and bound at
Manipal Technologies Limited, Manipal

This book is produced from independently certified FSC® paper to ensure responsible forest management.

To
Meghna–Sandeep,
Nidhi–Pallava,
Aditi–Amit,
Arushi–Sharad,
Ananth–Yuko,
Ajay–Quyen,
&
Arihant-Shree;
the shining stars of the next generation of my parents' family and living proof of a rising India.

CONTENTS

List of Abbreviations   xiii

Introduction   xvii

Part I
The Case for Free Trade

1. Losing the Barriers   3
2. Defending Free Trade   9
3. Why We Must Trade Freely: Five Reasons India Should Review Its Current Protectionist Policy   13
4. Liberalize Consumer Goods' Imports   17
5. The Korean Growth Experience   21
6. Without Trade Openness, There Is No Sustained Growth   25
7. Free-Trade Sceptics: Wrong Again   29

Part II
Recidivism in Trade Policy

8. Is India Returning to Protectionism?   35

9.	Anti-Dumping: Don't Shoot Ourselves in the Foot	40
10.	Dump the Anti-Dumping	44
11.	Import Substitution Masked under Security Concerns Still Won't Work	47
12.	Budget 2018: Return of Protectionism	51
13.	India's Trade Policy Folly	55

Part III

The Pitfalls of Import Substitution

14.	A Case for Import Substitution?	61
15.	Wrong Way to Make in India	66
16.	Don't Resurrect Failed Policy	70
17.	Giving Up on the World?	74
18.	Big Lessons from Small Nations	78

Part IV

Tariff Structure, Exchange Rate and Other Issues

19.	A Single Tariff Rate Is the Best	85
20.	Let the Rupee Depreciate	89
21.	Trade Policy Has No Clothes	93
22.	The Tyranny of the Balance-of-Payments Identity	97
23.	Take-off from the Coast	101
24.	How to Make Exports Boom	105
25.	The US Can't Do a Russia to China	109

Part V

Lessons from History

26. Self-Sufficiency Held India Back: Some Useful Economic History Lessons on How We Manage to Handicap Ourselves — 115
27. Nehru's Real Big Mistake: Heavy Industry Wrongly Got Priority in the 1950s. So, Even at 75, India Isn't Rich — 119
28. Let It Seek Its Own Level — 123
29. Custom That Costs Us Dear — 127

Part VI

India–US Trade Relations

30. India as a Scapegoat: US Action under Super 301 — 133
31. True Driver of India–US Partnership — 138
32. On Strengthening India–US Ties — 142
33. India Must Call the US's Bluff on Patents — 146
34. India Is Trump's Next Target in the Trade War — 150

Part VII

India–China Trade Relations

35. Is There Something Deeply Unfair about the India–China Trade Relationship? — 157
36. On China Trade Sanctions — 160
37. How to Distance from China? — 164
38. It's Yin-Yang Boomerang — 168

Part VIII
India and Multilateral Trade Negotiations

39.	The WTO and Developing Country Interests	175
40.	Narrowing Down the Seattle Round Agenda	180
41.	WTO Negotiations: Invest in Research	184
42.	Launching the Qatar Round	188
43.	India Arrives at the WTO	192
44.	Doha: Winners and Losers	196
45.	Defensive Play Simply Won't Work	199
46.	Making Sense of the Collapse in Cancun	210
47.	The World Terrorist Organization or a Godsend?	214
48.	The Challenge before Pascal Lamy	218
49.	Salvaging the Doha Agricultural Talks	222
50.	Hailing Hong Kong, Completing Doha	226
51.	A Historic Opportunity for India	230
52.	Closing the Doha Round	234
53.	How the US Has Weakened the WTO: The Multilateral Trading System Is Under Stress, Member Countries Must Repair It	238

Part IX
Preferential Trade Liberalization

54.	SAARC: Follow APEC, Not NAFTA	245
55.	A Misguided Idea	248
56.	Is This Free Meal Worth Having?	253

57. An India–China Free Trade Area? 257
58. RCEP as Winning Strategy 261
59. Staying out of RCEP Is Not in India's Economic Interest 265
60. Oz Is Just the Start: Australia FTA Shows India Is Now Confident on Trade. Aim Bigger, Including the Ambitious Deal with the US 270

Part X
Non-trade Issues in Multilateral Trade Negotiations

61. Patent Rights: Tripping on Facts and Falsehoods 277
62. Yes to IPRs, but Not under the WTO 282
63. How to Break the TRIPS Impasse 286
64. Curbing Child Labour: Rugmark Label on the Mat 290
65. The Return of Labour Standards into the WTO? 295
66. Seattle: Failure without Losers 299
67. Shoe Is on the Other Foot 303
68. Protectionism's Other Names: Traps India Should Avoid at G-20 307
69. Say 'No' at Copenhagen 311
70. A Thoughtless Tax: Carbon-Tax-Equalizing Tariffs Are a Bad Idea 315

Sources 319
Acknowledgements 323
Index 327

LIST OF ABBREVIATIONS

AB	:	Appellate Body
ACES	:	American Clean Energy and Security
ACP	:	Africa, the Caribbean and the Pacific
AD	:	Anti-dumping
AFTA	:	ASEAN Free Trade Area
AGOA	:	Africa Growth and Opportunity Act
APEC	:	Asia Pacific Economic Cooperation
APTA	:	ASEAN Preferential Trading Area
ASEAN	:	Association of Southeast Asian Nations
ATC	:	Agreement on Textiles and Clothing
BGMEA	:	Bangladesh Garment Manufacturers' and Exporters' Association
BoP	:	balance-of-payments
CAD	:	Current Account Deficit
CEZ	:	Coastal Economic Zone
DBT	:	Direct Benefit Transfers
DGTR	:	Directorate General of Trade Remedies

List of Abbreviations

DSB	:	Dispute Settlement Body
DSU	:	Dispute Settlement Understanding
ECB	:	External Commercial Borrowing
ECTA	:	Economic Cooperation and Trade Agreement
EEC	:	European Economic Community
EU	:	European Union
FDI	:	Foreign Direct Investment
FTA	:	Free Trade Area
FTAA	:	Free Trade Area of the Americas
GATS	:	General Agreement on Trade in Services
GATT	:	General Agreement on Tariffs and Trade
GDP	:	Gross Domestic Product
GSP	:	Generalized System of Preferences
GST	:	Goods and Services Tax
ILO	:	International Labour Organization
IMF	:	International Monetary Fund
IP	:	Intellectual Property
IPR	:	Intellectual Property Right
ISI	:	Import Substitution Industrialization
ISO	:	International Standards Organization
LDC	:	Least Developed Country
MEA	:	Multilateral Environmental Agreement
MEG	:	Mono-ethylene Glycol
MERCOSUR	:	Southern Common Market (or South American Trade bloc; the abbreviation is the Spanish version of the bloc)
MFA	:	Multi-Fibre Agreement
MFN	:	Most Favoured Nation
MMF	:	Man-Made Fibre
MSMEs	:	Micro, Small and Medium Enterprises
MTN	:	Multilateral Trade Negotiation

List of Abbreviations

NAFTA	:	North American Free Trade Agreement
NAMA	:	Non-Agricultural Market Access
NIEs	:	Newly Industrialized Economies
NMC	:	National Medical Commission
OECD	:	Organization for Economic Co-operation and Development
PLI	:	Production-Linked Incentive
PMP	:	Phased Manufacturing Programme
PSE	:	Producer Support Estimate
PTA	:	Preferential Trade Arrangement
PTA	:	Purified Terephthalic Acid
RBI	:	Reserve Bank of India
RCEP	:	Regional Comprehensive Economic Partnership
SAARC	:	South Asian Association of Regional Cooperation
SAFTA	:	South Asian Free Trade Area
SEZ	:	Special Economic Zone
SIL	:	Special Import Licence
SSG	:	Special Agricultural Safeguard
SSI	:	Small-Scale Industries
SSM	:	Special Safeguard Mechanism
TFP	:	Total Factor Productivity
TPA	:	Trade Promotion Authority
TPP	:	Trans-Pacific Partnership
TPR	:	Trade Policy Review
TWIN-SAL	:	Third World Intellectuals and NGOs: Statement Against Linkage
UAE	:	United Arab Emirates
UK	:	United Kingdom
UNCTAD	:	United Nations Conference on Trade and Development

UNFCCC	:	United Nations Framework Convention on Climate Change
UPA	:	United Progressive Alliance
UR	:	Uruguay Round
US	:	United States
USTR	:	United States Trade Representative
WTO	:	World Trade Organization

INTRODUCTION

PAUL SAMUELSON, THE FIRST American to win the Nobel Prize in economics, once said that protectionism is like skin disease—you cure it in one place and it appears in another. As a result, the fight against protectionism is a never-ending battle for trade economists. One might add that just like skin disease takes ages to cure, the elimination of protectionism is a slow process.

The chapters in this book, published mostly in Indian print media, from 1989 to 2023, testify to the truth of these assertions. India began its liberalization process in earnest in 1991, but even the removal of import licensing was not fully achieved till 2001. Then, between 1991 and 2023, tariff liberalization has seen reversal twice—first between 1996–97 to 1999–2000 and then again from 2018–19 onwards. Anti-dumping (AD) has been used extensively to exclude the imports of specific products from the most competitive sources.

As a trade economist, it has been my endeavour to push against the creeping protectionism and import substitution, and advocate for faster liberalization throughout the three decades since the process began. I wrote my very first opinion piece titled 'India as a Scapegoat: US Action under Super 301' in 1989 in *The Times of India* (Chapter 30). The context of the article was the looming threat of trade sanctions by the United States (US) as a counter to India's weak intellectual property rights (IPRs) regime and its high barriers to inward foreign investment, especially in the insurance sector. While criticizing the basis of the threat and arguing that India should refuse to yield to the pressure by the US, I concluded with the recommendation that India ought to seize the initiative for trade liberalization. I wrote:

> Even while rejecting US demands, India should take this opportunity to rethink foreign trade and investment policies. ... My view concerning our trade policies is that we have maintained very high tariffs for very long. Admittedly, tariffs are a major source of revenue for us. But lowering tariff rates that average 130 per cent will raise, not lower, revenue.

In the current context, this call for liberalization would seem rather timidly worded—but those were the days when hardly anyone, apart from the World Bank, International Monetary Fund (IMF) and rare economists such as Jagdish Bhagwati and T.N. Srinivasan, were pushing for trade liberalization in India.

Soon after the publication of this article, I joined the World Bank and worked there until the summer of 1993. Because the World Bank did not allow its staff members to write in the media, my next article on India's trade policy did not appear till July 1994. In the interim, beginning in 1991, India had changed policy course—it ended import licensing on capital goods and intermediate inputs while also opening up to foreign investment. But it had kept its strict licensing on consumer goods' imports. Therefore, my

1994 article in *The Times of India*, 'Liberalize Consumer Goods' Imports' (Chapter 4), appropriately made a case to end licensing on consumer goods' imports. Re-reading the article today, it is a matter of great personal satisfaction for me that I managed to touch on all the important arguments one would make given the context. So much so that if I were to rewrite the article today, it would still largely read the same. It is another matter that India did not give up import licensing on consumer goods for another seven years. And when it did do so, in 2001, it was as a result of a ruling by the World Trade Organization (WTO) declaring the measure as a violation of its rules.

While consumer goods' imports remained largely off limits till 2001, India steadily reduced its tariffs by compressing them from the top every single year between 1990–91 and 1995–96. With some exceptions—such as auto and auto parts, on which it continued to maintain high tariffs—the country lowered the top tariff rate on industrial goods from 355 per cent to 50 per cent. Then there was a pause in the top tariff rate with a special duty of 5 per cent introduced on all imports. This effectively raised the level of protection in the economy. In the following year, 1997–98, the top rate was reduced to 40 per cent, but since the 50 per cent rate was applicable mostly to consumer goods, which were subject to strict import licensing, this reduction did not result in any effective liberalization immediately. In the following two years, once again, there was no reduction in the top rate. Instead, the government introduced another 4 per cent special additional duty on all imports in 1998–99. I wrote against these reversals in liberalization in an article titled 'Is India Returning to Protectionism?' in *The Economic Times* in 1998 (Chapter 8).

The net impact of these changes was increased overall protection during the last four years of the 1990s. As already noted, these years also saw India emerge as a heavy user of AD, which resulted in the imposition of high AD duties on top of regular custom duties on imports from some of the most competitive suppliers in selected sectors. I felt sufficiently alarmed at the time that I wrote two articles, 'Anti-dumping: Don't Shoot Ourselves in the Foot' and 'Dump the Anti-dumping' in *The Economic Times* in 1998 and 2002 (chapters 9 and 10), respectively, to draw attention to this new development. Unfortunately, AD remains an important concern until date. As a result, the latest of my articles included in this book point to the damage AD has done over the last two decades to the development of the textiles and clothing industry in the man-made fibre (MMF) segment (Chapter 21).

Luckily, in 2000–01, India returned to the path of tariff liberalization, lowering the top industrial tariff rate to 35 per cent. No change in the top tariff rate took place the following year, which, nevertheless, saw the removal of import licensing on consumer goods due to the loss of the case in the WTO. Indians were finally free to import whatever they wanted, as long as they paid the custom duty and other border taxes. In the subsequent four years, the government reduced the top industrial tariff rate by 5 percentage points each year, bringing it down to 15 per cent in 2005–06. In the following two years, the country lowered the rate by another 2.5 percentage points each year. This brought the top rate down to 10 per cent in 2007–08 after which no reduction in the top rate has taken place.

While India's trade liberalization came to a standstill after 2007–08, the government continued to tinker here and there with tariff rates of individual products in the subsequent years through its annual Budgets and occasional notifications. These adjustments did not add up to a major change in the overall policy regime with the simple average of all industrial tariffs staying at 12 per cent until the mid-2010s. Sadly, however, the year 2018–19 saw a major escalation in tariffs. That year, as many as 42.3 per cent of all tariff lines went up with the average of all custom duties rising from 13.7

per cent to 17.7 per cent. The proportion of tariff lines attracting duty rates of 15 per cent or higher shot up from 28.7 per cent to 51 per cent (Chapter 29). The government's policy stance, expressed in the Budget speeches of the finance minister as well as other public policy statements, has also shifted towards import substitution. We have seen protection-related vocabulary of the yesteryears, exemplified by terms such as the 'actual user' condition, 'essential' imports and 'phased manufacturing programme (PMP)', return in the pronouncements of government officials. Two products—colour televisions and a certain category of tyres—have even been subjected to explicit import licensing, an instrument we have not used since 2001. These developments have led me to write a number of articles (chapters 15–18) in the last five years pointing to the dangers that this 'new import substitution' poses to India's growth prospects.

It is worth pointing out here, that despite everything I have mentioned above, the opening to the global economy has paid India handsomely. On the back of this liberalization and other economic reforms, India has seen a major upward shift in the growth rate while also experiencing a large reduction in abject poverty. I have systematically noted these gains of liberalization in my book *India Unlimited: Reclaiming the Lost Glory*. Purely in terms of the (GDP), from 2003–04 to 2019–20, the country has sustained an annual growth rate exceeding 7 per cent. The importance of openness to global trade in helping bring about these gains can be judged from the fact that the country's merchandise exports have gone up from $52.7 billion in 2002–03 to $330 billion in 2018–19. Correspondingly, merchandise imports have risen from $61.4 billion to $541 billion over the same period.

The decade of the 2000s also saw much activity in international negotiations on trade liberalization and rulemaking. These negotiations took both multilateral and bilateral forms. In the former category was the Doha Round, under which extensive efforts were made to liberalize trade in agriculture, industrial goods and services among 140-plus WTO members. These were contentious negotiations leading to extensive public debates throughout the 2000s. Unfortunately, the decade ended without progress in achieving an agreement and the Doha Round is considered all but dead now. Bilateral trade negotiations took the form of free trade area (FTA) agreements. These were usually between two or more countries who wanted to achieve free trade between themselves while maintaining trade restrictions on other trading partners. I wrote extensively on both subjects, generally favouring the multilateral form of liberalization and being critical of FTAs since they were discriminatory in nature. Only recently have I begun to see FTAs in a different light, principally because the prospects of multilateral liberalization have turned bleak, and India has yielded once again to the allure of protectionism and import substitution. My articles on the World Trade Organization and the Doha Round appear in Part VIII, and those on FTAs in Part IX.

A new element in both multilateral and bilateral trade negotiations in the 1990s and subsequently was the pressure to include non-trade issues such as labour, environment and IPR in trade agreements. This was a development that divided the WTO member countries along the north–south lines, since the developed (north) countries wanted to use the link to effectively force their labour, environmental and intellectual property (IP) standards on the developing (south) ones. By doing so, they stood to gain through reduced competitiveness of the latter. As such, unlike trade liberalization, which involves win-win bargains, the linkage led to benefits for one at the cost of the other. I wrote several articles attacking the demands for the linkage during the past two-plus decades. They are reproduced in Part X.

This book is divided into ten parts in all. In Part I, I have included seven chapters that come from a variety of angles to defend the case for free trade. Each of these chapters is written in the context of a country or a group of countries. Occasionally, when influential authors write sceptically or critically on the benefits of liberal trade policies, I have taken them to task, explaining why their arguments are specious. In each case, my end objective has been to inform the readers on the benefits of an open economy, especially with respect to international trade. The everlasting policy relevance of the theme of these articles is reflected in the fact that I wrote the earliest chapters in this part in 1994 and the latest in 2021.

In Part II, I have included articles describing India's episodic return to protectionism and import substitution even after having made a decisive break with the old autarchic regime. There are six articles in this part. Closely related, Part III includes five articles on import substitution. Many of these articles are of relatively recent origin and offer explanations for why the plausible-sounding case for import substitution is, in fact, wrong. At the heart of the case against import substitution is the fact that any efforts at it would move resources out of more efficiently performed activities into less efficiently performed ones. Unfortunately, few policy analysts grasp the essence of this argument, thinking that any substitution of imports by domestic production represents a net addition to the GDP. Many also continue to believe that import substitution promotes infant industries, notwithstanding the massive failures seen during the bygone era of the licence-permit raj. The illusion of 'this time it is different' continues to fog the vision of these defenders of import substitution.

In Part IV, I have included a set of trade policy-related issues, such as the efficient structure of tariffs when political or other factors rule out complete free trade, the critical role of the exchange rate in trade liberalization, the futility of custom duties as instruments of correcting the current account deficit (CAD), and the role of coastal zones with liberal land and labour policies in the growth of export-oriented manufacturing. In the last article of this part, I also discuss why trade sanctions have little chance of success when imposed on a large trading partner, such as China, even if they may yield some desired results when imposed on a smaller country like Russia.

In Part V, I have included a small number of essays in which I have either highlighted the role of past policy in holding back India's progress or drawn lessons from historical episodes. In the former category are two chapters on Jawaharlal Nehru–era policies focusing on self-sufficiency and heavy-industry development (chapters 26 and 27, respectively). In the latter category are chapters on the exchange rate and tariffs (chapters 28 and 29).

In Parts VI and VII, I have included chapters on India–US and India–China trade relations. The US and China are India's two largest trading partners, and trade relations with them have been subject to tensions at various points in time inviting commentary. This is particularly true of China, with which India has been running a large trade deficit for many years, whose manufacturing exports are a challenge to Indian industry and with which India also has an active border dispute. All these factors have led to calls for all kinds of trade restrictions by commentators and policy analysts in India.

Finally, as already described, Parts VIII to X contain chapters on the WTO and multilateral negotiations, FTA agreements, and non-trade issues in trade agreements. In the past two decades, India has had to grapple with a variety of issues on each of these fronts. Of particular importance in the current context is the subject of FTAs. Given the emergence of the country's friendly relations with the US, the European Union (EU), the United Kingdom (UK), Japan, Australia and United Arab Emirates (UAE) on the one hand and increased hostility towards China on the other, India has begun to engage more seriously in negotiations for FTAs with some countries in the former group. It has already signed FTA agreements with UAE and Australia, and expects to sign one with the UK as well.

Introduction

As already noted, the articles in this book were written over a period of three decades, with each of them having a specific context of its own. But they remain relevant today for two reasons. First, taken as a whole, they tell the story of the evolution of India's trade policy. In effect, they offer a window to the history of trade-policy changes, the factors driving them and their implications for the country's development and well-being. Second, the examination provided in one specific context is applicable to other similar contexts. Therefore, they have lasting analytic value.

In concluding this introduction, let me assert that though published in newspapers and policy magazines, the articles in this book are different from those published daily in vast numbers in these outlets. There are two reasons why I make this claim, with due humility, of course—as a scholar, I have a reputation to protect among my peers; therefore, I have always endeavoured to adhere to high standards of rigor. In most cases, I am careful to outline the argument or evidence underlying the propositions I offer. Even when space considerations force me to resort to assertion without providing the argument or evidence, I try hard to be sure that, if asked by a reader, I can offer those to her. I rarely write opinion pieces without spending two or three days researching the subject. Since this takes away time from my more scholarly research activity, I have limited my opinion pieces to no more than two a month.

Second, in writing these articles, I make an extra effort to ensure that I avoid the use of jargon, but without sacrificing the rigor of the argument. I have almost never sent first drafts of my articles to newspaper editors. In most cases, I revise them multiple times to achieve clarity of argument. Amita, my wife, generously reads almost all my articles in draft form, often multiple times, before I finalize them.

PART I
THE CASE FOR FREE TRADE

1

LOSING THE BARRIERS

11 August 2018

IN HIS ALL-TIME CLASSIC *Protection or Free Trade*—published in 1886—American political economist Henry George provides one of the wittiest and most persuasive defences of free trade. At the time he wrote, the world was in the midst of the First Globalization. Liberal trade policies had swept across the globe. Yet, his own country remained staunchly protectionist. Unsurprisingly, his axe fell on every conceivable argument that protectionists of his day offered.

In the book, George observes that protection implies prevention and defence. In this vein, protective tariffs prevent foreign goods from flowing into our country. Unlike a flood, earthquake or tornado, which are acts of nature, flow of goods is the result of human action. He asks, who are the people whose actions lead to this flow of goods?

Foreign sellers may well be the answer. George reasons, however, that this is erroneous because those sellers could not sell their products to our people unless our people wanted to buy them. Therefore, it is our own people whose actions cause the flow of these goods into our country. Protection thus prevents the protected from what they want to do; it defends them not against foreigners, but themselves.

At the time George wrote his treatise, free trade prevailed in most of the colonies as well. This was not a choice that the colonies themselves had made; indeed, it had been thrust upon them by self-interested colonial powers. Paradoxically, during the inter-war period, as the colonies acquired the ability to choose their own trade policies, they chose protection. Later, as they won their political freedom in the wake of the Second World War, they uniformly went for yet higher protection.

India followed this general pattern. Textiles and the iron and steel industries had sought, and got, high protection during the inter-war years. Endemic shortages during the Second World War led to the introduction of far more stringent import controls via import licensing. After Independence, when a balance-of-payments (BoP) crisis broke out in 1958, the country adopted foreign-exchange budgeting. This change paved the way for the emergence of a near-autarchic trade policy regime. Those old enough to remember life during the 1960s through to the 1980s would testify to the hardships this regime brought to daily lives. No consumer goods could be imported under any circumstances, and even raw materials and machinery imports required producers to jump through numerous bureaucratic hoops.

Indian producers partially won their freedom in 1991 when the government decided to remove import licensing on raw material and machinery. But they experienced fuller freedom only after the government significantly lowered tariffs. The Indian consumer had to wait even longer. For, import licensing on consumer goods ended only in 2001, after the WTO ruled against it. Our commerce ministry lost the case in Geneva, but our consumers smelled freedom.

With trade thus liberalized, alongside other reforms, India saw its per capita income rise by more during the first seventeen years of the twenty-first century than during the entire twentieth century. With GDP at $2.6 trillion in 2017–18, India is now the sixth-largest economy worldwide. In less than ten years, we will be the third-largest economy, behind only the US and China. The pre-British glory days, when India and China together accounted for more than half of the global economy, are within our grasp.

Fulfilling this promise will of course require sustained reforms and commitment to openness. Today, with imports having expanded to more than one-fifth of the GDP, bureaucratic temptation to return India to import substitution through higher protection is high. But the wisdom that George imparted to late nineteenth-century US remains valid for today's India.

Demands for protection are frequently made on infant industry grounds. George urged the America of his time to stand firm against these demands. He reasoned:

> All experience shows that the policy of encouragement, once begun, leads to a scramble in which it is the strong, not the weak; the unscrupulous, not the deserving, that succeed. What are really infant industries have no more chance in the struggle for governmental encouragement than infant pigs have with full-grown swine about a meal-tub.

George argued that when offered, infant industry protection goes, not to industries capable of eventually surviving without protection, but to industries that can survive only in this way. He noted that the struggle for existence, which drives out unprofitable industries, is the best determinant of which industries are needed under prevailing circumstances and which are not. For rare industries that genuinely deserve support, his prescription was a subsidy conditional upon success.

George went on to remind his countrymen how infants protected in the early days of the American republic still remained protected and continued to claim infancy:

> The infant boys and girls of that time (when protection was originally granted) have grown to maturity, become old men and women, and with rare exceptions have passed away. But the "infant industries", for which a little temporary protection was then timidly asked, are still infants in their desire for encouragement. Though they have grown mightily, they claim the benefits of the "Baby Act" all the more lustily ...

George's words aptly describe our own auto industry, which has been fully shielded from foreign competition since Independence on infant industry grounds and continues to enjoy prohibitive tariffs till today.

Separately, today, India also faces the question of whether it should retaliate against recent tariffs on steel and aluminium by the US. Predictably, George advised against an eye-for-an-eye approach to trade policy. Coincidentally, he made his argument by recourse to long-standing US tariffs on none other industry than iron. He reasoned that these tariffs inflicted far greater injury on the US than on any individual trading partner such as Great Britain. The latter was able to compensate for the loss of exports to the US due to high US tariffs by diverting its exports of iron to other countries. But the

US did not have the option to soften the blow to itself from its own tariffs. George wrote:

> For the effect of duties on iron and iron ore and of the system of which they are part, has been so to increase the cost of American productions as to give to Great Britain the greater part of the carrying trade of the world, for which we were her principal competitor, and to hand over to her the trade of South America and of other countries, of which, but for this, we should have had the largest share.

'And in the same way,' he concluded, 'for any nation to restrict the freedom of its own citizens to trade, because other nations so restrict the freedom of their citizens, is a policy of the biting off one's nose to spite one's face order. Other nations may injure us by the imposition of taxes, which tend to impoverish their own citizens ... But no other nation can thus injure us so much as we shall injure ourselves if we impose similar taxes upon our own citizens by way of retaliation.'

Decades later, Cambridge economist Joan Robinson stated the point more eloquently, quipping that just because others throw rocks into their harbour, that is no reason to throw rocks into our own.

I can think of only one circumstance under which retaliatory tariffs by India could advance its national interest: they persuade the US to withdraw its tariffs in a reasonably short period of time. If retaliation ends up being just that, we would have piled a bigger injury to ourselves on top of the initial smaller injury inflicted by the US.

A necessary but not sufficient condition for retaliation to persuade the US to withdraw its tariffs is that all major exporters of steel and aluminium retaliate against it. But with the EU and the US in conciliatory talks, prospects for serious joint retaliation are dim. The inescapable conclusion, therefore, is that our interest will be best served by bargaining away retaliation for more valuable concessions from the US in areas in which it can offer them at low cost to itself.

2

DEFENDING FREE TRADE

22 November 2000

MATHEMATICIAN STANISLAW ULAM ONCE asked Economics Nobel Laureate Paul Samuelson whether he could point to an idea in economics that was universally true and not obvious at the same time. Samuelson's response was the 'principle of comparative advantage', according to which two countries necessarily benefit from engaging in free trade with each other provided their relative production costs are not identical. Being based on a mathematical relationship, the principle easily passes the test of universal validity. And centuries of assertions by politicians, journalists and policy analysts directly contradicting the principle testify to its subtle nature.

If you are among free trade sceptics, consider the following parable.

During the 1970s, a trade economist was invited to visit China. As he toured the country, he noticed that construction workers invariably used shovels. He could not resist suggesting to his host that importing a few bulldozers and replacing shovels with them could drastically cut costs. The host was horrified and reminded him that such a change would lead to huge unemployment. In that case, retorted the trade economist, you may as well replace the shovels with spoons!

This parable dramatizes the fallacy underlying the twin arguments that freeing up imports and substituting capital for labour lead to unemployment. Thus, for example, when I recently wrote that we must free up the imports of used cars, L. Ganesh (*The Economic Times*, Letters, 6 November) was quick to assert that this would lead to unemployment: '… half a million people cannot all move to the United States of America to find jobs there'.

The problem with such arguments is that they focus exclusively on employment in the liberalized sector. They entirely ignore the fact that to import more, you must export more. The employment lost in the inefficient import-competing sector is regained in the more efficient export sectors. This is why economists generally agree that aggregate employment is determined primarily by macroeconomic policies; trade and tax policies only determine the allocation of resources.

Likewise, substituting capital for labour may lower employment in a specific sector but not the economy as a whole. Indeed, if such substitution leads to sufficiently large efficiency gains, as the use of shovels over spoons definitely would and of bulldozers over shovels might, employment may rise even within the sector in which capital substitutes for labour. Due to increased profitability, the sector may expand so much that the total employment in it rises even as employment per unit of capital declines.

Of course, just as we cannot blame free trade for increased (aggregate) unemployment, we should not credit it with the taming of inflation. While freer trade lowers the prices of importable goods, it also raises the prices of exportable goods. All Indians are aware of the contribution of exports to at least temporary spikes in onion prices and hence the price level. Even when increased competition due to trade liberalization lowers the price level overall, it is a one-time reduction rather than a reduction in the inflation rate. Ultimately, the rate of inflation is determined by macroeconomic variables; trade and tax policies mainly influence relative prices.

An argument against free trade that has gained some currency in recent years in developed countries is that due to low wages, poor countries enjoy an unfair advantage against them. But this is silly since higher wages in developed countries reflect higher productivity. Symmetrically, developing countries can claim that developed countries enjoy an unfair advantage due to the availability of cheap capital, skilled labour and superior technology. But that too will be silly since these differences are the very basis of gainful trade. If we were to artificially eliminate the differences in technology and factor prices, in the absence of economies of scale, no basis for gainful trade would be left.

The argument against free trade that is more difficult to counter is that it may lead to adverse income-distribution effects. In the US, it has been argued that the expansion of labour-intensive imports during the last two decades has led to increased wage inequality between skilled and unskilled workers. There are at least three problems with this argument, however. First, developed countries spend less than 2 per cent of their income on the imports from developing countries, which can hardly lead to the observed 30 per cent reduction in the wages of unskilled relative to skilled workers. Second, technological change that is biased in favour of skilled labour is the more plausible explanation for the increased wage inequality. Finally, in the ultimate, income distribution concerns are best addressed through adjustment assistance, training programmes and social safety nets. The overall benefits from trade should not be sacrificed in perpetuity. After all, if there is a technological breakthrough, such as the handling of soft material by robots, which can potentially eliminate the need for labour in the apparel industry, we will not ban its application on the grounds that it worsens income distribution. Why should trade be any different?

The income-distribution argument has also been invoked in India in the context of liberalization. The argument, based on evidence of questionable quality, is that liberalization has led to increased poverty. I have argued systematically in a previous column (*The Economic Times*, 24 May 2000) that this is an ill-conceived argument. For one thing, even based on faulty data, states that have grown rapidly do show a continued reduction in poverty. In addition, rapid growth, which trade liberalization and other economic reforms seek, is the best hope for the removal of poverty. Without that, we will lack resources to provide for education, health and other poverty-reduction programmes.

Of course, the centuries-old tradition of misguided arguments against free trade is not about to come to an end. We will continue to hear about the damage trade does to the environment, labour rights, employment, technological upgrading, foreign exchange reserves, poor people, children, women, consumers, tribal communities, rural life, animals and so on.

And that is just as well for trade economists!

3

WHY WE MUST TRADE FREELY: FIVE REASONS INDIA SHOULD REVIEW ITS CURRENT PROTECTIONIST POLICY

18 November 2021

IN VIEW OF INDIA'S turn to import substitution and protection, it is worth asking why economists view trade openness as one of the most critical elements in a country's development policy. There are at least five sources through which free trade contributes to a country's development.

First, we have the conventional trade theory rooted in the principle of comparative advantage. Freeing up trade moves a country towards specialization in products in which its production costs in terms of output foregone of other products are the lowest, and away from products in which its production costs are the highest compared to its trading partners. It then exchanges a part of its output of low-cost products for high-cost products. This brings gains from efficient specialization and exchange.

Second, we have the insights from the New Trade Theory for which economist Paul Krugman was awarded the Nobel Prize in Economics in 2008. When production activity is subject to economies of scale, trade allows each country to specialize in a handful of products. In doing so, it allows each country to take advantage of scale economies and lower the costs of production of products it continues to produce. It can then benefit by selling a part of the output of these products for those it ceases to produce.

Third, trade serves as the conduit for access to the most productive technology worldwide. Sometimes, this technology may be embodied in machines that must be imported. At other times, it may be embodied in imported products and can be accessed by reverse engineering. Given that new technologies are being developed continuously by countries around the world, engaging in trade freely offers the best avenue to accessing them.

Fourth, engagement in the global economy exposes a country's entrepreneurs to competition against the best in the world. Such intense competition keeps them continuously on their toes and offers an opportunity to learn from their peers. This is not unlike the game of cricket in which international competition in test matches and T20 games helps produce more and more world-class players.

Finally, free trade benchmarks the economy against the best in the world. If the country is then unable to compete effectively in the world markets, it is a sign that its domestic policies, regulations and infrastructure require tweaking. In effect, exposure to the best in the world is an effective instrument for exposing domestic policy distortions and poor infrastructure. In contrast, protection hides these weaknesses.

Two relatively recent, mutually reinforcing developments have made free trade even more critical than in the past. One, as a result of advances in transportation and communication technologies, costs of moving goods and information over long distances have come crashing down. And two, technological advances have given rise to more complex products of mass consumption while also making it possible to break down the production processes of old and new products more finely than in the past.

These two developments have meant that it is now possible to specialize production activity not by product but by components and activities. Product innovation, product design, and production and assembly of the numerous components can all take place in different locations based on cost advantage. This phenomenon had existed in the past as well—for example, production of clothing could be broken down into fibre, fabric, design, cutting and stitching, but its scale has grown manifold in recent years. For example, the iPhone is made of some 1,600 components, which are supplied by 200 firms located in 43 different countries.

This development has serious implications for the efficient pattern of specialization. In the past, high transport costs allowed countries to minimize production costs by specializing in entire products, such as clothing, and trading them for other products, such as steel. But today, cost minimization mandates specialization in specific components of different products or their assembly by different countries.

If a country is abundant in labour and the assembly of products is a labour-intensive activity, it must specialize in this activity across a large number of products rather than targeting 100 per cent domestic value added in a few of them until it turns labour-scarce. Likewise, a country that is rich in human capital is better off focusing on innovation and design, leaving manufacturing of components and assembly to countries that have a cost advantage in those activities.

This reasoning reveals the folly of policies such as India's PMP, tried even in the pre-reform era with disastrous consequences. To be sure, by erecting high enough custom duties on components and an even higher custom duty on the fully assembled smartphone, any country can indigenize the product in its entirety.

But what good is such 100 per cent indigenization if it makes the smartphone so costly that only a few captive domestic consumers with sufficient income would buy it? Is the country not better off capturing a large slice of the massive world market in the assembly or a few selected components in which it is the most cost-effective? China has understood this principle well. Even with 10 per cent value added *per* Apple device, 100 million–plus devices it produces contain a lot of *total* value added of Chinese origin.

4

LIBERALIZE CONSUMER GOODS' IMPORTS

23 July 1994

INDIA'S TRADE REFORM HAS had a significant impact on our exports and foreign investment. In the first ten months of 1993–94, exports grew by 21 per cent in dollar terms. Annual direct foreign investment has risen to $1.5 billion from $100–200 million in the pre-reform period. And foreign portfolio investment, virtually nil three years ago, has reached $3.5 billion.

If we are to realize the full benefits of the changes already made and eventually acquire the status of an Asian tiger, further reforms are urgently needed. Our ability to act today will determine whether or not we prosper tomorrow. In the area of import policy, two major tasks remain: liberalization of consumer goods, and further compression and rationalization of tariffs. Though liberalization of consumer goods' imports has been controversial at present, the case for it is impeccable. First, at its current rate of Rs 31.45 per dollar, the rupee is highly undervalued. Left to the market, it will surely appreciate—and the dollar will depreciate—to Rs 26–28 per dollar. Because such appreciation will undermine the competitiveness of our exports, the RBI has defended the current exchange rate by purchasing several billion dollars in return for rupees during the last year. Unfortunately, this solution is only temporary. The expansion of the money supply needed to defend the dollar at the current exchange rate is inflationary and will eventually erode the competitiveness of our exports. A partial way out of this dilemma is to liberalize consumer goods' imports, which will prop up private demand for dollars and release the pressure on the RBI to buy them in return for rupees.

The second reason for the liberalization of consumer goods' imports follows from the usual efficiency considerations. In the name of curbing luxury consumption, we have for long penalized the consumers and protected domestic producers of sub-standard products. Today, it is difficult to buy a toaster in India which functions flawlessly for even six months or a sharpener that does not damage the pencil before sharpening it. The availability of high-quality foreign goods will make the consumers more discriminating and force domestic producers to upgrade the quality of their products. A dramatic example in this context is that of Ambassador and Fiat cars. In the 1970s, the same models of these cars were sold as those in the 1950s. Revolutionary advances in the world automobile industry in this period left our automobile manufacturers untouched. It was not until the Maruti arrived on the scene that the consumers got taste of a world-class car. That discovery made the consumers more demanding and sent the manufacturers of Fiat and Ambassador immediately to the drawing board.

Third, opponents of liberalization of consumer goods' imports often argue that it will benefit the rich who will divert resources from investment into conspicuous consumption. This argument is wrong for at least three reasons.

First, restrictions on imports largely have an impact on the form of conspicuous consumption, not its magnitude. Faced with the ban on consumer goods' imports, the rich in India have gone on to spend excessively on palatial houses, other non-tradable goods and locally made tradable but non-traded consumer goods. The more daring have obtained foreign consumer goods through illegal channels.

Secondly, today only a small minority of potential consumer goods' imports can be labelled as luxuries. The use of TV, refrigerator, stereo, toaster, oven and blender is no longer limited to a privileged few. Finally, even if we wish to curb the consumption of certain luxury products, the right instrument is a consumption tax, which does not discriminate between domestic and foreign sources of supply.

It is often argued that liberalization of consumer goods' imports will wipe out the domestic consumer goods industry. This is not true. It is true that liberalization will change the composition of the consumer goods industry, but it will not cause the latter to shrink. Under the anti-trade regime in the pre-reform era, we devoted a much larger proportion of our resources to capital goods' production than countries like China, South Korea and Indonesia. Because our comparative advantage is in labour-intensive manufactures, the reform will eventually move resources into this sector, composed largely of consumer goods. And trade will not be one-way: while we will import foreign varieties of TVs, VCRs, stereos, automobiles, shoes and textiles, we will export—in larger quantities—domestic varieties of these products.

The process of liberalization of consumer goods' imports has already been initiated through two channels. Under baggage rules, passengers coming from abroad are allowed to import many consumer goods on payment of a 100 per cent duty. In addition, beginning from October 1992, the government has been giving a special import licence (SIL) to large exporters. Depending on the size of the exporter, the value of the SIL varies from 3 to 10 per cent of the total export earnings. The licence is tradable freely and entitles the holder to import several consumer goods included in a positive list.

Though these steps are in the right direction, they are still in the old spirit of liberalization by stealth. The time is now ripe for an extension of the bold approach of the present government to consumer goods. Accordingly, we must abolish licensing on consumer goods, subject them to a current top tariff of 65 per cent and use a non-discriminatory consumption tax to curb the consumption of luxury goods.

Regarding the appropriate level and structure of tariffs, the government has accepted the recommendation of the tax reforms committee that there be four tariff rates in all—a maximum rate of 40 to 50 per cent for consumer goods, 30 per cent for intermediate inputs, 20 per cent for capital goods, and a minimum rate of 5 to 10 per cent. Though this structure is a vast improvement over what exists today, it is not entirely satisfactory. First, the top rate of 40 to 50 per cent, with other rates much lower, leaves a very high degree of effective protection on consumer goods. Secondly, from a political economy standpoint, it is not prudent to have an excessive variation in tariff rates across (the board) commodities. In a democracy, firms lobby politicians and officials to obtain as high a level of protection as available. Our own past experience in this regard is not encouraging. Under the structure recommended by the committee, any firm whose product is even remotely a consumer item will lobby for and obtain the top rate of 50 per cent. Tariffs will escalate and real resources will be wasted in lobbying activities. Therefore, it would be best to have relatively few tariff rates, all within a narrow band.

5

THE KOREAN GROWTH EXPERIENCE

25 April 2001

IN THE 1950s, INDIA and South Korea had approximately similar levels of per capita incomes. In the following two decades, Korea grew at rates far exceeding those of India, achieving a much higher per capita-income level than the latter.

During the same decades, Singapore, Taiwan and Hong Kong grew at rates even higher than that of Korea. The precise source of the success of these countries, sometimes called the Asian tigers, has been a subject of considerable controversy among scholars. At least three alternative views have emerged.

Jagdish Bhagwati, Anne Krueger, Ian Little, T.N. Srinivasan and the late Bela Balassa have taken the view that outward orientation and pro-market policies were the primary forces behind the stellar performance of these economies.

These authors generally downplay the role of interventionist policies and argue that export subsidies neutralized the anti-trade bias introduced by import barriers, yielding domestic relative prices that more or less corresponded to the world prices.

The second view, associated with Larry Westphal and Howard Pack, also recognizes the importance of outward orientation, but assigns a more substantial role to industrial policy, especially in affecting technical change in selected industries.

The third and final view, associated with Alice Amsden, Dani Rodrik and Robert Wade, considers industrial policy central to the Korean success and downplays the role of outward orientation. Amsden goes so far as to assert that industrial policies that propelled these countries to such high rates of growth essentially amounted to 'getting prices wrong'.

According to Westphal and Pack, a central element in Korea's trade strategy was to permit exporters to trade at world prices. They were allowed to import all inputs and sell all exports at these prices.

In addition, targeted infant industry promotion played a crucial role in Korea's success. At their inception, targeted industries were granted absolute protection in the domestic market via import controls. At the same time, using export targets, the government insisted that the firms export a swiftly growing proportion of their output at world prices.

The Amsden-Rodrik-Wade view regards the role of the government in promoting investment as much more central. Rodrik notes that since exports were only 5 per cent of the GDP in 1960, they could hardly serve as the engine of growth. Moreover, since the relative price of exports in Korea showed no positive trend, export incentives cannot be credited with export growth. He argues that, on the contrary, export expansion was itself the result of an investment boom, which the government of Korea was able to engineer by solving the so-called coordination failure problem. Rodrik's view clearly conflicts with the Westphal-Pack view, which considers activist export policies central to Korea's growth experience.

The Korean Growth Experience

But even accepting the Rodrik view at its face value, one cannot downplay the role of outward-oriented policies. The boom in investment demand hypothesized by Rodrik could not have translated into a miracle had Korea chosen inward-looking policies. Thus, no matter which of the three views we accept, trade openness turns out to be a necessary ingredient in the success of South Korea.

What can we say about the role of infant industry protection? Both the Westphal-Pack and Amsden-Rodrik-Wade schools assign significant importance to infant industry promotion in Korea. Wade argues, '(T)he balance of presumption must be that government industrial policies, including sectoral ones, helped more than hindered. To argue otherwise is to suppose that economic performance would have been still more exceptional with less intervention which is simply less plausible than the converse.'

Little questions Wade's reasoning. He contends:

> Since the less interventionist Hong Kong, Singapore, and Taiwan grew faster than Korea, it is unclear why Wade thinks it simply less plausible that less intervention would have been better, given also the widespread failure of government industrial policies elsewhere. I find it simply more plausible that Korea grew fast despite its industrial policies, than because of them.

Little argues further that productivity growth in the most capital-intensive sector, which was the object of industrial policy promotion, was less than half that in the most labour-intensive sectors in Korea. Electrical goods, rubber, leather and plastic products, furniture, and clothing and footwear all showed above-average productivity growth.

Thus, the contribution of infant industry protection to Korea's growth is at best controversial and at worst negative. But even if one accepts it to be positive, there are two reasons why it is safer today to err on the side of non-intervention.

First, the experience with interventions on behalf of infant industries in South Asia has been uniformly negative. There are no studies to be found suggesting that infant industry protection in this region had even moderate success, especially after 1965. The inefficiency of the Indian auto industry, protected for long by appeal to both the infant industry and economies of scale arguments, stands out in this respect.

Second, the government has much better prospects for contributing positively to growth when the economy is small and just initiating the process of development. Recall that in the initial years, even the Soviet Union was a success story. As development proceeds, however, the expansion of demand for education, health, infrastructure, legal institutions, regulation and macroeconomic stability is likely to limit severely the government's ability to make wise decisions on behalf of new infant industries.

Moreover, once the economy has grown large and diversified, organizational diseconomies of scale set in and the government's ability to 'manage' it declines as was witnessed in the Soviet Union and, to a lesser extent, China and India.

6

WITHOUT TRADE OPENNESS, THERE IS NO SUSTAINED GROWTH

23 April 2003

RECENT ATTACKS ON GLOBALIZATION have also translated into attacks on the wisdom of outward-oriented trade policies that developing countries have embraced with increasing frequency. Free trade sceptics question the ability of liberal trade policies to stimulate growth. As a corollary, they also blame growth failures on the surge of imports resulting from increased openness. Furthermore, they view outward-oriented trade policies as detrimental to the fate of the poor.

Are the sceptics right? The answer is a categorical no. In so far as developing countries are concerned, there is compelling evidence that openness is a necessary condition for rapid growth. There are few developing countries that have grown rapidly on a sustained basis during the post-Second World War era without simultaneously experiencing rapid growth in their exports and imports. Because openness by itself is not sufficient to promote growth—macroeconomic stability, policy credibility and perhaps other policies must usually accompany it—one can surely find examples of countries opening up without experiencing growth. But this is quite different from saying that openness is either inessential or detrimental to growth when it does happen.

In the same vein, countries that have achieved significant poverty reduction are generally those that have grown rapidly and have, in turn, been open to trade. The most obvious examples are the Newly Industrialized Economies (NIEs) including Hong Kong, Singapore, the Republic of Korea and Taiwan, which have entirely eliminated poverty according to the dollar-a-day poverty line. On the other hand, countries such as India that remained autarchic and grew at less than 1.5 per cent in per capita terms until the late seventies experienced little reduction in the trend poverty ratio. Both India and China achieved significant poverty reduction only after they began to dismantle autarchic policies and began to grow rapidly.

In my own recent research, I have analysed the data for a large number of countries for thirty-eight years spanning from 1961 to 1999, made available by the Global Development Network. I divide these data into two nineteen-year periods and identify, for each period, what I call growth 'miracles' and 'debacles'. The former are defined as countries that grow at 3 per cent or more in per capita terms and the latter are those experiencing a decline in the per capita income. I find that miracle countries invariably experience a very rapid expansion of exports and imports while debacle countries rarely do.

Thus, consider the period 1961–80. These years are commonly identified with import substitution. Yet, the remarkable fact is that virtually all miracle countries during this period rapidly expanded their exports and imports. The countries in this group came from virtually all continents, including Latin America, which is often described as having led the developing world in the area of import substitution. Brazil, which grew at 4.6 per cent between 1961 and 1980, expanded its exports and imports at 8.1 and 7.6 per cent, respectively, over the period. Among countries that grew at 3.6 per cent or more, the lowest recorded growth rate of imports was 7.2 per cent for Tunisia, which grew at 4 per cent in per capita terms. Even as we go down the list, there are only two countries that registered relatively low growth rates of imports: Mauritius and Kenya with import growth, of 3.8 and 3.6 per cent, respectively.

If we look at growth debacles, the weight of evidence is hugely against trade being the culprit. Out of the seven debacle cases on which we have data on trade, only two show significant growth in imports. In the other cases, declines in per capita terms are accompanied by an import growth of less than 2 per cent.

This pattern is repeated during 1981–1999. The key difference is that the number of miracle countries in the latter period is smaller and that of the debacle countries larger. But remarkably, the total population enjoying miracle growth rates at the beginning of the first period at 356.5 million was considerably smaller than that at the beginning of the second period at 2.1 billion. The popular belief that the 1980s and 1990s were lost decades of development while, 1960s represented the golden period of growth is too simplistic. While it is true that the population experiencing a decline in per capita incomes during 1980–1999 was vastly larger than in 1961–1980—partially due to the implosion of the Soviet Union, and East and Central European countries—the developing country population experiencing rising living standards during 1980–1999 was also much larger on account of China and India growing at 8.3 and 3.8 per cent, respectively.

Critics often capitalize on the observation that openness by itself does not always lead to the resumption of growth to ask rhetorically: why should a country take the painful decision to liberalize if it is not going to immediately result in increased incomes? But this misses the point. Our ability to predict when and what will trigger the process of growth in a country is limited. What we do know, however, is that openness is almost always essential for it. Therefore, it makes sense to be ready with an open trade regime should the opportunity knock at the door.

The point is duly illustrated by the contrasting post-war experiences of Korea and India until the late 1970s. Increased savings rates offered both countries growth opportunities, but only Korea was able to take advantage of it. With its emphasis on producing everything domestically, including machinery and raw materials, India choked off the growth potential it had created for itself.

Critics may still persist that even if fast growth in trade volumes accompanies fast growth in incomes, how can we be sure that lower trade barriers accompany the latter as well. Admittedly, evidence of the direct relationship between trade barriers and income growth has been more controversial, but if one must choose a policy variable to allow trade to grow faster, the reduction in trade barriers is likely to be the prime candidate.

7

FREE-TRADE SCEPTICS: WRONG AGAIN

25 January 2006

THANKS TO A HANDFUL of vocal free trade sceptics among economists, pro-free trade economists never have to fear being rendered redundant.

In a recent article in the *Guardian* (12 December 2005), Larry Elliott writes that according to Harvard economist Dani Rodrik, the experiences of Vietnam and Mexico illustrate why liberal trade policies contribute precious little to economic prosperity.

Take Mexico and Vietnam, he (Rodrik) says. One ... has had a free trade agreement with its neighbour across the Rio Grande. It receives oodles of inward investment and sends its workers across the border in droves. It is fully plugged into the global economy. The other was the subject of a US trade embargo until 1994 and suffered from trade restrictions for years after that. Unlike Mexico, Vietnam is not even a member of the WTO.

So which of the two has the better recent economic record? The question should be a no-brainer if all the free trade theories are right – Mexico should be streets ahead of Vietnam. In fact, the opposite is true. Since Mexico signed the North American Free Trade Agreement (NAFTA) deal with the US and Canada in 1992, its annual per capita growth rate has barely been above 1 per cent. Vietnam has grown by around 5 per cent a year for the past two decades. Poverty in Vietnam has come down dramatically: real wages in Mexico have fallen.

Like the other arguments against trade liberalization by Rodrik, this one also appears plausible at first sight but collapses in the face of careful scrutiny. Thus, we begin with a closer examination of Vietnam.

To be sure, Vietnam has been a huge success. Its GDP grew at 5.2 per cent during the three-year period spanning 1989–1991. In the following six years, 1992–1997, the growth rate jumped to 8.8 per cent. The Asian crisis saw the rate decline some, but the economy still managed to clock a rate of 5.8 per cent during 1998–2000. As one would expect, this rapid growth helped 'pull up' vast numbers out of poverty. The proportion of those living in absolute poverty fell from 78 per cent to 37 per cent between 1988 and 1998.

If Vietnam had achieved this impressive growth in the absence of low or declining protection, it would indeed offer a serious indictment of pro-free trade economists. But it did no such thing: Vietnam's exports of goods and services as a proportion of the GDP grew from 31 per cent in 1991 to 55 per cent in 2000. Because the rise took place during a period of very high GDP growth, the growth rate of exports of goods and services was truly impressive: 28 per cent during 1991–2001.

Sceptics would, no doubt, counter that this export growth proves nothing since the causation may have been running in the reverse: from GDP growth to export expansion. While there is no doubt that there is a two-way causation between export and GDP growth, one has to be in Alice's Wonderland to argue that openness was not crucial to the expansion of Vietnam's trade. No amount of GDP growth can produce any export growth if a country effectively outlaws trade. In order for water to flow, the tap must be open. True, as water pressure grows, water would flow at a faster rate, but you would take full advantage of the increased pressure only by opening the tap further.

To put the argument positively, trade policies in Vietnam underwent significant liberalization along virtually all dimensions including external trade and investment during the period under consideration. Under the old regime, trade was primarily with the Soviet bloc countries. And it was regulated by shipment-by-shipment licences and import and export quotas using a multiple exchange rates system.

Reforms resulted in all foreign transactions being done in convertible currencies by 1993. The multiple exchange rates were unified in 1989 and a series of devaluations helped eliminate the general bias against the traded goods. Import and export controls were relaxed, and trade progressively moved from the licence-based to tariff-based regime. By 1995, export quotas had been removed on all products except rice and import quotas were limited to six items. Steps were taken to liberalize foreign investment throughout the 1990s.

What do we make of the lack of WTO membership and the US trade embargo? Traditionally, the large majority of the WTO members have granted their 'Most Favoured Nation' (MFN) tariffs to non-members in the expectation that the latter would eventually become WTO members.

As a result, non-members have not been hugely disadvantaged as long as they themselves play by the WTO rules. The main exception for Vietnam was the US, which subjected it to a trade embargo until 1994. But such embargoes are almost never successful in preventing determined exporters unless they are applied by virtually all countries, as was done against South Africa under the apartheid. With the huge European and Asian markets open to them, Vietnamese exporters were not constrained on the demand side.

While Vietnam, thus, bolsters, rather than undermines, the case of pro-free trade economists, what about the poor performance of Mexico? Here, it bears reminding that careful pro-free trade economists have always pointed to low or declining trade barriers as a necessary though not sufficient condition for rapid growth. Slow growth may result despite a liberal trade regime because of the absence of a variety of complementary factors, such as macroeconomic stability, good governance, sound infrastructure and a competitive exchange rate.

The question we must ask is whether Mexico's performance would have been better had it been closed to trade, foreign investment and outward flow of labour. Would Rodrik advise Mexico to close its borders to the flow of goods, foreign investment and labour flows?

One final word: a country greatly enhances its chances of producing world-class cricketers such as Sachin Tendulkar if it opts to play test cricket. By limiting its team to state, district or college-level cricket, the country is likely to condemn its players to mediocrity. Entrepreneurship is no different.

PART II
RECIDIVISM IN TRADE POLICY

8

IS INDIA RETURNING TO PROTECTIONISM?

19 September 1998

IN HIS BUDGET SPEECH in June 1998, when finance minister Yashwant Sinha announced an 8 per cent across-the-board special additional duty on imports, the reaction to it was sharp and swift. With one voice, analysts and columnists decried the duty as a 'swadeshi' tax and, within a week, forced the minister to scale it down to 4 per cent.

Though Mr Sinha took much heat for administering a setback to India's trade reform, the fact is that his predecessor, P. Chidambaram, had sabotaged the reform process much earlier. In his maiden, 1996–97 Budget, Mr Chidambaram had already begun to reverse Manmohan Singh's reforms with the introduction of a 2 per cent across-the-board special custom duty. At the time, few observers paid attention to this reversal, presumably because the duty was low and viewed as temporary. But instead of removing the duty, within six months, Mr Chidambaram issued an executive order raising it to 5 per cent.

Mr Sinha's special additional duty—aptly abbreviated as SAD—applies not only to the border price but also to all existing custom duties. Because the latter are as much as 50 per cent of the border price in some cases, the true incidence of the duty can be as much as that of a 6 per cent custom duty.

Taking into account Mr Chidambaram's 5 per cent special duty, the custom duty on all imports has, thus, gone up by 9 to 11 percentage points since Mr Singh left office.

Against this increase in protection, the main liberalization has been the reduction in the highest custom duty from 50 per cent to 40 per cent announced in the 1997–98 Budget. But since that rate applies mainly to consumer goods whose imports are largely banned, the liberalization is of no immediate consequence.

An understanding of the source of this enormous reversal of our tariff reform holds the key to bringing the reform back on track.

Though the media has almost unanimously christened Mr Sinha's duty a 'swadeshi' tax, the real reason behind it is the same as that behind Mr Chidambaram's special duty: a derailment of the revenue equation which had begun in 1994–95 but became more acute in the subsequent years.

To keep inflation under control, a key concern of a reforming finance minister is to hold the line on the budget deficit. Because large cuts in expenditures are politically infeasible, he must ensure that tariff reductions do not lead to large revenue losses.

This is a challenging task in a country such as India where trade taxes have traditionally accounted for almost one-third of tax revenues.

At the beginning of our reforms, import licensing was pervasive and tariff levels extremely high. When tariffs are lowered from such high levels and accompanied by a removal of import licensing, significant revenue losses are unlikely. Any losses in the revenue from reductions in tariff rates are offset by a large expansion of the quantity of imports.

But once the removal of licensing had been accomplished and tariff rates had come down to the levels where they have been in the last few years, further reductions in them were bound to affect the tariff revenue adversely.

To carry on trade reforms, a finance minister had to find an alternative source of revenue. According to most public finance experts, this source is the excise duty. Because excise duty applies equally to domestically produced and imported goods, it is the most efficient instrument of raising revenue.

For a variety of reasons, successive finance ministers have found it difficult to increase excise duties.

First, the pressure from business lobbies is almost always to reduce excise duties.

Second, in the public perception, all duty reductions have come to be identified with reforms.

Third and finally, under the Indian Constitution, the Centre must share excise duties with states, but not tariffs.

Therefore, the convenient course for a finance minister, conscious of a pro-reform image, is to announce reductions in excise duties with a thunder and, when necessary, raise tariffs by stealth.

The failure to garner enough revenue from excise duties to sustain trade reform can be seen from the data available in various issues of the Economic Survey.

During 1990–1993, excise duties averaged 4.6 per cent of the GDP and accounted for 42 per cent of the total tax revenue. By 1995–96, despite a hefty 12.5 per cent growth in industrial output, they had fallen to 3.6 per cent of the GDP and 36.1 per cent of the total tax revenue. In 1997–1998, these shares fell further to 3.4 and 33.4 per cent, respectively.

At the time Mr Chidambaram took office, in proportionate terms, custom duties had already declined significantly. As a proportion of the GDP, they fell from 3.9 per cent in 1990–91 to 3.2 per cent in 1995–96. As a proportion of the total tax revenue, they fell from 36 per cent to 32 per cent over the same period. When Mr Sinha took office, these figures stood at 2.9 and 28.7 per cent, respectively. The only way to carry forward tariff liberalization for these ministers was to raise excise duties, a task in which they both failed.

If Mr Sinha is serious about reclaiming the trade reform for the country, he must resist pressures from the industry for lower excise duties and also explain to the public that when tariffs are reduced, increases in excise duties overall are entirely consistent with reforms.

Without it, he will not only be unable to reclaim the trade reform but also be forced to continue to rely on one-time sources of revenue such as the sales of public-sector enterprises and Mr Chidambaram's Voluntary Disclosure Scheme.

A casual review of the changes in trade and tax policies during the 1990s suggests that the systematic approach to first-generation reforms during the early to mid-1990s has been replaced by a less integrated, ad hoc approach in more recent years.

Despite its many shortcomings, the Tax Reforms Committee report provided a broad scheme within which tariff and tax reforms were carried out in the early stages.

No such overall framework appears to be guiding the current policy changes.

To place tax and trade reforms back on track, Mr Sinha should call upon the Tariff Commission (or appoint a second Tax Reforms Committee) to outline an integrated approach to the second-generation tax and tariff reforms. In addition to addressing the revenue issue more carefully, the Commission must reassess the course of trade and tax policy reforms over the next six to eight years. For example, the final levels of tariffs recommended by the

Tax Reforms Committee were far too high and dispersed. By the standards achieved in most of the major developing countries in East and Southeast Asia and Latin America, both the level and dispersion of these tariff rates must be reduced. The Commission should determine how further compression of duties should be achieved over the next six to eight years.

Quite independently of the revenue link between tariff and tax reform, the tax system is also in dire need of a new blueprint of reforms.

Constant tampering with the rates of rebate to raise revenues has already made a mockery of the MODVAT system. The unification of excise tax rates even as recommended by the Tax Reforms Committee remains a distant goal. The anomaly with respect to the sharing of excise duties but not customs duties between the Centre and states also remains to be tackled.

Then there is the matter of the states having the right to collect sales tax on goods but not services.

Though many of these issues are being currently addressed in various fora, the approach remains ad hoc and fragmented.

And if the implementation is also ad hoc and fragmented, we can be sure to see further hikes in custom duties the moment these reforms lead to a decline in total revenues.

9

ANTI-DUMPING: DON'T SHOOT OURSELVES IN THE FOOT

30 June 1999

AN OMINOUS DEVELOPMENT ON the trade-policy front in recent years has been the rise of AD actions. Till 1992, we had never imposed AD duties. But by early 1998, when the WTO carried out our second Trade Policy Review (TPR), we had initiated as many as 45 AD cases, covering eighteen products. In eleven cases, definitive duties had been imposed. In only two cases, petitions got thrown out due to a ruling of no injury to the local industry. This trend has remained unchanged in the last year, with several new products being subject to AD actions.

Under the criteria laid down in the General Agreement on Tariffs and Trade (GATT), it is relatively easy to prosecute foreign firms for dumping. The AD authority has to only show that the foreign firm has sold the product at prices below what it charged in its own domestic market and that such sales have resulted in injury to the local industry. The standard of proof for establishing injury is low.

Anti-Dumping: Don't Shoot Ourselves in the Foot

Trade economists regard AD to be the most pernicious instrument of protection. Its use is economically justified only if dumping is predatory, meaning that the offending firms sell the product below cost with the objective of driving other firms out of the market and then raising the price to the monopoly level.

In modern times, with so many potential sources of supply around the world, the probability that a small number of firms can establish the monopoly price is extremely low, if not zero. The US firms selling steel in India must compete against the firms from not merely India but Europe, Japan, Korea and China as well. To successfully establish the monopoly price, they must stamp out competition from all these sources.

Leaving aside this unlikely case, if foreign firms wish to sell a product to us below cost, we should gladly take it. From the national welfare standpoint, we should want to pay less for foreign goods, not more. And it should not matter whether the low price is the result of sales below cost or the discovery of a cheaper method of production. Nor should it matter that the price is lower than what the firms charge in their domestic market.

While the consumers and the country as a whole benefit from cheaper supply of foreign goods, inefficient domestic firms that produce similar goods lose. If these firms are politically powerful, they successfully lobby the government to take AD actions against the more efficient foreign suppliers. And given the weak GATT rules, prosecution is relatively easy.

Prior to the reforms initiated in 1991, protection to domestic firms was provided on demand through strict licensing and tariffs that sometimes exceeded 300 per cent. The economic reforms of the 1990s did away with licensing, except in the case of consumer goods, and slashed tariffs considerably. The highest tariff rate came down to 40 per cent (with some reversal in the form of special additional duty) and the import-weighted average tariff rate to 25 per cent. It is this liberalization and concomitant benefit to the consumers that anti-dumping measures now threaten to reverse.

Even in rare circumstances when a compelling case for temporary protection can be made, two factors make AD the least desirable instrument. First, under the GATT rules, foreign firms can avoid AD duties if they sell goods in our market at prices at least as high as those they charge in their own markets. This gives the firms an incentive to charge us higher prices than otherwise.

Second, AD is a highly targeted and discriminatory instrument. To provide protection to domestic firms, it targets the most efficient foreign suppliers. After all, it is these firms that are likely to be most competitive.

A less costly means of providing temporary protection is the use of conventional safeguards permitted under GATT Article XIX. These measures do not discriminate among foreign suppliers and are, thus, consistent with the MFN principle.

AD measures were invented by and accommodated into GATT Article VI at the initiative of developed countries. Until as late as 1990, just four developed countries accounted for 80 per cent of all AD actions: Australia, Canada, European Communities and the US. Today, having substantially done away with tariffs and quotas, developing countries have become significant players in this game, however. They already account for as many as two-thirds of the new AD actions taken annually worldwide.

The destructive nature of AD becomes especially apparent when we consider the use of AD measures against our own exporting firms in foreign markets. Recall that a key benefit that developing countries have negotiated under the Uruguay Round (UR) Agreement is the elimination of the Multi-fibre Agreement (MFA) by 2005. This means that starting in 2005, developing countries will no longer face quotas on their exports of textiles and clothing in developed country markets. A key fear of developing countries today is that as MFA quotas are removed, developed countries will replace them with AD measures. This will nullify the major benefit developing countries negotiated under the UR Agreement.

An argument is sometimes made that AD actions by developing countries against developed country firms may be the only way to convince developed countries of the ills of this practice and, hence, to persuade them to outlaw it from GATT. While there is some truth in this argument, we must remember that to date the majority of AD actions by developing countries have been taken against other developing countries. Moreover, in pursuing this strategic approach, developing countries that indulge in AD do hurt themselves. Therefore, on balance, exercising restraint and using conventional safeguards when necessary will best serve our interests.

The ideal long-term solution to the evil of AD lies in seeking tighter rules on AD in the next round of trade negotiations. At present, the US has said that it will not negotiate these rules. But this may simply be a negotiating tactic. Past experience shows that when the price is right, the US does not walk away from negotiations.

10

DUMP THE ANTI-DUMPING

7 May 2002

Having carried out fifty-one anti-dumping investigations between July and December 2001 alone, India now has the distinction of being the top user of this lethal weapon against foreign goods. With thirty-five, sixteen and fifteen cases, the US, Argentina and the EU, respectively, rank distant second, third and fourth.

For trade economists, the question 'Should anti-dumping be dumped?' is a no-brainer. The WTO members should jointly agree to outlaw the use of this self-destructive weapon. But should they fail to do so, countries should unilaterally discard it from their arsenals. When a country resorts to anti-dumping to promote the interests of narrowly defined producer interests, it inflicts a disproportionately large injury on the rest of its citizenry. The net effect on the country is positively harmful.

Anti-dumping is economically defensible only if dumping is predatory, meaning that the offending firms sell the product below cost to drive other firms out of the market and then earn supernormal profits by raising the price to the monopoly level. But with so many potential sources of supply around the world in modern times, the probability of a small number of firms establishing the monopoly price is virtually zero. The Chinese firms selling bicycles in India must compete against firms from not merely India but also from Japan, the EU, Korea, Thailand, Mexico and Brazil.

Unfortunately, the WTO rules do not subject dumping to this high standard for the purpose of sanctioning anti-dumping duties. Instead, they define dumping as selling at 'less than fair value', where 'fair value' is often measured by the price charged by the firm in its domestic market.

It is easy to show, however, that this definition suffers from a serious internal inconsistency. Thus, suppose American and European firms are selling identical tyres at identical prices in identical quantities in the Indian market. Since the impact of these imports on India is identical in all respects, it makes no sense to treat them differently. Yet, if the US firms happen to charge a higher price for the tyres sold in their domestic market than that in the Indian market while the European firms do not, the former will be charged with dumping but not the latter!

Anti-dumping measures were accommodated as safety valves originally into the GATT and subsequently into WTO to encourage member countries to liberalize tariffs and quotas. It was felt that in their absence, import-competing interests would simply block the liberalization of these conventional measures of protection. The option of anti-dumping reassured the import-competing interests by offering temporary relief in case of import surges following liberalization.

This justification remains unpersuasive for two reasons, however. First, anti-dumping is a highly targeted and discriminatory instrument. To provide protection to domestic firms, it often targets the most efficient foreign suppliers. A less costly means of providing temporary relief is available through the conventional safeguards permitted under the GATT Article XIX and the UR Agreement on Safeguard Measures. These measures, invoked recently by the US to provide protection to the steel industry for a period of three years, are broadly non-discriminatory.

Second, foreign firms can avoid anti-dumping duties if they sell goods at prices at least as high as those they charge in their own markets. This fact gives the firms an incentive to charge higher prices in their export market than otherwise and undermines the benefits of free trade.

Many pro-free trade economists had hoped that the Doha Round would help tighten the rules on the use of anti-dumping. But with developing and developed countries both becoming heavy users of it, the constituency for this reform has shrunken considerably. In addition, the US is simply opposed to a serious reform of this instrument. As a result, the negotiating mandate on anti-dumping rules in the Doha Ministerial Declaration has been worded such that it leaves little room for meaningful reform.

11

IMPORT SUBSTITUTION MASKED UNDER SECURITY CONCERNS STILL WON'T WORK

23 January 2013

WHEN THE END TO investment and import licensing, and substantial tariff reductions, led to only modest acceleration in GDP and trade in the 1990s, critics derided the reforms for having made little difference. But that changed in the 2000s. Reinforced by major additional reforms in the late 1990s and early 2000s, growth of the GDP and trade saw a massive shift. Trade expanded so fast that despite a rapidly rising GDP, it climbed from 27 per cent of the GDP in 1999–2000 to 56 per cent in 2011–12.

But whereas a rising share of manufactures in the economy has led the economic transformation in every other successful country, this share has remained unchanged at around 16 per cent in India during the last twenty years. The causes of this disappointing performance of manufacturing are to be found in the lack of complementary reforms in factor markets—labour and land—and the inability of the government to build infrastructure. But misdiagnosis of the problem has led the government to stealthily, but dangerously, seek the expansion of manufacturing by nudging the economy back towards the dirt road of import substitution, which it had abandoned in 1991.

The driving force behind this shift is the 2011 manufacturing policy that aspires to raise the share of manufactures from 16 per cent to 25 per cent of the GDP and create 100 million jobs in ten years. Sadly, the policy lacks a credible roadmap for labour and land market reforms, and indirectly encourages various ministries to seek avenues to replace imports by domestic production instead.

The policy has found expression, for example, in the side conditions accompanying the recent opening up of single-brand retail to 100 per cent and multi-brand retail to 51 per cent foreign direct investment (FDI). In both cases, foreign retailers must source 30 per cent of their purchases locally from small and medium firms. Most analysts have paid almost no attention to this 'import-substitution' feature of the policy package on FDI in retail.

Even more disconcertingly, draft regulations issued by the Ministry of Communications and Information Technology, which could soon become official policy, would require that 30–100 per cent of twenty-four information technology products purchased by all government departments, government licensees and their managed service providers to be of domestic origin.

To fulfil the 'domestic-origin' qualification, the product in turn must contain 25–45 per cent domestic value added in 2013–14. The requisite domestic content is to rise over time to eventually reach 65 per cent.

There is no doubt that the production of manufactures in India has lagged. But their promotion by encouraging inefficient domestic production through higher prices that will follow the partial shutting down of imports rather than through reforms that would bring domestic costs of production down is counterproductive. There is now evidence that restrictions on imports practised for decades were costly and that trade liberalization has led to significant productivity gains in terms of reduced costs, improved quality and increased product variety. Adding labour and land reforms to the liberalization already in place will magnify these gains many times over.

The draft regulations offer national security as the reason for domestic sourcing. But they forget that protectionism could paradoxically compromise national security by putting in place substandard domestically made equipment.

My generation of Indians can scarcely forget the suffering (we endured) from low-quality bicycles, fountain pens and phones that were then available. The joke was that fountain pens had been designed to work more like fountains than pens.

The proposed regulations are also certain to run into difficulty at the WTO. While purchases by the government in India are not subject to WTO discipline, those by firms are. From repeated references to security considerations in the draft regulations, it may be hypothesized that the government intends to argue its case on national security grounds. But the chances of success are dim. Few countries have imposed similar restrictions on private purchases of the products listed in the draft regulations. That fact is going to weigh heavily with the WTO dispute settlement process.

American and other foreign firms and governments are upset by the proposed rules. But they need to do soul-searching of their own.

Open markets are a two-way street. In recent years, American and foreign firms have increasingly acquiesced to, even encouraged, protectionism in their own home markets. Few American firms raised their voice against the punishing fees America slapped on

H1-B visas or the denial of government contracts to firms that outsourced work abroad.

It is difficult to believe that the characterization of firms that outsource services from abroad as Benedict Arnolds (or traitors) by John Kerry, soon to be the secretary of state of the US, and repeated denunciations of these firms by President Barack Obama would not encourage similar sentiments elsewhere. The privilege of world leadership comes with responsibilities.

While the Indian government needs to rethink its slide into import substitution, the draft regulations must also be a reminder to the US government and companies that protection at home is a double-edged sword that encourages protection in partner countries.

12

BUDGET 2018: RETURN OF PROTECTIONISM

12 February 2018

WHEN THE GOVERNMENT OF India raised custom duties on a number of products in December 2017, as an eternal optimist, I took the view that this had been done for revenue reasons. But increases in duties on a long list of products ranging from kites and footwear to cellular mobile phones and motor vehicles in 2018 have ended that optimism. Indeed, revenue secretary Hasmukh Adhia has explicitly stated that the duties have been levied not to raise revenue, but to provide protection to micro, small and medium enterprises (MSMEs). Adhia adds, 'We have a phased manufacturing programme in electronic manufacture industry for which increasingly we will be putting more duty on the final product, then on second level of spare part and third level of spare part.'

The clear message from the revenue secretary: stay tuned, more tariff hikes are on the way.

For those of us old enough to remember the India of the 1960s to the 1980s, this is déjà vu. Thanks to ultra-high protection and tight internal regulation, India was condemned to a per capita growth rate of less than 2 per cent from 1950–51 to 1990–91. Imports as a proportion of the GDP, which did not even once touch the 10 per cent mark during the four decades, fell to as low as 4.1 per cent in 1969–70. Exports were consistently lower yet.

It was not until 1991 that a new generation of political leadership, which appreciated the damage protection and regulation had done, came along. Supported by an enlightened bureaucracy, this leadership went on to systematically liberalize the economy.

With substantial liberalization under Prime Ministers P.V. Narasimha Rao and Atal Bihari Vajpayee, India became the first democracy to achieve 8 per cent–plus growth for nine years beginning in 2003–04. The top industrial tariff rate fell from 355 per cent in 1990–91 to 10 per cent in 2007–08, and imports as a proportion of the GDP expanded to 30 per cent and exports to 24 per cent by 2011–12.

Sadly, a new generation of bureaucrats seems to have now replaced its more enlightened predecessor. It is on course to erect the wall of protection all over again.

French economist Frédéric Bastiat wrote as far back as 1845 that protectionism appeals to many because its favourable effect on the output of the protected sector is immediately visible while the damage it does is spread throughout the economy and requires deeper probing.

Consider, for example, the steel industry. We have come to its rescue through anti-dumping duties, tariffs and pressure on railways to buy steel domestically, preferably from public sector units. There is little doubt that these policies give fillip to our steel industry. But they also raise the price of steel, which undermines the pace of expansion of railways and hurts the consumers of products using steel, such as kitchen utensils, cutlery, refrigerators, bicycles, motorcycles, farm machinery and automobiles. The higher costs also lead to job losses in these products.

The same goes for increased protection to mobile phones. It helps local mobile producers, but raises the price that the consumers pay. Some consumers are entirely priced out, undermining progress towards digital India. American philosopher George Santayana wrote in his 1905 book, *Reason in Common Sense*, 'Those who cannot remember the past are condemned to repeat it.' We had pursued with vigour the PMP during the heydays of licence-permit raj.

Under it, investment licence to a firm was granted only on the condition that it would progressively replace imported components with domestically sourced ones. Once the agreed deadline for indigenization passed, the firm would not be given import licence for the components. The policy was a total failure and the New Industrial Policy, 1991, relegated it to the dustbin of history.

The argument that protection would help the MSMEs also needs to be carefully scrutinized. Did we not do nearly everything to promote our small-scale enterprises in the past? Until 2001, we had a near ban on the imports of most products produced by them. The enterprises also had the exclusive lock on the production of most of the items they produced via the small-scale industries (SSI) reservation. We followed these policies for 50 years and yet produced no notable success. In the end, both import ban and SSI reservation were ended as a part of our reform programme.

When our producers of even the most labour-intensive products such as garments, footwear and furniture, and wholly traditional items such as kites and rakhis are unable to outcompete foreign suppliers on our own soil, there has to be something seriously wrong with our domestic regulatory policies. Unless we work on a direct removal of these hurdles, we will keep hurting our own consumers through higher tariffs without preparing our entrepreneurs to challenge the competitors in the global marketplace, which is what is ultimately needed to build the New India.

Defenders of the revival of protection would probably argue that this time it is different, because the economic environment today is not the same as that under licence–permit raj in the 1970s and 1980s. But haven't we heard this before? Didn't our bureaucrats tirelessly tell us prior to 1991 that the experience of Singapore, South Korea and Taiwan didn't apply to us because we are different?

13

INDIA'S TRADE POLICY FOLLY

25 July 2018

TRADE OPENNESS TODAY FACES both external and internal challenges in India. Externally, tariff hikes on aluminium and steel imports by the US invited retaliation by us, at least as a last resort. We also face challenges of secondary sanctions arising out of the US sanctions against Iran and Russia. Internally, bureaucratic forces have regrouped to return India to import substitution.

This column is exclusively about the latter internal challenge. Despite repeated assertions that 'Make in India' is about making for the world, in reality, it is the 'Make in India for India' view that is winning. The first significant tilt in this direction came with the extensive tariff hikes in the 2018–19 Budget, which the revenue secretary later defended as necessary to promote import substitution. True to his word, he went on to deliver additional tariffs subsequently.

To top it all, we have now appointed a taskforce headed by the Cabinet secretary aimed at cutting imports of items that India can produce at home. It may be recalled that the key elements of our 1991 reforms were to end import licensing on all products other than consumer goods, two back-to-back devaluations of the rupee, an end to investment licensing and opening to foreign investment. During the subsequent two decades, the process of import liberalization was deepened with the complete dismantling of the import licensing regime in 2001 and a decline in the average industrial tariff from 113 per cent in 1990–91 to 12 per cent in 2007–08.

That liberalization brought us handsome rewards. Between 2003–04 and 2011–12, India's GDP grew 8.2 per cent annually leading to a massive fall in poverty. Alongside, imports of goods and services expanded from $85 billion in 2002 to $642 billion in 2011–12. The expansion of exports and remittances from $92 billion to $518 billion over the same period helped sustain these imports.

What was the connection between rapid growth in the GDP and the expansion of imports and exports? As we liberalized trade, we produced and exported more and more of those products for which our production costs were lower than our trading partners, and imported more and more of those products for which our production costs were higher. To use the economist's jargon, we specialized in and exported products in which we enjoyed a comparative advantage and imported products in which we lacked a comparative advantage.

This same explanation also goes a long way (though it is not the whole story) towards explaining why our performance was so abysmal during the first three-and-a-half decades after Independence. During those decades, we kept tightening our import regime more and more, and pushing the economy into producing goods in which we lacked a comparative advantage.

Sadly, our current turn to import substitution threatens to return us from the turnpike on which we have been travelling all these years to the dirt road. To be sure, with imports and exports of goods and services at 21.6 per cent and 19.6 per cent of the GDP respectively in 2016–17, we are far more open today than in the 1950s when we first experimented with import substitution. For this reason and because the response to any policy change takes time, we will not feel the impact of our mistake immediately. But if we stay on the current course, we will eventually find ourselves on the dirt road. Then, no matter how powerful the engine of our vehicle, we will slow down.

There is no wisdom in producing at home products that we can buy abroad at a lower cost using our export earnings. It is best to let a doctor do what he does best and a nuclear scientist do what she does best. It is a trap to think that the doctor can also do what the nuclear scientist does and vice versa. The same principle applies to nations.

Rather than appoint a taskforce to find ways to curb imports, our strategy should be to appoint a taskforce to devise strategies to expand exports and to do so on a war footing. That is precisely what President Park Chung-hee—who made South Korea what it is today—did. After he embarked upon an export-oriented strategy, he personally presided over many hundred meetings each year to ensure that bottlenecks facing exporters were promptly removed. In less than a decade, Korea's exports rose from just 3.5 per cent of the GDP in 1963 to 21.3 per cent in 1972. And Korea grew 9.5 per cent annually during that same decade.

Mathematician and nuclear physicist Stanislaw Ulam once teased economics Nobel laureate Paul Samuelson, asking whether he could name 'one proposition in all of the social sciences which is both true and non-trivial'. Samuelson was dumbfounded at the time, but later wrote that his answer should have been the principle of comparative advantage. 'That it is logically true need not be argued before a mathematician; that it is not trivial is attested by the thousands of important and intelligent men who have never been able to grasp the doctrine for themselves or to believe it after it was explained to them.'

No wonder, generation after generation of bureaucrats have tried to defy this immutable principle and time and again produced outcomes that only go to prove its truth.

PART III
THE PITFALLS OF IMPORT SUBSTITUTION

14

A CASE FOR IMPORT SUBSTITUTION?

25 September 2002

TAKING ISSUE WITH MY conclusion in the 22 May column that the Indian industry needs further trade liberalization, labour-market reforms, an end to the SSI reservation, effective bankruptcy laws and privatization to catch up with China, my friend Professor Dani Rodrik of Harvard University writes in a personal note:

> Most of the countries of Latin America did all of that, and the result was a rate of industrial growth (and TFP expansion) that is way below the levels experienced under ISI (import substitution industrialization). The least that India can do is to learn from this experience and not assume that all the good things will follow as soon as trade liberalization, deregulation and privatization takes place.

Rodrik is among a handful of thoughtful critics of trade liberalization and deregulation who ground their views in serious scholarly research. Therefore, one cannot summarily dismiss his advice.

So how does one respond to Rodrik? To begin with, there are serious limits to applying the Latin American experience to India. Since the early 1970s, Latin America has been repeatedly subject to devastating macroeconomic crises. The worst India has seen is the BoP crisis of 1991.

To place this contrast in perspective, while a 20 per cent inflation rate is synonymous with the absence of inflation in Latin America, it defines the absolute upper limit of tolerance in India. Four years ago, insufficient appreciation of this difference landed the then chief economist of the World Bank, Joseph Stiglitz, into hot water at a conference in Colombo.

Drawing on research, based principally on Latin American data, Stiglitz argued forcefully that the additional benefit from fighting inflation was zero once it had been brought down to 20 per cent. That sent the South Asian policymakers present at the conference into fury: how could Stiglitz not know that in South Asia 20 per cent inflation was equivalent to death for the poor?

But leave this qualification aside and examine the case for ISI made out by Rodrik in his recent book, *Making Openness Work*. He presents evidence showing that the years 1960–73 define the golden period of growth for developing countries, with thirty countries growing at 3 per cent or more in per capita terms. In contrast, growth rates plummeted during 1973–84 and 1984–94. The decline was especially pronounced in Latin America (columns 2 and 3 of the accompanying table) and Africa.

Growth Rates in the Latin American Countries That Grew 3 Per Cent or More Between 1963–1973*

	Per Capita GDP		Exports in Real Terms	
Country Name	1960–73	1973–84	1960–73	1973–84
(1)	(2)	(3)	(4)	(5)
Brazil	4.7	1.7	7.8	8.0
Dominican Republic	3.8	1.7	4.7	1.9
Mexico	3.2	2.0	6.5	13.6
Costa Rica	3.0	0.2	10.5	3.0
Trinidad and Tobago	3.0	2.5	7.1	-0.6
Jamaica	3.0	-2.6	4.9	-2.0

* Barbados and Panama also grew at rates exceeding 3 per cent in per capita terms during 1963–1973, but had to be omitted from the table due to unavailability of export data.

Source: Rodrik, Dani, *Making Openness Work* for growth rates of GDP and author's calculations for growth rates of exports.

Rodrik argues that ISI policies during 1960–73 'spurred growth and created protected and therefore profitable home markets for domestic entrepreneurs to invest in. Contrary to received wisdom, ISI-driven growth did not produce tremendous inefficiencies on an economy-wide scale'.

For the debacle that followed 1973, including the failure of ISI during the rest of the 1970s, Rodrik points to macroeconomic instability as the villain. For the instability itself, he blames external shocks including 'the abandonment of the Bretton Woods system of fixed exchange rates, two major oil shocks, various other commodity boom-and-bust cycles, plus the Volcker interest-rate shock of the early 1980s'.

What is wrong with this story? For starters, during 1960–73, industrial countries grew far more rapidly than during 1973–94 and they progressively opened their markets. Both factors helped spur growth in developing countries. While the more open economies of East Asia benefited more, the less open economies of Latin America also benefited from the open and growing markets in industrial countries (column 4 of the table). But this is not all.

If ISI is to be credited with stimulating growth in Latin America, at the minimum, we must be able to establish this persuasively for Brazil, by far the largest economy of the continent. To be sure, Brazil did register the second-highest growth of the continent during 1960–73. But evidence hardly credits ISI for it. Thus, during 1960–73, Brazil's exports and imports grew at the impressive annual rates of 7.8 and 8.9 per cent, respectively, in real terms. More importantly, trade policy specialists on Brazil describe the period between 1965–73 as one of 'cautious outward-looking trade policy liberalization' and 1974–80 as one of 'renewed inward-looking policies'. During the former period, Brazil corrected the real-exchange-rate overvaluation, introduced several export incentives to reduce the anti-export bias and lowered average legal tariff for manufacturing (including surcharges) from 99 to 57 per cent and for agriculture from 53 to 34 per cent.

The case for ISI as the key to growth in Latin America during 1960–73 is, thus, seriously undermined. But we are still left with Rodrik's criticism that trade liberalization and privatization during 1980s did not produce significant growth response there. To address this concern, we must once again begin by recognizing the role of the slow growth in industrial economies and its impact on Latin American exports (column 5 of the table).

But beyond that, Rodrik's own explanation for why ISI failed to deliver during the 1970s—macroeconomic instability—must be invoked. If ISI is to be rescued from culpability during the

1970s by appeal to macroeconomic instability, symmetry demands that trade liberalization and privatization be acquitted of the charge of ineffectiveness during the 1980s as well since the same macroeconomic instability prevailed then.

The critical question one must still answer from the policy perspective, however, is why the East and South Asian economies escaped macroeconomic instability during the 1980s while Latin American economies fell prey to it. Here the principal villain would seem to be short-term capital mobility, which the latter had largely embraced by the early 1980s while the former had not. The collapse of the fixed exchange rates and oil crises affected all oil-importing economies symmetrically, but the Volcker interest-rate shocks impacted Latin America asymmetrically.

Given that India enjoys the necessary macroeconomic stability and is some distance from embracing short-term capital mobility, the prediction that good things will follow trade liberalization and privatization is a safer bet than the alternative.

15

WRONG WAY TO MAKE IN INDIA

13 December 2017

IN THE IMMEDIATE POST-SECOND World War era, following the- then consensus view, nearly all emerging independent countries chose the path of import substitution to achieve industrialization. But by the early to mid-1960s, Singapore, Taiwan and South Korea had broken away from this consensus, and switched to export-oriented strategies.

They soon achieved growth rates of 8–10 per cent for the following two to three decades. India chose to stay on course, deepening import substitution yet further. Our imports as a proportion of the GDP dropped to just 4 per cent in 1969–70 from the peak of 10 per cent in 1957–58.

By the mid-1960s, we had banned consumer goods' imports, which took away the pressure on domestic producers to supply high-quality products. The 'domestic availability' condition additionally denied our producers access to world-class raw materials and machinery whenever equivalent domestic products, no matter how poor in quality, were available.

Quality of our products plummeted and they failed to compete in the global marketplace. Poor performance of exports in turn created foreign exchange shortages, which led to yet greater tightening of import controls. This vicious cycle took its toll on growth, with per capita income rising at the paltry annual rate of 1.5 per cent during 1951–81.

The only way to break this cycle of import controls leading to poor export performance and poor export performance forcing yet tighter import controls was to do away with import controls and let the rupee depreciate sufficiently to incentivize exporters and producers of import-competing products. That is exactly what we did beginning in 1991.

The process was gradual but steady and credible. With top-quality products, beginning to flow into the country, consumers became more and more discriminating, and producers could access world-class raw materials, machinery and technology.

This change eventually brought vast improvement in the quality of our products allowing exports to grow alongside imports. Most dramatically, our expanding exports could readily finance the imports of millions of mobile phones that were critical to the success of the New Telecom Policy that the Vajpayee government implemented during 1999–2003.

Our exports of goods and services multiplied six-fold from just $75 billion in 2002–03 to $450 billion in 2011–12. Many today argue that our commitment to the WTO Information Technology Agreement, which bound us to zero custom duty on information technology products, denied us the opportunity to manufacture the millions of mobile phones that our citizens bought. I would argue that a protected mobile market would have killed the mobile revolution instead.

While adding at most a small quantity to domestic production, it would have denied access to inexpensive but decent-quality mobile phones to millions of our consumers. We were much wiser to export what we were good at to pay for the mobile phones we imported.

Today, we are in danger of forgetting the lesson we have learnt the hard way. Thanks to the reforms under Prime Ministers Rao, Vajpayee and Modi, we are now a $2.3 trillion economy and our imports stand at $450 billion. Unfortunately, however, the latter fact has created renewed temptation for a return to import substitution to make a success of Make in India.

What better way to get there than to replace this large volume of imports by domestic production, so goes the argument. Is this market not ours for the taking? Sadly, this line of reasoning can take us back to ruin yet again. Let me explain why.

When we think of replacing imports with domestic production, we are invariably thinking this would be a net addition to Make in India. This is a false premise. The equivalent reduction in exports is almost sure to accompany the reduction in imports. This is because macroeconomic stability requires the Reserve Bank of India (RBI) to maintain the exchange rate at a level that keeps the CAD (total imports minus total exports) to around 1–2 per cent of the GDP. With rare exceptions, RBI has adhered to this policy since we adopted flexible exchange rates.

Put another way, if foreigners cannot sell their goods to us, they will not have the revenues to pay for the goods they buy from us. If we cut back on their goods, they will have to cut back on ours. Even the large decline in our oil import bill during 2015–16 was accompanied by a near-equivalent decline in our exports. What is added to Make in India through import substitution will get subtracted by losses in exports.

The key to the gains from international trade is that we export products that we produce at the lowest cost and import those that our trading partners produce at the lowest cost. In this way, we maximize the gains from trade. Import substitution, which relies on raising barriers against imports or subsidizing our products, undermines these gains.

Only if import substitution is the result of increased efficiency of our producers does it add to the gains from trade. If politics compels us to intervene to help producers, the least damaging course is to do so on behalf of those able to export to world markets.

In doing so, we are likely to assist producers on the verge of becoming competitive against the best in the world. In contrast, the risk in import substitution is that we may end up propelling sectors in which we are among the costliest producers.

16

DON'T RESURRECT FAILED POLICY
22 July 2020

IN THE WAKE OF the Galwan events, a consensus has emerged that India needs to distance itself from China in its international trade. There are three possible policy-driven avenues to this goal: tariffs that apply to imports from China alone; tariffs on all imports of products of which China is the principal current supplier; and more favourable treatment of imports from non-China sources through free trade agreements.

The first of these options will require invoking the national security clause of WTO rules, which India can justifiably do given the hostilities on the border. But it will most surely invite retaliation by China, which may include restrictions on its exports to India of products that only it can supply or supplies at costs far below those of the next best alternative. Given the fragility of our own economy today, this is not a desirable route.

The third alternative is non-disruptive and supportive of India's growth and jobs imperative. It will take time, patience and some hard negotiation, but it is the option that India must exercise. If the agreements are forged and strengthened with entities such as the EU, the UK, Japan, Australia, Canada, and eventually, the US, they will complement our strategic relationships.

But it is the second option that seems to find the greatest favour in India at present. For it nicely fits into the broader import substitution instincts of many in India, both in the government and outside. But hard-nosed economic analysis and critical assessment of available evidence reveal it to be the most treacherous route.

For starters, import substitution industrialization (ISI), which entails progressive replacement of imports by domestic production, is precisely the strategy we had pursued until 1991. That year, we finally recognized its total failure and switched to outward orientation. Those seeking its revival argue, however, that it will be different this time. Rather than take them for their word, let us examine whatever evidence exists.

We embraced ISI in the electronics industry nearly six years ago. Where do we stand today? Imports of electronic goods shot up from $32.4 billion to $55.6 billion between 2013–14 and 2018–19, while exports have inched up from $7.6 billion to $8.9 billion over the same period. Predictably, protected and subsidized, several mobile phone assembly firms have come up, but they have not added up to a vibrant electronics industry. Nearly all locally owned firms are small by global standards, with not one that is about to turn into a powerhouse of exports.

Undeterred, we are proceeding with PMP, under which the production of some of the components used in mobile phones will be encouraged. In public policy, memories are so short that past mistakes get repeated. Accordingly, it is appropriate to remind (everyone) that the PMP road is also one on which we have travelled before, during the licence-permit-raj era.

Then, we used to make indigenization of the product a condition of the licence. For instance, licence for assembling tube lights was given on the condition that imports of specified components would be permitted for a specified period after which they would have to be sourced domestically. The programme failed and we abandoned it alongside licensing in 1991.

A return to PMP in mobiles in today's context will entail raising tariffs and giving subsidy on the components that less-efficient domestic producers will replace. That will, of course, raise the cost for mobile assembly firms that have sprung up in the last six years. So we will have to either provide them yet higher protection or let them go out of business.

Instinctively, governments want to pursue ISI in products in which imports account for the largest proportion of domestic consumption because that is where domestic suppliers have the greatest scope for substituting imports. But one must ask why imports have the largest share in domestic consumption of those products. The most likely answer is that those are the products in which domestic producers have the greatest cost disadvantage. So ISI ends up concentrating on precisely those products in which the country is least efficient, a sure-fire recipe for failure.

ISI has a further problem that predisposes it to failure. It encourages domestic production through tariffs and output subsidies. Both factors attract small-scale firms focused on making quick, risk-free profits with no plans to become exporters. On top of this, the policy itself has a tendency to build a bias in favour of the entry of small firms when it comes to domestically owned firms, as is the case with the recent production-linked incentives (PLI) scheme.

If a country feels compelled to pursue industrial policy, it has far better chances of success if it targets products that are already exported or on the verge of becoming exports. Such a strategy benchmarks domestic firms against the best in the world.

Since the luxury of sustained large export subsidies (as opposed to high tariffs under ISI) is not there due to possible retaliation or countervailing duties by importing countries, making a success of such a policy automatically forces the government to address the reform of domestic policies. It feels a greater compulsion to remove bottlenecks such as high land and electricity prices, labour market inflexibilities and infrastructure bottlenecks.

17

GIVING UP ON THE WORLD?

17 August 2020

SINCE THE SECOND UNITED Progressive Alliance (UPA) government, India has come a long way on the road to reforms. The Insolvency and Bankruptcy Act, goods and services tax (GST), direct benefit transfers (DBT), National Medical Commission (NMC) Act, Ayushman Bharat Yojana, slashing of corporate profit tax, commercial mining in coal and agricultural marketing reforms are some key examples. The pipeline of reforms to come includes such major measures as the National Higher Education Commission Act, public enterprise policy and electricity reforms.

Sadly, however, the scope of benefits of these reforms is being considerably limited by our policy mistakes in one important area: international trade. Here, we are deviating from the road of steady liberalization that we had adopted in 1991. We travelled down this road till 2007, stopped, and have now taken a U-turn to begin travelling in the reverse direction.

I have no doubt that eventually India will transform itself into a modern urban industrial economy. The critical question is whether we want to do it in 100 years or more as nearly all Western industrial economies did or in two to three decades, as the economies of East Asia have done. If the latter, we need to reconsider our trade policy.

Empirically speaking, there is no country that has achieved rapid transformation by being inward-looking as opposed to outward-oriented. Governments of rapid transformers may have intervened here and there, but the broad fact remains that those interventions did not interfere with their expanding trade in any substantive way. Moreover, those interventions slowed down rather than accelerated growth. I have documented these trends at length in my recent book *Free Trade and Prosperity*.

A key advantage of maintaining an open trade regime is that it benchmarks our firms against the best in the world. A commitment to openness forces us to ask what changes to domestic policies must we make to remove the disabilities that handicap our firms vis-à-vis the best in the world. But when we give up openness and use import protection to help our firms withstand foreign competition, we are not addressing the fundamental source of the disability. Such a policy may enable our firms to compete in the domestic market, but, with fundamental sources of disability left unaddressed, it will not make them competitive in the global economy.

Import protection as the path to global competitiveness is a non-starter. We need look no further than our own auto industry that punishes our consumers and, despite a prohibitive wall of protection for seventy years, remains dependent on the same crutches.

The reason why import substitution looks so attractive to many is that they only see what is visible to the naked eye: the addition of output in the protected sector. They do not see what requires deeper vision: output subtraction in other sectors. One simple way to see the subtracted output is to recognize that a nation's resources at any point in time are limited. When a protected sector such as auto expands, it takes away resources from other sectors. Its expansion is not a positive-sum activity.

Even more concretely, take the volume of investible resources available at any point in time. By definition, these are given by the nation's own savings plus the CAD. The latter determines the volume by which foreign capital complements domestic savings. With the domestic savings rate a given and the CAD held at some target level (often 1 to 2 per cent of the GDP) by the RBI, the total investible resources in any year are fixed. Therefore, if protection allows the auto industry to expand by investing more, it leaves less investible resources for some other sectors. There is no free lunch.

An alternative way to see the same point is that the RBI manages the exchange rate to maintain the CAD at some target level. Therefore, any effort to curtail the imports of one product through import substitution would either expand imports of another set of products or contract exports.

Once we recognize that the notion that we can add to the GDP by simply replacing imports with domestic output is a fallacy, we can come back to look at the productivity effects of import substitution versus export orientation. Import substitution typically attracts inefficient firms by creating quick rents. Domestic firms that enter the market have no plans to eventually capture the world markets. They see an assured, almost risk-free market behind a protective wall. Our own experience in the electronics industry in the past six years illustrates this point.

During this period, not a single domestic firm that promises to turn into an export powerhouse has entered the market. And the pace of expansion this sector has shown even inclusive of foreign multinationals places us closer to the time path followed by Western industrial nations rather than East Asian ones.

If we want to capitalize on the vast benefits our numerous reforms promise, it is critical that we do course correction on trade policy. To use an analogy from our favourite sport, could we have produced the long stream of world-class cricket players such as Sachin Tendulkar, Virat Kohli, Yuvraj Singh, Saurav Ganguly and the just-retired Mahendra Singh Dhoni without playing test cricket? The same goes for world-class firms.

18

BIG LESSONS FROM SMALL NATIONS

(With Deepak Mishra)

14 September 2021

IN 2015, TURNING ITS back on trade liberalization, India decided to promote the mobile phone industry through import substitution. The eventual goal of the switch was to make a success of 'Make in India for the World'. Have we turned a corner as seems to be widely believed?

Imports of telephones had risen from $3.2 billion in 2009 to $7.5 billion in 2014, and have fallen to $2.2 billion in 2020. Alongside, exports had fallen from $3.5 billion in 2009 to $0.6 billion in 2014 and have risen to $3.0 billion in 2020.

No doubt, these numbers testify to a significant expansion of domestic production of telephones since 2015. But the success is rather modest when measured against what Vietnam, a country less than one-tenth of India's size, has achieved. From just $0.9 billion in 2009, its telephone exports rose to $21.5 billion in 2014 and to $31.2 billion in 2020. Its electronic goods exports stood at $122 billion in 2020 against India's $12.8 billion.

How has Vietnam achieved this success? Whereas Indian leaders routinely express regret at having signed free trade agreements (FTAs) even with countries accounting for a minuscule proportion of the country's trade, tiny Vietnam has boldly embraced such economic giants as China and the EU in free trade arrangements. It also has FTAs with every single Asian country of any significance.

In today's world of crisscrossing supply chains, even small tariffs can have big effects. The iPhone contains 1,600 components supplied by approximately 200 firms spread over 43 countries. With tariffs piling up on tariffs as components cross multiple country borders for processing from one stage to the next, even small custom duties at each border crossing can add up to large cost escalations. FTAs among countries playing host to suppliers eliminate this problem.

If the objective of the policy is to simply eliminate or drastically reduce imports, import substitution can surely do it. A rising tariff not only allows progressively less efficient producers to add to supply, it also prices out more and more consumers. This is exactly how we held imports strictly below 10 per cent of GDP for four decades till 1991.

But it is an entirely different matter if the objective is 'Make in India for the World'. A hypothetical example best explains why.

Suppose, absent any custom duties, the landed cost of an imported smartphone is $100 and that of all the components contained in it $90. Local manufacturers able to assemble the components into a smartphone at a cost of $10 per handset or less can then compete against imports.

Assume, however, that these manufacturers supply only a small part of the total demand with imports filling the gap. Suppose next the government imposes a custom duty of 20 per cent. This raises the cost of an imported smartphone to $120. Since the components can still be imported for $90, manufacturers can now compete against imported smartphones even if their assembly cost is up to $30 per handset. This is three times the assembly cost at which they could compete in the absence of the tariff. The 20 per cent tariff on the smartphone has thus provided a hefty 200 per cent protection to assembly activity.

But the story does not end here. No sooner the assembly activity has seen an expansion, politicians and bureaucrats want to double their 'success' by going for domestic production of components. In India, we long ago invented the concept of PMP towards this end.

The PMP in our example would provide protection to components next. Assume this is done via a 20 per cent custom duty on all components. The tariff would undoubtedly encourage domestic production of components, but it would also raise the cost of components for producers assembling them into smartphones by $18 per handset. The $20 margin that the original tariff on the smartphone had created has now shrunk to just $2.

Therefore, most of those who had entered assembly activity to make a quick buck after the imposition of the original tariff would be rendered uncompetitive. But no government would allow them to go under lest its policy be judged a failure. Instead, it would raise the tariff on the smartphone to 38 per cent or more to eliminate the 'disability' that the tariff on the component imports created. A vicious cycle of escalating tariffs thus follows.

The high tariff brings smugglers into business who pocket custom duty due on legal imports as their profit. In parallel, official import data understate true imports, overstating the success of import substitution. The biggest losers are the consumers, who must now pay higher prices, with some of them priced out of the market or forced into switching to inferior-quality smartphones.

Producers that enter production activity in response to high protection are likely to be predominantly rent-seekers rather than risk-takers. It is a mistake to think that they would eventually turn into export powerhouses. On the other hand, risk-taking producers that enter production activity with an eye on the global market would have done so even absent protection. They are happy to share in the spoils offered by protection, but do not depend on them. It is these producers who would make a success of 'Make in India for the World'.

PART IV
TARIFF STRUCTURE, EXCHANGE RATE AND OTHER ISSUES

19

A SINGLE TARIFF RATE IS THE BEST

18 June 2003

THE 2002–03 BUDGET SET the goal that by 2004–05, India will have only two tariff rates for non-agricultural goods: 10 per cent covering raw materials, intermediates and components, and 20 per cent for final products.

With less than a year left before this goal is translated into policy, it is timely to ask if this is the best course our trade policy can take.

Begin by considering the existing tariffs. In spite of the reform and rationalization of trade policy for more than a decade, our tariff regime remains messy. The 2003–04 Budget ostensibly brought the peak tariff on non-agricultural goods down to 25 per cent. But according to Arun Goyal of the Academy of Business Studies, more than 15 per cent of all tariff rates still remain higher than the official peak rate. In terms of the complexity of the tariff structure, the situation is even grimmer: Goyal counts as many as twenty-three tariff-bends in existence currently.

According to the latest WTO TPR of India, 2002, tariff rates on chemicals and photographic supplies ranged from 0 to 170 per cent, and those on transport equipment from 3 to 105 per cent in 2001–02. The situation is not much different today, with the multi-billion-dollar automobile industry receiving protection well in access of the 25 per cent peak rate.

In economic terms, there is little rationale for this tariff structure. It is essentially the result of two sets of forces. One, some sectors such as chemicals and automobiles are politically powerful, and have therefore managed to evade the tariff compression applied to other sectors during the past decade. And two, there remains the misconception among policymakers that somehow final goods must be protected at tariff rates higher than those applied to raw materials and intermediate inputs. This latter fact has meant that tariffs on final goods have been compressed lesser than those on inputs. The process has been somewhat arrested recently, however, with tariff reductions limited largely to products subject to the 'peak' tariff rate, which happen to be final goods, and some of the lower tariff rates applying to intermediate inputs raised as a part of the rationalization process.

What should be our next step? I will argue that rather than move to the two-part tariff with the plethora of exceptions still continuing to apply, we must switch to a single uniform tariff rate of 15 per cent except in the handful of the cases where it might be contrary to our WTO obligations. This will involve raising the tariff rates on up to 4 per cent of the items that are currently subject to tariff rates below 15 per cent.

Before I consider the merits of this proposal, let me comment briefly on its feasibility on the revenue front. It can be argued that a 15 per cent uniform tariff can raise as much revenue as a two-part tariff consisting of a 10 per cent rate on raw material and intermediate inputs and a 20 per cent rate on finished goods. But even if tariff revenue under the former happens to be less than that under the latter, it should not stand in the way of the reform. Consistent with the practice in recent years and the recommendations of the Kelkar Committee, we must keep moving to the more efficient and broad-based sources of revenue. The eventual goal should be to rely on domestic taxation rather than trade taxes for revenue purposes.

The adoption of a uniform tariff brings several advantages. First and foremost, it takes politics out of trade policy. When the government is willing to offer protection at different rates, industrial lobbies have a field day. Those politically more powerful, such as the automobile and chemical sectors, manage to lobby for sweetheart deals at the cost of the consumers. But once the rule is that all will receive equal degree of protection, the incentive for any single industry to lobby diminishes dramatically. Simultaneously, the government has a logical defence against the demands of specific industries for higher protection: because it must raise the tariff for all if it does for one, its hands are tied.

The single tariff rate also has the advantage of transparency and administrative simplicity. It eliminates the prospect of a higher tariff through classification of one's product as finished rather than intermediate. It also does away with all kinds of exemptions. According to the TPR of India, 2002, there are more than 100 kinds of exemptions in our tariff code currently, with each running into several pages. The Review concludes, 'The use of such exemptions not only increases the complexity of the tariff, it also reduces transparency and hampers efficiency-increasing tools such as computerization of customs.'

Critics of the uniform tariff idea may argue that it fails to minimize the distortion cost of raising revenue. In a strict sense, this is correct. The theory of optimal taxation tells us that under some technical assumptions, goods with inelastic import demand should be subject to higher tariffs than those with elastic demand.

The problem with this criticism, however, is that the actual tariff structure has little relationship to this theoretical ideal. The relevant counterfactual is not the optimal tariff structure based on various elasticities on which we lack information but the one actually in place. Compared with that structure, the uniform tariff is a vastly superior alternative.

The single uniform tariff is also superior to the two-part structure that admits no exceptions and exemptions. A tariff structure that levies 10 per cent tariff on raw materials and 20 per cent tariff on final goods grants excessively high effective protection to the latter. For example, suppose the free trade price of a cell phone is $100 while its components cost $80. The two-part tariff raises the prices of the cell phone and its components to $120 and $88, respectively. This allows the domestic value added in cell phone assembly from $20 to $32 signifying an effective protection of 60 per cent!

20

LET THE RUPEE DEPRECIATE

17 October 2018

AN EPISODE FROM THE 1950s illustrates that a failure to use the exchange rate as an instrument of macroeconomic adjustment can be costly. With the exchange rate fixed at 4.76 rupees per dollar during the 1950s, the rupee was overvalued relative to foreign currencies. This made India's goods expensive relative to foreign goods and resulted in the import bill consistently exceeding export revenues. The gap had to be covered by running down scarce foreign exchange reserves. By early 1958, the reserve had almost run out.

Rather than devaluing the rupee to properly align the prices of domestic and foreign goods, the then government resorted to what is known as foreign exchange budgeting. Beginning with the second half of 1958, every six months, the finance ministry began preparing a detailed budget of how the expected foreign exchange revenues over the following six months would be allocated across different ministries.

That process multiplied the complexity and cost of investment licensing: no licence for investment in a project could now be given unless the finance ministry allocated the foreign exchange necessary to buy foreign machinery and inputs. With high inflation making Indian goods progressively more expensive relative to foreign goods, export revenues shrank and import demands expanded leading to progressive tightening of import controls.

It took India another three decades to accept that the exchange rate was a key tool of macroeconomic adjustment. With reforms launched in 1991, it adopted a flexible exchange rate system with the RBI intervening in the foreign exchange market only to smooth out short-term fluctuations. As a result, value of the rupee has changed from Rs 17.50 per dollar in 1990 to Rs 74 today. This depreciation has been crucial for maintaining both overall macroeconomic stability and a robust growth during these years.

Nevertheless, the recent episode of rupee depreciation has rekindled the debate on the role of the exchange rate in the adjustment process. To understand why this depreciation became necessary, begin by noting that the post-1991 opening up of our capital account was initially limited to FDI and equity investment. But this changed in recent years with the government opening the door wider and wider to financial capital flows. These flows are far more liquid than FDI and equity investments, and can enter and exit the country fast in response to changes in interest rates abroad.

Following the 2008 global financial crisis, interest rates in the US progressively fell, leading foreign investors to move more and more funds into Indian debt. Since these funds helped keep the interest rate on the government debt low, the government found it attractive to progressively liberalize the cap on them. In parallel, Indian corporates also sought and got progressively greater access to lower-interest external commercial borrowings (ECBs).

As long as interest rates in the US remained low, these capital inflows produced a happy outcome for the government, foreign investors investing in Indian debt and Indian corporates borrowing abroad. Steady inflows of capital also kept the rupee from depreciating, which ensured high dollar returns to foreign investors and a low rupee cost of servicing ECBs for Indian corporates.

But an upward turn in the interest rates in the US recently jolted this happy equilibrium. Not only did the availability of foreign financial capital suddenly dry up, but also several years of accumulated investment in Indian debt sought to exit. Foreign institutions that could recall loans given to Indian corporates did so as well. Some foreign investors in Indian equities also sought exit to earn the higher interest rates at home.

These exits required the conversion of massive volumes of rupees into dollars over a short period. That put downward pressure on the value of the rupee. The only way that RBI could have maintained the original value of the rupee was by selling as many dollars from its reserves as demanded by exiting investors at the original exchange rate.

Such defence would have been unwise for two reasons. One, whereas the depreciation discouraged exits by effectively increasing the cost of converting rupees into dollars, a stable rupee would have led to much larger exits, heavily depleting RBI's foreign exchange reserves. And two, with private actors instead of the RBI supplying dollars to exiting investors, dollars available for imports shrank. That forced a much-needed adjustment in the current account.

Much has been made of the oil price hike in the current episode. No doubt, the price hike added to the difficulties of foreign exchange management. But it was no more than a sideshow. Absent oil price hike, the rupee depreciation would have been less but not by a wide margin.

The worst of this episode is perhaps behind us. While we did not learn from a similar episode in the summer of 2013, we must not let this repeat episode go to waste. We must reassess the wisdom of opening the economy wider and wider to financial capital inflows. Using low-cost foreign financial capital may seem attractive but this lunch is not free. Eventually, when the inflows reverse, which they inevitably do, the economy does pay for it and rather heavily.

21

TRADE POLICY HAS NO CLOTHES
10 March 2023

Employment potential of India's textiles and clothing industry remains grossly underrealized. Its share in the total workforce remains low at 3.6 per cent and of agriculture high at 45.5 per cent.

While the well-recognized policy constraints originating in land, labour and electricity markets, and the logistics sector remain critical, as a recent paper by economists Abhishek Anand and Naveen J. Thomas emphasizes, trade-policy interventions too have contributed to the underperformance of the sector. The damage has been particularly serious in the MMF segment.

The textiles and clothing industry consists of several products: raw materials used to produce fibre, fibre, yarn, fabric and clothing and accessories. Among these products, clothing and accessories offer the greatest potential for employment and output. In 2021, world exports of clothing and accessories by themselves amounted to

$508 billion, while those of fibre, yarn and fabric together summed to only $174 billion.

Within the MMF segment, the subject of this article, viscose- and polyester-based fibre, yarn, fabric and clothing are the major contributors. Technically, viscose itself is plant-based, but since its conversion into fibre requires processing with a heavy dose of chemicals, it is included in the MMF segment. Polyester fibre is produced from polyester, which is itself produced by polymerizing purified terephthalic acid (PTA) and mono-ethylene glycol (MEG).

To be competitive, producers of clothing and accessories must be able to buy fabric at globally competitive prices. Such access in turn depends on either low, possibly zero, custom duty on the imported fabric or the existence of a vibrant and globally competitive domestic fabric industry. Unfortunately, neither alternative has been available to producers of MMF clothing and accessories producers in India.

Until a year ago, with rare exceptions, basic custom duty on MMF fabrics was set at 25 per cent. Currently, this duty stands at 20 per cent which is still very high, considering the low margins on which clothing and accessories manufacturers operate. No doubt, the duty is set at this level to provide protection to fabric producers. But, alas, such protection undermines an activity that has a huge output and employment potential.

The problem would be less serious had a vibrant MMF fabric industry emerged behind this protective wall. But this too has failed to materialize partially because of repeated renewals of large AD duties on imports, which make polyester and viscose yarn overly expensive for weavers who convert it into fabric.

PTA and MEG, the key ingredients in the production of polyester fibre, are highly capital-intensive products. The same is also true of viscose staple fibre. Furthermore, production of these items is heavily concentrated in the hands of a very small number of large and highly influential business houses. Vertically integrated, these business houses produce not only fibre and raw materials going into them but also yarn, fabric and clothing.

During the last two decades, with enormous legal resources at their command, the business houses have heavily lobbied the government for AD duties on the imports of raw materials, fibre and/or yarn in the MMF segment. Unfortunately, the Directorate General of Trade Remedies (DGTR), which is tasked with conducting AD investigations and recommending AD duties, has been much too eager to oblige them. Until recently, the finance ministry, the decision-making authority, has invariably gone along with DGTR recommendations. As a result, though subject to a five-year sunset clause under WTO rules, AD duties have been repeatedly renewed. That in turn has made producers of downstream products—fabric and clothing—uncompetitive. Uncertainty associated with each renewal also discourages new investments in the downstream products.

Recently, the government has begun to take a tougher stand and let many AD duties expire. Notably, it ended the duty on PTA in February 2020 and on viscose fibre in August 2021.

But this has not deterred the business houses from filing yet more applications for AD investigations. As a result, positive recommendations from DGTR for AD duties on MEG and viscose fibre are already awaiting decision by the finance ministry.

If we are to develop a vibrant MMF segment, and join the world clothing and textiles industry, which has moved heavily in this direction in recent decades, the government must give a clear signal to the business houses that they cannot hold the downstream industry hostage to their inefficiency. The purpose of AD duties is to give producers temporarily injured by highly competitive imports space to do necessary repairs. Five years is long enough to do such repairs. But when producers keep claiming injury for two decades, it is a sure sign of fundamental inefficiency and not temporary injury.

From a national welfare standpoint, it makes no sense to trade a small number of jobs in the highly capital-intensive upstream products such as PTA, MEG, and polyester and viscose fibre and yarn for many, many more jobs in the downstream weaving and clothing industry.

Finally, AD duties are only a part of the problem. Indian weaving and clothing industries are highly fragmented in both MMF and natural fibre segments. And India needs both segments to flourish to create good jobs for the masses. Seen this way, the exclusion of natural-fibre-based clothing industry from the PLI scheme is a mistake worthy of correction.

22

THE TYRANNY OF THE BALANCE-OF-PAYMENTS IDENTITY

9 March 2013

INDIA'S CAD HAS BALLOONED, reaching 4.6 per cent of the (GDP) in 2011–12. While the latest Economic Survey advises cutting gold and oil imports, the Budget speech emphatically points to larger capital inflows as the solution.

Both the survey and the speech couldn't be more wrong. Restricting gold or oil imports will not change the total imports or the CAD. And bringing more foreign capital will *increase*, not reduce, the latter.

The reason for these outcomes lies in what I call the tyranny of the BoP identity. In its simplest form, the identity says that the current account deficit (CAD) must equal net capital inflows (K) minus additions to RBI foreign exchange reserves (R): CAD = K – R.

By definition, CAD is the total value of imports minus the sum of the total value of exports and net foreign remittance. Capital inflows include investment by foreign entities in Indian stocks, bonds and companies, increases in NRI deposits, government borrowing abroad, and external commercial borrowing (ECB).

A simple international transaction illustrates why no country can escape the BoP identity. Suppose Goldman Sachs invests $100 million in the Indian stock market. This generates K = $100 million in the BoP identity. Because stocks can only be purchased in rupees, some entity must convert the dollars into rupees. There are three possibilities.

First, the RBI may buy the $100 million, placing equivalent rupees in the hands of Goldman Sachs. The transaction enhances the RBI foreign exchange reserves by $100 million and therefore R = $100 million. The net effect of the Goldman Sachs investment is K − R = 0 and CAD = 0.

Second, Goldman Sachs buys the rupees from an Indian bank. The bank may in turn either invest the $100 million abroad or sell them to someone else who does the same. In either case, the action results in K = − $100 million, exactly offsetting the inflow associated with the purchase of Indian stocks by Goldman Sachs. On net, we have K = 0, R = 0 and CAD = 0.

Finally, after buying $100 million from Goldman Sachs, the bank sells them to an importer. Dollars are used to affect imports leading to K − R = $100 million and CAD = $100 million. The bottom line is that if there is positive net capital inflow, either the RBI must buy the associated dollars or the CAD will rise by the equivalent amount. No nation can escape this fate.

Now return to consider the CAD in India. India began the decade of the 2000s with a modest CAD in 2000–01, which turned into a surplus in the following three years and then into a modest deficit again until 2007–08. But beginning in 2008–09, the year of a global financial crisis, the CAD became significantly larger, skyrocketing to 4.6 per cent of the GDP in 2011–12.

The Tyranny of the Balance-of-Payments Identity 99

What changed beginning in 2008–09? Throughout much of the 2000s, capital inflows had built up and the RBI had simultaneously bought the associated dollar inflows, building its reserves. From 2000–01 to 2007–08, $252.5 billion worth of foreign capital flowed into India on a net basis and the RBI absorbed $236 billion of the associated dollar inflows by accumulating reserves. This left a paltry $16.5 billion for the CAD to absorb over the eight-year period.

But beginning in 2009, India had a changed RBI. Perhaps yielding to the US' exhortations against currency manipulation (mostly aimed at China), it virtually stopped intervening in the foreign exchange market. From 2008–09 to 2011–12, $183.8 billion worth of capital flowed into the country, but the RBI reserves actually fell by a modest sum of $6.4 billion. As a flip side, cumulative CAD over just four years ended up being $190.2 billion.

RBI defenders might argue that with the rupee nominally depreciating against the dollar and inflation raging, purchases of dollars by the RBI would have led to an even larger depreciation of the rupee. But the rupee depreciation did not begin until June 2011. The RBI had plenty of opportunity to buy dollars prior to that date. Moreover, the large capital inflows were a self-inflicted wound: the RBI has deliberately progressively loosened its hand on the ECB.

There is one final point concerning exports. One increasingly sees official statements these days, including in the Economic Survey, that India cannot count on expanding exports due to a stagnant world economy. Such export pessimism is both misplaced and self-defeating. In 2011, India's share in the world merchandise exports was a minuscule 1.7 per cent compared to China's 10.4 per cent. India has vast scope for export expansion just by increasing its *share* in global exports.

In fact, in expanding exports, India faces a far smaller political challenge abroad than China did ten or more years ago. Whereas

China had to wipe out the domestic apparel, footwear and toy industries in the US and Europe to get where it got and deal with the associated political backlash, India only has to displace some of the Chinese exports into these markets. Export expansion through increased share is entirely feasible even within a stagnant global economy provided we have the courage to undertake the necessary internal reforms making the policy environment friendlier for labour-intensive manufacturing.

23

TAKE-OFF FROM THE COAST

19 February 2016

IT IS GENERALLY AGREED that a key element in the transformation of India is the creation of a large number of good jobs. While micro and small enterprises provide lots of jobs, given their low average labour productivity, they are able to pay relatively low wages. Economists Rana Hasan and Nidhi Kapoor of the Asian Development Bank find, for example, that manufacturing firms with less than twenty workers employed 73 per cent of manufacturing workforce but produced only 12 per cent of manufacturing output in 2010–11.

With such a large share in employment but a small share in output, these firms could pay only a fraction of the average wage paid by larger firms, which is itself low in India when seen in the international context. There is compelling evidence that productivity and wages rise with the size of the enterprise.

Large firms are able to attain higher levels of productivity by exploiting scale economies. They also operate predominantly in the highly competitive world market, which forces them to continuously improve product quality and adopt cost-cutting technologies. Their presence also enhances the efficiency of small and medium firms because these later must either become their ancillaries or compete against them.

Unfortunately, large firms are missing in India in precisely the sectors where they are needed the most: employment-intensive sectors such as apparel, footwear, electronic and electrical products, and a host of other light manufactures. These are products in which China has done well, thereby generating a large volume of good jobs for its workers. In 2014, China exported $56 billion worth of footwear, $187 billion worth of apparel, and $782 billion worth of electrical and electronic goods.

The corresponding exports by India were $3 billion, $18 billion and $9 billion, respectively. The single most important key to China's success in manufactures has been its decision to go for the large world market, which today stands at $18 trillion.

In 1980, when China's GDP was less than $500 billion at today's prices and exchange rate, it began by establishing four very large Special Economic Zones (SEZs) along its southeast coast. Shenzhen, one of these four SEZs, was then at best semi-urban with a population of 3,00,000. Attracted by its low wages and business-friendly environment, investors from Hong Kong and Taiwan flocked to it.

Its coastal location allowed these investors to operate in world markets unhindered by poor infrastructure in the hinterland. Today, Shenzhen has a population of 11 million, a gross city product of $265 billion and a per capita income of $24,000. Though originally Cantonese, it speaks Mandarin because the bulk of its population migrated from other parts of China. Most of the major multinational firms have a presence in Shenzhen. Rapid growth has sent Chinese manufacturing wages shooting up—they now stand at Rs 5 lakh per year.

Unsurprisingly, many multinational firms from China are looking for alternative lower-wage locations. With its large labour force, India is well positioned to become home to these firms. But this requires the creation of a business-friendly ecosystem in locations that can serve as export bases for these firms. It is here that India can leverage the Sagarmala project of the prime minister.

It can create a handful of Shenzhen-style Coastal Economic Zones (CEZs) on its coasts next to deep-draft ports. The CEZs must cover a large area (Shenzhen spans 2,050 sq. km), and have some existing infrastructure and economic activity. They must also provide a business-friendly ecosystem including ease of exporting and importing, swift clearances, and speedy water and electricity connections.

They must also offer urban spaces to house the local resident workforce. For firms that create a threshold level of direct employment (for example, 50,000 jobs), a tax holiday for a pre-specified period may be considered. The incentive may be offered during a short window of three to four years to reward the firms that take early initiative.

An important advantage of locating the zones near the coast is that they would attract large firms interested in serving the export markets. These firms would bring with them technology, capital, goods management and links to world markets. They would help create an ecosystem around them in which productive small and medium firms would also emerge and flourish.

Initially, the number of these zones must be limited to two or three. This would help ensure that limited resources are not diluted, and many sector-specific zones and clusters can emerge within each of them to fully exploit economies of scale and agglomeration.

Simultaneous creation of too many zones would spread the available public resources thinly while also diffusing economic activities with potential synergies.

As initial zones succeed, more may be subsequently launched. This is not unlike the software industry, which initially concentrated in Bengaluru but subsequently spread to other towns. One final point is worth noting. Given the vast size of the world market and our tiny share (1.7 per cent) in it, there remains vast scope for the expansion of exports even if the global economy remains stagnant. Slow growth of the world economy is not an insurmountable barrier to export-led growth.

24

HOW TO MAKE EXPORTS BOOM

26 June 2019

PRIME MINISTER NARENDRA MODI has made exports a high priority. Indeed, India would do well if it gave them the highest priority and pursued their success in mission mode. No nation has sustained growth rates of 9–10 per cent for two or more decades without succeeding in global markets. China's share in global merchandise exports rose from 2 per cent in 1991 to 12.4 per cent in 2012. These two decades saw China fully transform from a primarily agrarian to a modern industrial economy.

Today, India's share in global merchandise exports remains low at 1.7 per cent. In 2000, when China's GDP was no more than India's today, it already accounted for 4 per cent of global merchandise exports. Sustaining high growth and creating good jobs will require a strategy centred on building an export-friendly ecosystem in the country.

The starting point for this strategy is shedding three of our current obsessions: import substitution, micro and small enterprises, and a strong rupee. Import substitution has never produced sustained rapid growth anywhere. On their own, micro and small enterprises can provide low productivity, subsistence wage employment to the multitude, but they cannot be the source of high productivity, well-paid jobs without successful medium and large enterprises around them.

A strong rupee keeps imports artificially cheap for our citizens and our exports artificially expensive for foreigners. The resulting trade deficit then tempts policymakers to slap tariffs on imports.

The first step in building a trade-friendly ecosystem has to be a realistic exchange rate. We reaped the benefits of this approach in the 2000s. By letting the rupee depreciate steadily from Rs 17.1 per dollar in 1990–91 to Rs 47.7 per dollar by 2001–02, we created a highly competitive environment for producers of our exportable goods as well as those competing against imports, which were being liberalized alongside.

Our exports boomed during the following decade, with exports of goods and services as a proportion of GDP rising from 12.9 per cent in 2001–02 to 24.1 per cent in 2011–12. With rapidly expanding exports, we could also expand imports, which rose from 14.7 per cent to 30.8 per cent of the GDP over the same period. Recall that this was the period during which the cell phone revolution took place in India. Without the export growth, we could not have imported cell phones and this revolution would have stopped dead in its tracks.

Unfortunately, however, higher inflation in India than in trading partners without a commensurate nominal depreciation of the rupee has left Indian products up to 15 per cent more expensive than their foreign counterparts since 2014. An econometric study by Sajjid Chinoy and Toshi Jain finds that this loss of competitiveness has had a negative effect on India's exports. In the coming years, if the US tariffs on China lead to a depreciation of its currency and India continues to hold on to the strategy of a strong rupee, it would compound the problem of loss of competitiveness of our products vis-à-vis China.

Getting the exchange rate right is only the beginning. We also need to maintain a liberal trade regime in which exports and imports can flow freely without the uncertainty of interventions that disrupt market processes. Arbitrarily raising tariffs and bringing AD suits may benefit producers of some products, but they hurt the economy as a whole. They replace less costly imports with more costly domestic products while also, more subtly, undermining exports. When imports decline because of higher tariffs and AD duties, the RBI allows the rupee to appreciate, making our exports abroad more costly.

Free flow of exports and imports also requires trade facilitation. Unnecessary clearances, delays at ports and high transport costs add to the costs of exports. In ease of doing business rankings, India still continues to have a low ranking on cross-border trade, which measures the time and cost associated with the logistical process of exporting and importing goods.

Finally, and above all, sustained export growth requires an ecosystem in which medium and large firms can flourish. This requires flexible labour and land markets. Contrary to the impression conveyed in the media, progress was made in labour market reforms during the last five years. Of particular importance is the provision of fixed-term contracts, which allows firms to let workers go on the expiry of the contract.

But more needs to be done. For example, the temptation to fix the minimum wage at excessively high levels needs to be resisted, as it would lead even small firms to become micro to escape ultra-high minimum wages. India is also unique in the entire world in setting rising minimum wages with rising levels of skills. This practice must be ended.

Buying land remains a challenge for large firms due to the existence of land parcels that remain in dispute within any large contiguous land area. Only an amendment of the current draconian Land Acquisition Act can solve this problem.

Absent these reforms, we must experiment with Autonomous Employment Zones that cover large areas of 500 square kilometres or more and have considerable autonomy to implement flexible land and labour laws. Like Shenzhen in China, some of these zones could be close to the coast to become export hubs.

25

THE US CAN'T DO A RUSSIA TO CHINA

2 June 2022

ECONOMIC SANCTIONS AGAINST RUSSIA have led many commentators to draw attention to the so-called dollar dominance. They contend that the dominant role played by the dollar as the international medium of exchange, store of value and unit of account not only bestows large benefits on its issuer, the US, but also imparts the latter disproportionate economic power over other countries.

Closer examination reveals, however, that the benefits of dollar dominance to the US are vastly overstated, while the claim that it imparts the latter considerable power over other countries is outright wrong. Sanctions against Russia have derived their power not from the dominance of the dollar but from the much larger economic size of the countries imposing those sanctions. When it comes to economically large countries such as China, the sanctions lose much of their power despite the same dollar dominance. Symmetrically, a large country such as China is in a position to exercise considerable economic power over smaller countries even if its currency is insignificant internationally.

The fact of continuing dollar dominance along multiple dimensions has now been well documented. International trade is predominantly invoiced in the dollar. Between 1999 and 2019, the currency accounted for 96 per cent of trade invoicing in the Americas, 74 per cent in the Indo-Pacific and 79 per cent in the rest of the world other than Europe. The dollar also dominates international banking: 60 per cent of foreign currency deposits and loans have been consistently held in this currency since 2000. The percentage of foreign currency debt denominated in the US dollar has also remained stable at around 60 per cent since 2010.

Most importantly, the dollar enjoys the most confidence as a store of value. As a result, countries hold their foreign exchange reserves principally in the dollar. As of 2021, dollar-denominated official foreign exchange reserves accounted for 60 per cent of all reserves. Yet another indicator of the confidence in the dollar is that nearly half of the dollar banknotes issued by the US—approximately $950 billion worth at the end of March 2021—are held by foreign investors.

This ubiquity of the dollar is what has led many to think that the dollar generates a vast volume of benefits for the US while also giving it a huge amount of power over other nations. Yet, as economist Paul Krugman has lucidly explained, the only tangible benefit to the US comes from foreigners holding banknotes worth $950 billion. For this amount constitutes interest-free loans by foreigners to the US. Beyond it, argues Krugman, benefits of dollar dominance are not obvious. One may think that it allows the US to run large current account deficits, but Australia and the UK have been running larger deficits. The conjecture that dollar dominance allows the US to borrow money cheaply also turns out false: Britain and Japan borrow at yet lower interest rates.

The idea that dollar dominance imparts the US the power to inflict injury on other nations through sanctions also turns out to be false. Had the British pound or Euro been the dominant currency, as long as the US and its allies cooperated in the same way, the sanctions against Russia would have had the same effect. Russia is simply not large enough to effectively retaliate. Where it has the benefit of size, as in the oil and gas markets, Western countries found themselves without leverage.

An alternative way to see why it is country size rather than the dominance of the dollar that matters is to ask whether the US and its allies could use sanctions as effectively against China as against Russia. A moment's reflection shows that the answer is in the negative. The US would have to think twice before initiating such action. True, it has the ability to block China's official foreign exchange reserves of which two-thirds or approximately $2.1 trillion are held in Western government bonds. But the catch is that such an action would invite China to seize $3.6 trillion in direct investment and $2.2 trillion in portfolio investment by foreigners in China.

Sanctions against Chinese financial institutions pose a similar dilemma. Four of the thirty systemically important banks are Chinese. The US and its allies could not impose sanctions on them without risking large damages to their own financial institutions which have lent vast sums to the latter. Nor would such action be without risk to global financial stability.

On the other hand, despite the yuan having almost no standing as an international currency, China enjoys considerable power to inflict injury on other smaller countries. To give just one example, it accounts for 40 per cent or more of all imports of parts and components used in electrical and electronic goods by each of

Australia, Japan, India and South Korea. These countries do not have symmetric power to retaliate since, taken individually, none of them account for a similarly large share of Chinese imports. What all this boils down to is that the outcomes of the current sanctions against Russia are no guide to potential sanctions by Western countries against China in the event that the latter attempts a takeover of Taiwan.

PART V
LESSONS FROM HISTORY

26

SELF-SUFFICIENCY HELD INDIA BACK: SOME USEFUL ECONOMIC HISTORY LESSONS ON HOW WE MANAGE TO HANDICAP OURSELVES

3 March 2021

IT HAS GONE VIRTUALLY unrecognized that the goal of economic self-sufficiency single handedly held the Indian economy back for nearly four decades. All else, including the licence-permit raj, SSI reservation and heavy presence of the public sector was either a by-product of this goal or sideshow.

Prime Minister Jawaharlal Nehru viewed economic self-sufficiency as necessary for the preservation of political freedom. He held that depending on imports for railways, aeroplanes and guns amounted to being slaves of foreign countries. 'Whenever these countries wished they could stop sending these things … we would thus remain slaves.'

Unfortunately, there was an inherent conflict between such self-sufficiency and productive efficiency. In the 1950s India, both the income and the savings rate were extremely low. That translated into meagre savings. With ample labour supply available, the key to fast development therefore lay in the conversion of these savings into the most productive investments. Self-sufficiency stood in the way of such conversion.

Self-sufficiency required rapid expansion of the economy into a diverse set of products ranging from bicycles to automobiles to railways to aeroplanes, their components and metals and machinery necessary to manufacture the products and components.

Broadly, manufactures could be divided into two categories: capital-intensive products such as those just mentioned that had to be produced by large-scale enterprises and labour-intensive products such as clothing, footwear, kitchenware and furniture that could be produced by small-scale enterprises, referred to as the 'cottage industry' in the contemporary nomenclature. Given the need for diversification, it was only natural that the scarce savings be reserved exclusively for large-scale enterprises with cottage industry relying on its own internal savings.

The compulsion to spread the scarce savings over as many products as possible even within the capital-intensive category meant that each of these products was allocated just enough capital to operate on the minimum technologically feasible scale. This scale was generally significantly smaller than the one at which counterpart enterprises in other parts of the world operated. At this scale, production in India was inherently costly relative to that in other countries. Survival of the enterprises then required prohibition of imports through strict import licensing.

Instruments deployed to allocate scarce savings included the manufacture of certain heavy-industry products in the public sector using revenue resources and investment licensing for the private

Self-Sufficiency Held India Back

sector, whereby any investment in plant and machinery exceeding Rs 1 million (revised to Rs 2.5 million in 1964) came to require a licence issued by a government agency.

To exclude light manufactures from accessing scarce savings, initially the government adopted a policy of denying licences for their large-scale production. Later, in 1967, it adopted the SSI reservation policy, under which it drew up a long list of labour-intensive products and reserved them for exclusive manufacture by enterprises with Rs 1 million or less in investment in plant and machinery.

Under this system, India became uncompetitive against foreign products even in the labour-intensive manufactures. With investment in plant and machinery limited to Rs 1 million, costs and quality of even these products could not match their foreign counterparts. They too had to be protected via import licensing.

With imports shut down and investment licensing blocking entry of new domestic enterprises, all sources of competition were eliminated. Inefficiency from a lack of competition was thus piled on top of the inefficiency of scale.

Even so, with imports strictly controlled and domestic output limited by licence, products such as steel, scooters, automobiles and cement had the potential to generate large profits for those lucky enough to get licences. Price controls were adopted as the solution but that created shortages of the items. Distribution controls requiring a government-issued permit to procure the items followed.

From a development standpoint, industry came to be divided into a formal, capital-intensive sector and an informal cottage-industry sector. Capital got concentrated almost entirely in the former and labour in the latter. Hardly any attractive job opportunities opened for unskilled workers except in the public sector. India remained primarily agricultural with 66 per cent of the workforce trapped in that sector till as late as 1987–88.

Efficiency required the allocation of scarce savings to light manufactures allowing them to achieve scale and product quality necessary to compete in the vast global economy. That would have created jobs for the unskilled at decent wages and facilitated rural-urban migration. Resulting rising incomes would have led to rising savings and provided investible funds for investment in progressively more capital-intensive products. Diversification could, thus, have been achieved over time. This is precisely the strategy South Korea, Taiwan and Singapore followed in the 1960s and 1970s.

The proverbial dualistic structure with capital concentrated in formal, capital-intensive sectors and labour in the informal, SSI sector has continued to haunt India to date. The rise of the services sector has only reinforced this structure by concentrating skilled labour in formal employment and unskilled labour in self-employment or micro- and small-services enterprises.

Hardwired for it, our successful entrepreneurs, who walk away with much of the available bank credit, remain disinterested in investing in labour-intensive light manufactures. With policy makers focused on either capital- and skilled-labour-intensive sectors or micro and small enterprises as well, medium and large enterprises in light manufactures remain orphans.

27

NEHRU'S REAL BIG MISTAKE: HEAVY INDUSTRY WRONGLY GOT PRIORITY IN THE 1950s. SO, EVEN AT 75, INDIA ISN'T RICH

19 August 2021

AS INDIA ENTERS ITS seventy-fifth year of Independence, we must set the goal of bringing genuine prosperity to all by the hundredth year. But the occasion is also an opportunity to introspect why India did not achieve this goal already. After all, seventy-five years is a long time and some countries have become prosperous in less than this time.

It is commonplace to trace our economic failure during the first several decades to Nehruvian socialism. But this begs the question: precisely which features of it? Superficially, one may point the finger at Nehru's push for a progressively larger share of the public sector in the ownership of the means of production so that profits will translate into public revenues rather than private wealth.

While this intrusion of the public sector was surely a factor, it was not the real key to the failure. Instead, it was Nehru's decision to front-load his development model with highly capital-intensive, heavy industry at a time when investable capital was highly scarce.

Nehru's socialism is often likened to Fabian socialism, which rejects the revolutionary doctrines of Marxism and takes a more moderate approach to it. What is less well known is that till at least 1936, Nehru had subscribed to a far more radical form of socialism, bordering on communism. In this phase, he had come to the view that imperialism inevitably resulted from capitalism since capitalist nations needed colonies as the sources of raw materials and markets for finished products. It followed that socialism worldwide was the only way to defeat imperialism and that international trade inevitably gave rise to imperialist tendencies. 'We wanted neither to be victims of an imperialist power nor to develop such tendencies ourselves,' he wrote when explaining the rationale for economic self-sufficiency as an objective for a post-Independence India in *The Discovery of India*.

The conventional approach to seeking self-sufficiency while industrializing the nation would have been to follow the import-substitution industrialization (ISI) model. This would have entailed protection to assembly activities in the first stage, components production in the second stage, machines necessary to produce components and assembly activities in the third stage, and machines to produce machines in the fourth stage.

But Nehru never saw protection as the means to industrialization or self-sufficiency. In his thinking, the twin objectives had to be achieved by adjusting the production basket to the consumption needs of people. But a decision still had to be made regarding the sequence in which to phase out the production of final products, components and machines over time. Here Nehru went for exactly the opposite of the sequence that the ISI model recommended.

He placed heavy industry consisting of products such as steel and machines at the beginning of the process.

In a speech delivered in 1956, as India embarked upon the path-setting second five-year plan, Nehru outlined his approach thus:

> Previously people's idea of industrialization was one of increasing the output of consumer goods, with consequent employment. The idea now is, ... we must start from the heavy, basic, mother industries. ... We must start with the production of iron and steel on a large scale. We must start with the production of the machine which makes the machine.

Nehru saw heavy industry as essential for self-sufficiency as well. In a speech in 1953, he had argued, 'One thing is clear to me that if we do not develop heavy industry here then we either eliminate all modern things such as railways, airplanes and guns ... or else import them. But to import them from abroad is to be the slaves of foreign countries.' He expressed these views in numerous speeches throughout his tenure as prime minister.

The strategy brought with it many unintended consequences. All available capital was reserved for heavy industry. Given the meagre amount of capital, the scale of production in each product line within heavy industry still remained sub-optimal. In parallel, light manufactures were relegated to household and small enterprises where they too remained subject to production at sub-optimal scale. With higher inflation at home than abroad and a fixed exchange rate, most products soon became uncompetitive against their foreign counterparts and had to be protected through strict import licensing.

Heavy industry created few jobs for the unskilled. Simultaneously, the demand for light-industry products and services remained constrained by domestic incomes, which grew at a snail's pace.

The result was a painfully slow transition of workers from below-subsistence agriculture into industry and services. The proportion of workforce in agriculture, which stood at 69.7 per cent in 1951, remained stuck at 69.5 per cent in 1961 and 69.7 per cent in 1971. No reduction in poverty was achieved.

Though India began dismantling the Nehru model in 1991, the journey away from it has been slow due to the intellectual legacy and inherited industry structure. Socialist-era patronage produced intellectuals who, as educators, have continued to hardwire the future generations of bureaucrats and politicians in the old ideas. Entrepreneurs, likewise, invest where they have tasted success and few of them have done so in large-scale manufacturing of light manufactures, where the potential for well-paid jobs for the masses lies. That has meant continued slow pace of transformation.

28

LET IT SEEK ITS OWN LEVEL

27 September 2022

THE RBI HAD FOUGHT hard to hold the value of the US dollar below ₹80 in recent months using up nearly $45 billion of its foreign-exchange reserves since 1 July. But it finally yielded to the pressure stemming from the latest interest-rate hike by the Federal Reserve Board of the United States with the dollar attaining the value of ₹81 on 22 September. Many analysts view this rise of the dollar and the corresponding fall of the rupee as a sign of weakness in the Indian economy. But such inference is not only wrong but also encourages policymakers to rally behind a strong rupee when the national economic interest might well be served by allowing it to weaken.

To understand how damaging wrong choices on the exchange rate can be, it is instructive to briefly digress to a historical episode going back to the 1950s. During the Second World War, the strong performance of Indian exports and tight controls on imports had allowed India to accumulate a large volume of foreign exchange in terms of the pound sterling, which came to be called the sterling balances.

After the war, as India embarked upon its ambitious five-year plans, it had to resort to money creation to finance part of the expenditure, which resulted in inflation rates exceeding those of its trading partners. With the nominal exchange rates fixed at the time, the higher inflation rates made Indian products uncompetitive relative to foreign ones. Imports became more attractive while simultaneously exports suffered.

Evidently, this created a deficit in India's balance of payments, which had to be financed by drawing on the sterling balances. The availability of these balances proved a big blessing since they allowed the country to import not just machinery and raw materials required for industrialization but also consumer goods to soften the blow of inflation. Unfortunately, however, the sterling balances ran out by the end of 1957–58 and India came face-to-face with its first serious BoP crisis.

At this point, India had two options: devalue the rupee to make Indian goods more competitive vis-à-vis those of its trading partners or clamp down on imports by stricter enforcement of import licensing which had been in place since the world war. At the time, devaluation was widely viewed as equivalent to admission that the economy was fundamentally weak. Therefore, there was no political constituency whatsoever for it. Therefore, strict import licensing buttressed by exchange control became the default choice.

Many of the problems associated with the licence-permit raj that followed in the 1960s and beyond had their origins in this fateful policy choice. Even then, the government found itself compelled to devalue the rupee subsequently in June 1966. But it was too little too late by then and, moreover, the policy was ill-timed. Two back-to-back droughts effectively overwhelmed any positive effects that the devaluation could have had.

Though the current policy environment is very different from that in the 1950s, the lessons of this episode remain relevant. The origins of the pressure on the rupee today are to be traced not in higher inflation rates at home but in the rising interest rates in the US in the face of a high degree of international mobility of financial capital. Attracted by these high interest rates, financial capital in India seeks to flow to the US and puts downward pressure on the rupee.

As in the 1950s, India, specifically the RBI, has two options in the face of these capital outflows. One, just as it used sterling balances to meet the demand for imports in the 1950s, it can draw upon its stock of foreign-exchange reserves to finance capital outflows at the prevailing exchange rate. And two, it can make it attractive for the private agents to supply the necessary dollars by letting it appreciate (and the rupee to depreciate).

If the RBI chooses the first strategy while its trading partners choose the second, Indian goods become uncompetitive vis-à-vis those of the latter. As in the 1950s, exports would suffer and the temptation to increase protection against imports would rise. Additionally, there is the risk that as happened with the sterling balances in the 1950s, our foreign-exchange reserves will drop and undermine the ability of the RBI to credibly stabilize future exchange-rate fluctuations.

While the RBI has used a mix of these two options to date, it has relied more heavily on the first than is the case with several of its trading partners. Consequently, its reserves have seen a significant depletion while Indian goods have experienced a loss of competitiveness vis-à-vis those of the latter. Most recently, the RBI seems to have concluded that the US war on inflation and therefore its interest-rate hikes and pressures for financial capital outflows from India are likely to continue for some time. Hence, it has shifted the mix of the policies towards the second option. This is a welcome shift since maintaining the competitiveness of Indian goods both at home and abroad as well as safeguarding the foreign-exchange reserves are essential to sustaining the current growth momentum in the economy.

29

CUSTOM THAT COSTS US DEAR

11 August 2022

AN EXAMINATION OF CUSTOMS-DUTY rates beginning in 2011–12 confirms the general impression that they saw an uptick beginning in 2014–15. Increases in the duty rates, which had applied to less than 1 per cent of all tariff lines in earlier years, jumped to 3 to 4 per cent beginning that year. But the real break in the policy came in 2018–19. That year, a massive 42.3 per cent of all tariff lines went up, the average of all customs duties increased from 13.7 per cent to 17.7 per cent, and the proportion of tariff lines bearing 15 per cent or higher duty rates shot up from 28.7 per cent to 51.0 per cent.

The year 2018–19 thus marked a clear switch from liberalism to protectionism. The then finance minister explicitly noted the shift in the Budget speech of 1 February 2018 stating:

> In this budget, I am making a calibrated departure from the underlying policy in the last two decades, wherein the trend

largely was to reduce the customs duty. There is substantial potential for domestic value addition in certain sectors ... To further incentivize the domestic value addition ... I propose to increase customs duty on certain items.

To fully appreciate the gravity of such a massive change in trade policy without any analysis, discussion or debate, it is useful to look back at the history of tariff setting in India. For entirely selfish reasons, the British government had followed a policy of complete free trade in India beginning in 1882. When revenue needs forced it to impose a 5 per cent duty on imports in 1894, it simultaneously levied an equivalent excise tax on like products produced domestically, thereby eliminating any protective effect of the import duty. The government thus made a sharp distinction between protective and revenue roles of custom duties.

The idea of protective duty as a means to promote domestic producer interests in India first gained acceptance in the report of the Indian Fiscal Commission of 1921–22. The commission recommended the grant of such duty to an industry if it exhibited a natural advantage, was unlikely to develop without initial protection and was capable of withstanding foreign competition without protection eventually. It advised that a tariff board to which industries could petition for protective duties be set up.

The first Tariff Board was appointed in 1923 and the steel industry took the lead in petitioning for protection to it. Based on the board's recommendation, the government granted the industry protection but only for three years, which it later extended to another seven years. Subsequently, more tariff boards were appointed, and between 1923 and 1939, they conducted fifty-one investigations. They resulted in protection to thirteen narrowly defined products for limited periods and rejection of petitions in ten cases.

This practice of the grant of protection only after careful analysis effectively ended with the advent of the Second World War. The war brought with it strict and direct import controls enforced through licensing. Immediately after the war, the focus shifted to liberalizing the controls with an era of liberal trade policy ensuing.

Unfortunately, a BoP crisis in 1957–58 ended this liberal era. By the early 1960s, strict import licensing came to govern nearly all products. This regime ended the need for a tariff board–like entity. The Tariff Commission, which had been created in 1951 in the prevailing liberal policy environment, was formally disbanded in 1976.

During the licence-permit-raj era, the authority to set customs duties passed entirely into the hands of the revenue department of the Ministry of Finance. In the 1980s, it freely exercised this authority, converting the gap between the domestic and border prices of imports into customs duty. But once the 1991 reform eliminated import licensing, tariffs once again became effective instruments of protection. Recognizing this, the government revived the Tariff Commission in 1997, but it failed to effectively challenge the authority of the revenue department to set customs duties.

Fast forward to 2018–19 and you find the revenue department headed by a secretary with unshakable faith in import substitution. Alongside, you find the GST experiencing teething pains and therefore unable to deliver sufficient revenue to hold the fiscal deficit at the desired level. Hikes in customs duties covering a gigantic 42.3 per cent of all tariff lines without any analysis whatsoever follow.

A central principle of public finance is that customs duties should not form a revenue-raising instrument. Therefore, vesting the authority to impose customs duties solely in the revenue department constitutes a serious institutional flaw. Though the Tariff Commission continues to exist, it lacks the necessary expertise as well as the authority to materially influence the decisions of the revenue department.

In the early 1990s, India had introduced AD and safeguard mechanisms as responses to challenges posed by imports. For any existing industries, these instruments offer adequate remedies. Therefore, increases in customs duties should be strictly reserved for protection to new industries.

What about the high customs duties prevailing in many existing industries? The appropriate course here is their thorough review by an expert body to assess whether they are justified, and if so on what grounds and until when. After all, NITI Aayog now routinely conducts reviews of the Centrally Sponsored Schemes. Why should customs duties not be subject to a similar review?

PART VI

INDIA–US TRADE RELATIONS

30

INDIA AS A SCAPEGOAT: US ACTION UNDER SUPER 301

23 June 1989

THE STATED OBJECTIVE OF the recent Super-301 actions against India, Brazil and Japan by the US is to open markets and expand trade. Unfortunately, the result may turn out to be quite the opposite. The actions may unleash the worst global trade war since 1930.

The US Trade Act of 1974, which authorized the president to negotiate tariff reductions under the auspices of the GATT, also introduced Section 301, a provision for retaliation against foreign practices that 'unreasonably' restrict US exports. Between 1974 and 1988, approximately seventy cases arose under Section 301. Some of these cases were initiated by the US administration while others resulted from private petitions.

During the 1970s and 1980s, protectionist sentiment was on the rise in the US Congress. In spite of a president who was committed to free trade policies—or perhaps because of it—the Congress passed the Omnibus Trade Practices and Competitiveness Act in 1988. The new trade law considerably strengthened Section 301 of the 1974 Act. Accordingly, the United States Trade Representative (USTR) is required to identify priority foreign practices, which, if eliminated, will have the greatest benefit for the US commerce.

Investigation of policies of a country, which restrict US exports, is done under the Super 301 provisions of the 1988 Act. Action against policies, which deny American residents the protection of IPR (for instance, patents, trademarks and copyrights), is taken under the Special-301.

Unfair Traders

Ms Carla Hills, the current USTR, decided to use the power given to the office by the new Act. On 25 May, she declared India, Brazil and Japan to be 'unfair traders' under Super-301. Specific charges were brought against each country. Brazil was cited for maintaining a variety of non-tariff barriers including prohibition of import of 1,000 items. Japan was charged, inter alia, with forbidding American manufacturers of satellites and supercomputers from competing for government contracts. Interestingly, charges against India did not concern restrictive policies with respect to merchandise trade. Instead, we were cited for our restrictive policies with respect to foreign investment and an item on the invisibles account, namely, insurance. The USTR would like India to revise its policy of requiring government approval of foreign investment and to open its insurance market to foreign companies.

In addition to these Super-301 actions, the USTR also put eight nations on a 'priority watch list' for possible violation of IPR under Special-301. These nations are India, Brazil, Mexico, China, S. Korea, Taiwan, Saudi Arabia and Thailand. The USTR will reassess the situation on 1 November 1989 and may decide to cite some or all of these countries for violations.

Under the US law, the USTR must negotiate a separate agreement with each country cited within eighteen months of the announcement. The agreement must provide for the elimination of, or compensation for, the offending practice within three years. If an agreement is not reached or the agreement is violated, tariffs up to 100 per cent must be imposed on imports of selected items from the country concerned.

Even if India meets all US demands, economic gains to the latter will be negligible. India's GDP is less than 2 per cent of the GDP of the industrial market economies. The bilateral US trade deficit with India is less than 0.4 per cent of the total US trade deficit. Inclusion of India in the hit list is, therefore, almost contrary to the spirit of the 1988 Act, which seeks to identify priority countries where corrective action will confer the 'greatest' benefits for the US.

Additional Culprits

By all accounts, the principal target of the action was Japan. But, moving against Japan alone would have looked vindictive. Additional 'culprits' had to be found. The reason India became one of the culprits is perhaps that it is the best publicized case of a highly protective trade and investment regime. At the same time, India's significance for the US as a trading partner is minimal. Therefore, the potential loss to the US in the event of a trade war with India is practically nil.

Two additional factors worked against India. First, the US has been pushing hard for liberalizing trade in those services that it produces cheaply, like banking and insurance, while India has opposed this vehemently. It is demanding that if less-developed countries are to comply, the US and other developed countries must open their markets for labour-intensive services such as construction. Second, the long-run political relationship between India and the US has been less than warm. Moreover, there is no effective lobby in Washington to guard Indian interests. Not surprisingly, India has refused to negotiate with the USTR. Japan has done the same. If the two countries do not alter their position over the next eighteen months as is likely, the US may impose 100 per cent tariffs on imports of selected items from them.

The USTR has chosen to cite India for restrictive practices in precisely those areas where it is least capable of responding favourably. Liberalization of foreign investment is an extremely sensitive issue. Without a substantial change in the climate, any government will be taking a major political risk by substantially relaxing the current regulations. As regards insurance, this sector is nationalized in India. Opening the market to foreign companies will amount to denationalization of the industry, which raises rather complex economic and political issues.

EEC Policies

The US has lost moral ground due to the fact that it has chosen to put less developed and debt-burdened countries such as India and Brazil on the hit list but ignored the highly restrictive policies of the European Economic Community (EEC). It is reported that the EEC had threatened to retaliate if it was cited for Super 301. The inevitable inference is that the countries that have the power to retaliate effectively will be spared the wrath of Super 301.

Even while rejecting US demands, India should take this opportunity to rethink its foreign trade and investment policies. We must not lose sight of the fact that for some years now, the US has been the largest single importer of our goods. In 1987–88, 18.5

per cent of our exports went to that country. We should seize the initiative and make policy changes that are in our national interest. My view concerning our trade policies is that we have maintained very high tariffs for very long. Admittedly, tariffs are a major source of revenue for us. But lowering tariff rates, which average 130 per cent will raise, not lower, revenues. At present, there is a substantial evasion of tariffs via smuggling and fake invoicing. Lowering tariffs will undoubtedly reduce the incentive for evasion. High tariffs and other import restrictions have also encouraged inefficiency. For example, it was not till we allowed Suzuki to collaborate with Maruti to produce the state-of-the art automobile that we discovered the ills of the Fiat and Ambassador cars.

It is, of course, not wise for us to deregulate foreign investment at this stage. But the time is ripe for lowering the restrictions on trade at least to the point that they do not reduce revenues. There is also a desperate need to accelerate the simplification of procedures. The significant amount of resources and energy wasted in figuring complex procedures and evading regulations have become a major drain on the Indian economy.

31

THE TRUE DRIVER OF INDIA–US PARTNERSHIP

23 June 2010

FOLLOWING THE CONCLUSION OF the first India–US strategic dialogue, commentators in the Indian press have nearly uniformly expressed frustration with the lack of action under the Obama administration. To judge whether this dissatisfaction is grounded in reality, we must first ask whether each country has enough reason to invest in a close relationship with the other in the first place. From the Indian perspective, there seem to be sufficient reasons for an affirmative answer. Accounting for almost a quarter of the world's GDP, the US is by far the largest economy in the world. It is also the only superpower on the globe and likely to remain so in the foreseeable future. It is a democracy that values other democracies. And, finally, it is by far the largest single recipient of Indian exports of goods and services. If we seek rising economic prosperity and an increasing voice in world affairs, America is a good bet. An affirmative answer seems less clear-cut from the US perspective, at least on the surface. True, India is by far the world's largest democracy. But this cannot be a game changer by itself since it has been true for the last sixty years. At $1.25 trillion, the Indian economy is just a little more than 2 per cent of the world economy. Globally, it ranks a low eleventh in terms of economic size, ranking behind China and Brazil. Above all, India accounts for less than 2 per cent of the US exports and imports.

Seen in this context, the puzzle is not why the Obama administration is not doing more to promote ties with India but how India has come to command so much attention on the global stage. The main explanation of this puzzle lies in where the US sees India going in the next fifteen to twenty years.

In the last seven years, India has grown 11–12 per cent per year in real dollars. Based on the current dynamism in the economy, high and rising savings rate, a young population that is expected to grow younger and the past experiences of countries such as South Korea, Taiwan and China, India can be reasonably expected to sustain a 10 per cent growth in real dollars over the next fifteen years. This would turn the country into a $5 trillion economy and catapult it into the fourth, if not third, position worldwide, behind only the US, China and Japan. No forward-looking nation—least of all the US—would ignore an economy with such potential.

But this is not the only factor working in favour of a partnership with India. The vast numbers of highly successful Indians—a large majority of them first-generation immigrants—which they see around them also shape American perceptions of India. While the presence of Indians in the US is not new, their phenomenal success is. In the last fifteen years, their influence in the tech and finance industries and higher education has grown as that of no other single group. A year ago, when the microprocessor giant Intel decided to put its employees in its TV commercials, the first person it chose was Ajay Bhatt, the inventor of the USB port who had received his first engineering degree in the Maharaja Sayajirao University of Baroda. And to ensure that his Indian origins are not lost upon the viewers, it replaced the real Bhatt with an even more Indian-looking moustached actor! Complementing this feature is the presence of 1,00,000 students from India on the US campuses. The US leadership recognizes that these are not any 1,00,000 students. Instead, they are among the brightest young men and women anywhere who would be among the movers and shakers of tomorrow around the globe. And this flow is likely to continue. Therefore, as a country that looks ahead, the US has plenty of good reasons to seek a long-term partnership with India.

Therefore, it is no surprise that during the first India–US strategic dialogue, the US took great pains to counteract the impression that it lacked enthusiasm for India in any way. The secretary of state Hillary Clinton warmly wrote in *The Times of India* about what this partnership meant to her, and President Obama did the unusual by dropping in on the reception at the state department in honour of the visiting Indian external affairs minister S.M. Krishna.

How do we then explain the continuing frustration among the commentators in the Indian press? The answer perhaps is that outside of the highly complex security area, there is very little beyond the atmospherics that the governments can do to promote partnerships. Even commentators who deplore the US for failing to match its words with action and exhort it to move beyond symbolism do not offer a concrete set of actions they would like the latter to take. Demands for the removal of certain export controls and access to or the extradition of David Headley, which find frequent mentions, do not make a coherent agenda.

While the governments can make some contribution in areas of mutual interest such as research in agriculture and clean energy, cooperation in science and technology and higher education and possibly dialogue on trade and climate change issues, the bulk of the long-term relationship will be built on the business-to-business and individual- to-individual contacts outside of the government sector, as has been the case to date. The outsourcing relationship between the two countries did not have its origins in any US government decision to promote it. Nor did the American investors in India or Indian investors in America end up in their respective destinations because their governments placed them there. While continuing dialogue has signalling value, the ultimate key to achieving a true partnership remains sustained rapid growth that turns India into a $5 trillion economy in no more than fifteen years.

32

ON STRENGTHENING INDIA–US TIES

29 September 2010

BY ALL ACCOUNTS, LIKE Prime Minister Manmohan Singh, President Barack Obama is keen to strengthen India–US ties. Sadly, however, the recent actions by the US have only reinforced the feeling on the part of many in India that the president assigns significantly lower priority to India–US relations than his predecessor, President George W. Bush. This is unfortunate since the US interests in the region align most closely with those of India, at least from a longer-term perspective. Whereas China is already positioning itself as a rival, even belligerent, power, and the future of Afghanistan and Pakistan remains highly uncertain, India is a rising democratic power whose national interests are better served by a partnership rather than rivalry with the US.

Perhaps nothing gave a more negative signal to Indians than the recent decision by the president to play along with protection hawks among Democrats and sign into law an appropriations bill that the

Congress recently passed. Using the need for raising revenue to finance enhanced enforcement at the Mexican border as the excuse, the new law raises the fees on certain H-1B and L-1 temporary worker visa holders by $2,000 or more. While it is doubtful that the president's party would make any significant gains in the forthcoming elections from the protectionist rhetoric underlying the new law, the US has already lost considerable goodwill in India on account of it.

Under the UR Agreement, which brought into existence the WTO and the General Agreement on Trade in Services (GATS), one of the small concessions India had successfully negotiated with the US while agreeing to open its services market to foreign commercial presence was guaranteed access for 65,000 temporary foreign workers to the US market. The new appropriations law, passed with virtually no public discussion or debate, requires firms employing fifty or more workers and having 50 per cent or more of them on the H-1B visa to pay an extra fee of $2,250 for workers coming to the US under the L-1 inter-company transfer visa and $2,000 for those entering under the H-1B visa.

Facially, this provision is perhaps consistent with the national treatment commitment made by the US under the UR Agreement. This commitment forbids the US from discrimination in favour of the US companies with respect to the hiring of temporary workers. Since the new provision applies equally to the US and foreign companies that employ fifty workers of which 50 per cent or more are H-1B visa holders, facially the national treatment commitment is satisfied.

Yet, since India is perhaps the only country whose IT firms satisfy the criterion triggering the higher fee, the law has been seen in India almost uniformly as targeting it. Even substantively, it is questionable whether the national treatment commitment by the US is satisfied. The US companies such as Microsoft, Apple and

Oracle that employ talented foreign workers (often educated in the US universities) on H-1B visas have much easier access to the Permanent Resident visa. They are more easily able to shift their H-1B workers to this alternative visa and hold the proportion of their foreign H-1B visa workers well below 50 per cent, thus effectively escaping the law.

In his remarks on the Senate floor prior to the passage of the border security bill, Senator Charles Schumer who sponsored the bill stated, 'But recently, some companies have decided to exploit an unintended loophole in the H-1B visa program to use the program in a manner that many in Congress, including myself, do not believe is consistent with the program's intent.' The underlying political message of the Senator is that through the new legislation he intended to close this loophole. If such an objective was indeed achieved and the affected companies dropped their H-1B employees below the 50 per cent threshold, the legislation's very basis would come into question!

The purpose of the legislation is to raise revenue. If the companies changed their practice of relying on H-1B visas for more than 50 per cent of the workers, no additional revenue would actually be raised. Therefore, the claim that the law closes some real or imagined loophole in the existing rules is just that. Its real effect is to place Indian companies at a disadvantage and transfer some of their profits to the United States Treasury.

As President Obama plans his visit to India, it is important that he recognize the importance of containing measures that have at best small payoff in domestic politics and guaranteed fallout in friendly countries. Indeed, if the promotion of a warm relationship with India is a top priority, he must go a step further and drop the common US practice of insisting on matching concessions for every concession the US offers.

Following the visit to the White House by Prime Minister Manmohan Singh last November, some in the administration had pointed to the failure of India to bring anything to the table as the reason for the lack of substantive progress in India–US relations. This mindset must change. Every concession by the US need not be immediately matched by an equivalent or even bigger concession, especially when the player at the other end happens to be as yet a poor and developing country.

Ultimately, the payoff from a much stronger friendly democratic India in ten to twenty years in meeting the geopolitical challenges likely to be posed by the rapid rise of China as a rival power and the adverse developments in Afghanistan and Pakistan far outweighs any unmatched concessions the US might offer in the short term. That, in a nutshell, was the approach George W. Bush took when promoting his nuclear cooperation deal with India.

As a final point, it must be remembered that the real strength of the relationship will have to flow from business-to-business and person-to-person contacts. The governments can reinforce these contacts by resisting protectionist impulses.

33

INDIA MUST CALL THE US'S BLUFF ON PATENTS

4 March 2014

APART FROM THE DETERIORATION of the business environment generally, which impacts both domestic and foreign investors, retrospective taxation has figured most prominently in the media as the principal cause of growing scepticism among foreign investors. Entirely missing from the discourse has been an equally potent factor with wholly foreign origins: the hijacking of the economic policy dialogue between the US and India by pharmaceutical lobbies in the US. Big Pharma has convinced the US government that the country's interests are synonymous with its own. With its own list of grievances against trade restrictions in India, the National Association of Manufacturers, a lobby group of the US' manufacturers, has lent its support to the pharmaceutical industry.

Big Pharma is currently using its considerable clout to pressure the USTR into designating India as a 'priority foreign country' in its

India Must Call the US's Bluff on Patents

2014 Special 301 Report due on 30 April 2014. The designation is reserved for the worst offenders of IPR and triggers trade sanctions. If the USTR obliges, the immediate impact will be the withdrawal of tariff preferences enjoyed by India on $4.5 billion worth of its exports to the US. It is unlikely that in an election year, India will let such an act of hostility go unreciprocated. In all likelihood, it will retaliate through AD duties or outright increases in tariffs on imports from the US.

To understand what lies behind the discontent of Big Pharma, we must go back to the UR Agreement of 1994, which gave birth to the WTO. Pressed by its pharmaceutical lobbies, the US had demanded a uniform twenty-year patent on medicines and chemicals in all negotiating countries in the negotiations. The patent was to result in a twenty-year monopoly worldwide on the sales of new drugs by the firms innovating them. Because these firms were nearly exclusively from the rich world, most notably the US, the patent was to result in monopoly profits for these countries in all countries including the developing ones. Therefore, India had opposed the US's demand on behalf of the vast majority of the developing countries.

In the event, the US prevailed and the Trade-Related Aspects of Intellectual Property Rights (TRIPS) Agreement, which included the twenty-year patent protection, was incorporated into the UR Agreement. But India's efforts on behalf of the developing countries did not go to waste: India was successful in getting certain flexibilities inserted into the TRIPS Agreement. Under one such flexibility, a member country could issue a compulsory licence to a local firm for the manufacture of a patented drug if the patent holder's pricing or other actions resulted in the denial of access to the drug to most patients. Under another provision, countries were given the option to deny a patent to a drug that involved incremental innovation over an existing drug and provided no additional benefits.

Under the WTO agreement, India was required to bring its patent protection regime into conformity with the TRIPS Agreement by 1 January 2005. Accordingly, it adopted the Patents (Amendment) Act, 2005. It built the flexibilities it had negotiated into the legislation.

In the last nine years, India has used these flexibilities twice. First, in March 2012, it granted a compulsory licence to an Indian firm on an anti-cancer drug because the patent holder, the German multinational Bayer, had priced out more than 95 per cent of the patients. Second, in April 2013, India's Supreme Court upheld a 2006 decision by the Indian Patent Office denying the Swiss multinational Novartis patent on a drug. The Indian Patent Office and the Supreme Court argued that the patent would violate Section 3(d) of the Patents (Amendment) Act, 2005, which disallows patents to drugs representing incremental innovation and yielding no additional medical benefit over an existing drug.

A solitary compulsory licence and a solitary denial of a patent in nine years do not amount to much by themselves. But the reason they have worried pharmaceutical companies is that these instances may encourage a large number of other developing and even some developed countries to introduce similar provisions in their laws. That could severely restrict the companies' current ability to extend patents beyond twenty years through minor tweaking of drugs as their twenty-year patent expires.

Critics of the Indian patent law chastise it for flouting its international obligations under the TRIPS Agreement. When confronted with these critics, my response has been to advise them to urge the US to challenge India in the WTO Dispute Settlement Body (DSB) and test whether they are indeed right. But nine years have elapsed since the Indian law came into force; and, while bitterly complaining about its flaws, the USTR has not dared challenge it in the WTO. Nor would it do so now. Why?

There is, at best, a minuscule chance that the USTR will win the case. Against this, it must weigh the near certainty of losing the case and the cost associated with such a loss. Once the Indian law officially passes muster with the WTO, the USTR and pharmaceutical lobbies will no longer be able to maintain the fiction that India violates its WTO obligations. Even more importantly, it will open the floodgates to the adoption of the flexibility provisions of the Indian law by other countries. Activists may begin to demand similar flexibilities even within the US laws.

But what about possible action against India under the Special 301 provision of the US trade law? Ironically, this provision itself was ruled inconsistent with the WTO rules in 1999 and the US is forbidden from taking any action under it in violation of its WTO obligations. This would mean that it couldn't link the elimination of tariff preferences on imports from India to TRIPS violation by the latter. The withdrawal of preferences would, therefore, constitute an unprovoked unilateral action, placing India on firm footing for its retaliatory action.

34

INDIA IS TRUMP'S NEXT TARGET IN THE TRADE WAR

13 March 2019

JUST AS TENSIONS WITH China have started to ease, US President Donald Trump has opened a new front in his trade war: India. On 4 March 2019, he fired the first shot by notifying Congress of his intention to end the favourable treatment India has enjoyed under the Generalized System of Preferences (GSP). Negotiated during the 1970s under the auspices of the GATT, and later subsumed into the WTO, GSP allows many products from India and other developing countries to enter the US duty-free.

Trump's decision to end GSP did not come as a surprise. Despite close cooperation between the world's two largest democracies in defence and other areas, trade relations between them have been prickly for some time. They acquired an extra edge under Trump, who has sarcastically described India as 'the tariff king'.

Trump's favourite complaint is India's high tariff on Harley Davidson (bikes). But that isn't the only one. He's also irked that

India Is Trump's Next Target in the Trade War

the US runs a substantial trade deficit—to the tune of $27.3 billion in 2017—with India. Another problem is India's protectionist impulses, especially in agriculture. And during the last two years, the country also raised tariffs on several manufactured products, such as mobile phones and auto parts.

Further, India's IPR regime has been a source of concern for the US for a long time. Because of its restrictive patent law, the country has placed India on the 'Priority Watch List' of its Special 301 Report, which identifies countries that don't adequately protect IPR, multiple times—including in 2017.

Finally, India has recently made several decisions that have hurt the US tech companies. It passed laws requiring certain data to be stored locally, which adds to affected the US companies' operating costs. New e-commerce regulations have likewise prohibited online marketplaces from selling any products from companies in which the marketplaces have significant stakes. This has resulted in some short-run costs for Amazon and Walmart, which manage the two largest online marketplaces in India and sell millions of dollars' worth of products in which they hold indirect equity stakes. Finally, India is tightening the rules under which online content providers can operate.

India's list of complaints about the US is not nearly as long, but it does contain some significant concerns. For one, the country has long argued that US restrictions on H-1B visa workers have harmed the development of its software industry. India's concerns relate to long delays before visas are issued and the Trump administration's proposals to limit them to highly skilled workers and to deny work permits for spouses. Meanwhile, the US tariffs on steel and aluminium have hurt Indian exports of those products. Unlike Canada, China, Mexico, Turkey and the EU, however, India has refrained from taking retaliatory action so far. It has drawn up a list of twenty-nine products imported from the US—almonds, apples and phosphoric acid among them—on which it has threatened to raise duties. But it has postponed taking action multiple times. The latest deadline is set for 1 April 2019.

Finally, India fears collateral damage from the US sanctions against Iran and Russia. In both cases, the US has vowed to penalize third-party countries that do business with those two nations. So far, however, Washington has granted waivers that protect India, which is heavily dependent on defence equipment purchases from sanctioned Russian companies and oil imports from Iran, from getting dinged. But the waivers are only temporary, and the country has already had to reduce its oil imports from Iran and may eventually have to eliminate them altogether.

From an economic perspective, Trump's withdrawal of GSP won't make relations much worse. First, only a fraction of India's exports to the US enjoy GSP preferences to begin with. In fact, India estimates that the amount saved on customs duties thanks to GSP added up to just $190 million a year. Second, GSP was never going to apply to India's successful export products anyway. Once the value of exports of a particular product crosses a specified threshold—set at around $185 million currently—the country loses the GSP benefit on that product. In other words, it would be impossible for a country to become an export juggernaut on the back of GSP. Finally, under the WTO rules, GSP is meant to be unilateral, with no reciprocal concessions granted by the developing country. Yet, the US has repeatedly used the threat of withdrawal of GSP to pressure beneficiary countries on intellectual property (IP) and labour standards.

From a political perspective, though, Trump's move on GSP is dangerous. And it would be imprudent for the US to push India any further on trade issues. The country is in the midst of parliamentary elections, and the Indian government can ill afford to appear weak. It would likely deny concessions that it would be willing to grant under other circumstances. The government may even choose to retaliate to signal strength to the voters. Therefore, any aggressive action by the US runs the risk of triggering a trade war that would do little good for either side. From $20 billion in 2000, bilateral trade between the two countries has grown six-fold—to $126 billion in 2017. Cumulative FDI stands at around $45 billion from the US to India and $10 billion in the opposite direction. No wonder that, so far, Indian officials have been quite measured in their response to the impending withdrawal of GSP. But it is unclear how long such forbearance may last.

Once the Indian elections are over, the new government would do well to undertake a thorough review of all its trade policies and regulations. It should reassess the wisdom of the country's recent turn to protectionism and import substitution. Such policies were a central factor in India's economic failure during the first four decades after Independence. By contrast, openness to trade and foreign investment have paved the way to economic success in recent times.

In parallel, the US needs to appreciate that democracy places certain limits on India's leadership. Sometimes, New Delhi must accommodate political pressures that lead it to choose regulatory policies that are not to Washington's liking. In the interest of long-run partnership, it would be prudent to occasionally accommodate such behaviours. For example, India's decision in 2016 to open up online marketplaces to foreign investors resulted in Amazon and Walmart emerging as the two largest e-commerce platforms in the country within a short period. That in turn created political pressure to safeguard the interests of local small traders, who form a key constituency of the present government. New Delhi responded by reversing some of the original liberalization, but the net outcome remains an e-commerce sector that is more open to foreign investors.

From a long-term perspective, the two nations must keep in mind the vast potential for cooperation not just the defence, but also in trade. The US remains the richest and most robust economy in the world. India is predicted to grow 7 to 8 per cent annually on its path to becoming the third-largest economy in a decade. There is vast scope for win-win bargains between the two countries. With some patience, both can benefit as much from cooperation in trade in the coming years as they have in defence and related areas in the recent past.

PART VII
INDIA–CHINA TRADE RELATIONS

35

IS THERE SOMETHING DEEPLY UNFAIR ABOUT THE INDIA–CHINA TRADE RELATIONSHIP?

3 June 2013

ALTHOUGH INDIA AND CHINA granted each other the MFN status in trade relations in 1984, bilateral trade between the two countries rose to a modest $2.9 billion sixteen years later in 2000. But as growth in India accelerated to the 8–9 per cent range and industrial tariffs were slashed, the bilateral trade expanded at an astronomical pace, reaching $74 billion by 2011.

One would think that this change would be equally welcome in both Beijing and New Delhi. But it is not. The dominant view in the official circles and press in India is that there is something deeply unfair about this relationship. China exports to India two to three times what India exports to it. There is widespread belief that China engages in dumping its manufactured goods in the rapidly growing Indian market to the detriment of India. That view has found expression in the 154 AD cases initiated by India against China since 1995, by far the largest number of such cases by any member of the World Trade Organisation against another member.

But is this view grounded in proper analysis? Not by a long shot. For starters, the US merchandise imports from China are more than five times those of India and its bilateral trade deficit more than ten times that of the latter. Yet, at 112 cases since 1995, it plays a distant second to India in initiating AD cases against China.

Good economics tells you that you should worry about the overall balance in the current account, which includes trade in goods and services and remittances, and not any bilateral merchandise trade deficit. From a macroeconomic standpoint, there is nothing special about exporting goods over services or paying for imports from remittances. Even more importantly, macroeconomic stability requires long-run balancing of the overall current account and not that with every specific trade partner. If India gets the best prices for its goods and services in the US and Europe, those are the markets to which it should export. Symmetrically, if it can buy the goods and services it needs the cheapest from China, it should buy them from the latter. This is no different than what we do in our household decision-making: sell our services to the employer who pays the highest salary and buy goods from stores that sell them the cheapest. Indeed, restricting imports from China will do little to solve the problem of the overall CAD.

A different popular complaint is that India's trade with China exhibits a colonial pattern: it imports manufactured goods from China but exports raw materials to it. This is surely an important concern in terms of India failing to exploit its comparative advantage but not one for which we can hold China responsible. This is a wholly homegrown problem. Whereas China faces severe labour shortages and rising wages, India has a vast pool of labour in the informal sector that it can draw into the organized sector without significant wage increases and produce quality products that can outcompete the Chinese goods not only in our home market but third-country markets such as the US and the EU as well.

But because of our draconian labour laws, we have simply scuttled organized sector manufacturing of products that China exports in vast volumes. The most dramatic example is apparel. Today, China exports more than ten times the apparel India exports. Indeed, over time, the share of apparel in the total merchandise exports of India has dramatically shrunk from 12 per cent in 1993–94 to 5 per cent in 2011–12.

Highly constraining labour laws have meant that medium and large firms, which drive productivity, innovation and product quality, and also account for the bulk of the exports, have shied away from entering the apparel industry in India. In an important recent paper, Rana Hasan and Karl Jandoc show that whereas tiny firms with seven or fewer workers employ just 0.6 per cent of apparel workers in China, they account for a gigantic 85 per cent of apparel employment in India. At the other extreme, large firms with 201 or more workers employ 57 per cent of the Chinese apparel employees while medium-size firms with 51 to 200 workers employ another 31 per cent of them. The corresponding percentages in India are just 5 and 2. Two decades after the reforms were launched, there still remains something horribly wrong with the Indian policy framework.

A final Indian complaint is that China has obstructed Indian exports of pharmaceutical and software products. This is a wholly legitimate complaint and one behind which the Indian leadership should put its weight to seek better access to the Chinese market.

36

ON CHINA TRADE SANCTIONS

25 June 2020

AFTER DECADES OF PEACEFUL coexistence, China has turned progressively hostile in its territorial disputes with its neighbours including India. The most plausible explanation for this shift is the size of its economy. With the GDP at $14 trillion, it now feels economically secure and militarily powerful enough to pursue its long-standing geopolitical ambitions that include the acquisition of territories with strategic value.

The resulting incursions on the India–China border have led many in India to call for trade sanctions on China. The argument made is that at $77 billion, China's exports to India far exceed its imports from the latter at $19 billion in 2018. Therefore, trade sanctions by India can inflict far greater injury on China than the other way around. India's commerce ministry seems to read the situation through the same lens: post (the) Galwan Valley brawl, it has asked industry associations to identify non-essential imports from China for purposes of trade sanctions.

To be sure, border hostilities potentially give India room to invoke the national security clause in the WTO rules. This would allow it to impose tariffs on imports from China while exempting other trading partners. But do these sanctions serve India's interests?

Before addressing this question, it is worth asking a slightly different one: would China have chosen its current path of hostility had India been a $10 trillion economy? In all likelihood, it would not have. Rather than buy the animosity of a neighbour that is its near-equal in economic size as well as military might, it would have done everything to keep India on its good side and concentrated on realizing its other geopolitical ambitions.

But with India's GDP still less than $3 trillion, China is more than four times its size. This difference also means that India is militarily a lot weaker, placing it at a disadvantage in a prolonged conflict. The sooner India bridges this gap, the better for its national security vis-à-vis China and other hostile neighbours.

Return now to the trade sanctions question. In 2018, China's exports to India were only 3.1 per cent of its total exports. In contrast, India's exports to China were 5.8 per cent of its total exports. Chinese exports to India may be four times its imports from India in absolute terms but once we take the difference in economic size into account, India's ability to inflict greater damage on China begins to look suspect.

The argument against sanctions is reinforced by the fact that they would hurt not just China but India as well. Imports from China are 15 per cent of India's total imports. And contrary to the common claim that China exports only finished goods to India in return for minerals and raw materials, its exports include a significant volume of components and raw materials for a large number of critical industries. Any interruption of supplies of these raw materials and components will hurt output and employment in those industries.

India's present circumstances further weaken the case for sanctions. To begin with, India entered the COVID-19 crisis with its financial sector under great stress, a fact reflected in the plummeting of its GDP growth to just 4.2 per cent in 2019–20. COVID-19 has added to this fragility by disrupting both demand and supply.

Therefore, India's urgent economic problem is to rebuild the economy and return it to the 7.5 per cent growth trajectory on which it had been traversing before the disruption in the financial sector derailed it. Under such circumstances, piling up yet more disruption on the real economy through trade sanctions is hardly a wise step.

The final point is to ask what our end game is in imposing trade sanctions. In its trade war with even the largest economy in the world, the US, China has responded by retaliating forcefully. Therefore, it would be naïve to expect it to capitulate to our trade sanctions when we account for only 3.1 per cent of its exports. It will not only retaliate through tariffs on our exports but may also increase its border incursions. Having used up the trade sanctions weapon, we would be back to defending the border militarily and diplomatically only.

Rather than add trade warfare with no clear end-point target to the conflict with China, India would achieve its immediate security goals better by forging yet closer ties with the US, Japan and Australia. For the longer-term defence, it must focus attention on building the $10 trillion economy in the shortest possible time.

To accomplish this while also distancing the economy from China, India must aggressively pursue free trade agreements (FTAs) with friendly developed countries such as the United Kingdom, European Union and Canada, and woo multinationals to its shores. The FTAs would make India doubly attractive to multinationals.

Ideally, we should also forge an FTA with the US. Yet, I have resisted including it in the list above. The reason is that I remain sceptical that India would agree to open its agricultural sector to the highly competitive US agricultural exports or accept WTO-plus disciplines in areas such as labour, environment and IP, which are integral to the US FTA template. If India can overcome these hesitations, however, it will be icing on the cake.

37

HOW TO DISTANCE FROM CHINA?

18 July 2020

UNTIL RECENTLY, I HAD argued that while India should negotiate hard to get the best deal possible, its end goal should be to sign on to the Regional Comprehensive Economic Partnership (RCEP) consisting of India, China and fourteen other Asian countries. The economic argument was sound. The RCEP represents a vast market and India has low wages. Therefore, barrier-free trade within this market made India a very attractive destination for multinational enterprises currently operating in other RCEP countries but looking for an alternative location. Given its own fragmented goods and factor markets, and concentration of workforce in either self-employment or tiny enterprises, the benefits from having multinationals move to India, especially in labour-intensive sectors, were huge. The multinationals carried the potential to create an ecosystem that would create pressures for rapid increase in productivity.

The 15 June events in the Galwan Valley have, however, led me to change my mind. These events have brought home the lesson that China is not the US. Whereas the latter believes in peaceful coexistence and pursues a policy of enlightened self-interest, the former does not. As its economic and military might have grown, China has progressively revealed itself to be an aggressive and belligerent power that pursues narrowly defined self-interest. Whereas the US chose to promote shared prosperity in its dealings with China within a rules-based system for the past four-plus decades, China has sought to rewrite the rules of engagement in ways that may hurt other nations while benefiting itself. Its credibility to play by the rules to which it agrees within the RCEP framework is now in question. It can no longer be taken for granted that it will not use its economic leverage within the RCEP to pursue its geopolitical and strategic objectives even if it means violating the rules agreed upon within the arrangement. That casts a shadow of doubt on the value of the RCEP for India.

Beyond staying out of the RCEP, what should be India's trade and economic strategy vis-à-vis China? A natural extension of the argument I have made above would be that India should move away from trading with China. And a corollary then may be that India should simply begin restricting its imports from China by whatever means it can.

This is where much greater care is required. To be sure, where trade poses a direct threat to national security, there is little choice. For instance, if going with Huawei 5G standard could expose India to spying by China or to exclusive dependence on it for future supplies of spare parts and related equipment, we must look elsewhere for a 5G network and related equipment. The same goes for Chinese apps that make India vulnerable to spying by the Chinese government. In China, the line between the government and private sector is fuzzy.

But in areas where trade does not pose a direct threat to our security, any further distancing from China must be done on a piecemeal basis. There are at least three reasons for this prescription.

First and foremost, the Indian economy is in a rather vulnerable state at the moment. We went into the COVID-19 crisis with highly stressed financial markets. That stress has been reflected in the growth rate for the year 2019–20 being revised down recently to just 4.2 per cent. Pre-COVID-19, this is the lowest annual growth rate India has experienced since 2008–09, the year of the global financial crisis. COVID-19 has now administered by far the worst economic shock we have experienced in the post-Independence era. With the opening up of the economy after a strict lockdown, economic activity has just begun to pick up. With some luck, we may be able to return to pre-COVID-19 levels of activity in the second half of 2020–21. Under such circumstances, it would be imprudent for us to pile up an additional shock on the economy and put the fragile recovery into jeopardy.

Second, our merchandise imports from China account for almost 15 per cent of our total merchandise imports. But for China, these imports are just about 3 per cent of their total exports. Many of these imports are raw material and components that are used by our domestic industry. Any efforts to source them from other countries will only add to the cost of production at home and render us less competitive in the global marketplace.

Finally, rather than feel hurt by our sanctions against imports from it, China will likely derive satisfaction from the slowdown of our recovery that would result from the import restrictions. There is little reason to doubt that China now seeks a new global order in which it can be at the apex in one to two decades. Its more immediate goal, however, is to become the undisputed regional power in Asia. Any potential challenge to this goal can come only from India. Therefore, it is in China's interest to do everything to keep India from catching up with it economically. It would be naïve to imagine that its strategists have not thought about it. As such, by adopting policies that hit our own economy in the short run, and undermine our growth rate in the medium and long run, we only help advance China's strategic objectives.

To deal with China's threat, India needs its own long game. Two components of this game must be to progressively decouple from China and rapidly bridge the current gap in the size of our economies. To achieve the former objective without disruption, India must sign free trade agreements (FTAs) with the EU, and countries such as the UK, Canada and, eventually, the US. In this, we must learn from Vietnam. Less than one-tenth of India in population as well as economic size, this country has embraced free trade with such giants as China in the RCEP, the EU via the EU-Vietnam FTA and the US in the Trans-Pacific Partnership (TPP), though the US eventually withdrew from the latter arrangement. In contrast, we continue to fear competition against even much smaller countries such as South Korea, Singapore and Thailand, countries with whom we have signed FTAs that it now seems we would rather dispense with. We surely can be bolder.

To bridge the size gap with China, we need to create a policy environment that encourages the growth of medium and large firms. Tiny farms, tiny firms and self-employment where our workers are predominantly concentrated cannot deliver the high productivity that is so critical to launching India into a double-digit growth trajectory. Reforms are needed in land, labour and capital markets, school and higher education, and, above all, trade policy. Without them, we cannot arrest the ascendancy of China to the status of an undisputed regional power and thence to the top global power.

38

IT'S YIN-YANG BOOMERANG

3 January 2023

CALLS FOR TRADE SANCTIONS against China from not just the Opposition but also some among the supporters of the Bharatiya Janta Party are becoming louder by the day. The objective behind the more aggressive of such calls is to punish China for its transgressions on the India–China border, though some are also motivated by a desire to contain the bilateral trade deficit with it, a subject I do not consider here.

No one questions the desirability of cessation of any economic engagement with China that poses a direct threat to India's security. This has already been India's policy, especially post-Galwan, as exemplified by the ban on a number of apps including TikTok and enhanced scrutiny of new investments by Chinese firms in India. But when no such direct link exists and the objective is to settle the score, the case for disengagement is dubious.

The first question we must ask is whether the sanctions might not end up hurting us more than China. In 2021–22, merchandise imports from China, the subject of the calls for sanctions, accounted for 15.4 per cent of all merchandise imports by India. But they constituted only 2.8 per cent of all exports by China. Common sense would tell you that these ratios point to greater loss from sanctions to us than to China.

Two factors will likely soften the impact of the sanctions on both countries, though the conclusion that the loss will be proportionately larger for India is difficult to dispute. First, many of India's imports from China are critical inputs into its own manufacturing and services activities. As such, the domestic political economy would limit the sanctions to a fraction of the imports from China. Second, to the extent that India can import the sanctioned products from third countries while China can export them to the latter as well, the overall impact on either country will be smaller than if trade in the sanctioned products were to entirely cease. Taking the two factors together, one wonders whether the effect would be large enough to inflict significant injury on China.

But the matter is quite unlikely to end here since regardless of whether the injury to it is small or large, China would feel compelled to retaliate to send the message that it cannot be taken for granted. Indeed, that is exactly what it had done in response to the trade sanctions by the US.

One may be tempted to think that with India selling only 5 per cent of its exports to China, the latter has limited room for trade sanctions against it. But that would be a mistake of the highest order. China is aware that we import from it many items that form critical inputs into our manufacturing and services. As such, it will retaliate not by sanctioning its imports from us but by its exports of those items to us. For instance, export restrictions by it on active pharmaceutical ingredients, popularly known as the API, could have a crippling effect on our own pharmaceutical industry.

Finally, it is well and good for the proponents to make general noises about sanctions but can they name the specific products they would target? Once they are confronted with this question, they would find that they face Hobson's choice. To explain why, consider India's import basket from China.

In 2021, India imported $87.5 billion worth of goods. In order of declining value, the top six items were (i) electrical machinery and parts, sound recorders, television image and sound recorders, and accessories of these articles ($26.4 billion); (ii) nuclear reactors, boilers, machinery and mechanical appliances ($18.8 billion); (iii) organic chemicals including antibiotics and other APIs ($11.9 billion) (iv) plastics and articles thereof ($4.2 billion); (v) fertilizers ($2.7 billion); and (vi) optical, photographic, cinematographic, measuring, checking, medical or surgical instruments ($2.4 billion).

This list should suffice to demonstrate that selecting items for sanctions such that they will not majorly hurt our own population and yet inflict material injury on China is an infeasible proposition. Proponents of sanctions conveniently say that we can stop importing the final consumer goods which will ensure that our producer interests are protected. But how can consumer interest be excluded from the national interest? You surely cannot claim that the sanctions are in the 'national' interest while hurting the nation's consumers.

Today, the Indian economy has the potential to grow 7 to 8 per cent a year over the coming decade. Given this prospect, does it make sense for us to mindlessly engage China in economic warfare? We would do much better by shifting our trade gradually away from China and towards friendly countries through forces at work in favour of 'friendshoring' and speedy conclusion of free trade agreements with the United Kingdom and the European Union. Rather than precipitate a growth crisis by initiating a trade war, it is much better to patiently grow the economy to turn it into the world's third largest the soonest. The wealth accumulation will not only provide more resources for defence but also pave the way for forging partnerships with other powers looking for ways to confront the China challenge.

Finally, India will also need to continue with the reform agenda which must include trade liberalization, simplification of personal income taxation, implementation of the four labour codes already enacted by Parliament, making land markets more flexible, enactment of a modern higher education law, privatization of publicly owned banks and public-sector undertakings, and fiscal consolidation with the view to bringing the debt-to-GDP ratio down to 70 per cent from 85 per cent in five years. The country must also build more cities and modernize the existing ones. In the ultimate, transformation is all about moving the workforce substantially out of agriculture into industry and services, a transformation that is not possible without greater urbanization.

PART VIII
INDIA AND MULTILATERAL TRADE NEGOTIATIONS

39

THE WTO AND DEVELOPING COUNTRY INTERESTS

14 December 1998

THE UR AGREEMENT STIPULATES that, beginning 1 January 2000, the WTO members will launch a round of negotiations for trade liberalization in agriculture and services. With that date approaching, there is now a talk in international policy circles of a millennium round of multilateral trade negotiations (MTNs). In all likelihood, the next WTO ministerial conference, to be held in Washington, D.C. next year, will begin giving shape to the agenda for such a round. How should developing countries such as India approach this development?

Prior to the UR, developing countries had not participated actively in the MTNs. On the one hand, this fact gave developing countries a 'free ride' under the MFN rule of the GATT, now a key component of the WTO, a tariff reduction granted to one trading partner must be granted to all GATT members. But on the other hand, this non-participation encouraged developed countries to leave the sectors of greatest interest to developing countries out of the liberalization exercises. Indeed, they were able to maintain tight control of the sector in which developing countries have the greatest export potential, textiles and clothing, via the abominable GATT-sanctioned MFA.

All this changed in the UR Agreement, however. Developing countries participated actively in this MTN, accepting for the first time the GATT tariff bindings. Despite this switch, in the post-UR era, developing countries have largely played a reactive role in shaping the WTO agenda. Therefore, it makes more sense to adopt a joint, proactive approach that pushes common developing-country interests at the WTO ministerial conference in Washington, D.C. next year.

The first element in this approach should be to place on the forefront proposals for trade liberalization in not just agriculture and services, as required by the built-in UR agenda, but also industrial goods. There are many reasons why the inclusion of industrial products in this round should be an integral part of developing Asia's strategy.

First, starting with TRIPS and Trade-Related Investment Measures (TRIMs), developed countries have increasingly focused attention at the WTO on what is essentially a non-trade agenda. The clearest example of this approach is the attention given to the inclusion of labour and environmental standards into the WTO agenda. Thanks to a concerted action on the part of the developing countries and the support from some key developed countries, the issue of labour standards has now been delegated to the International Labour Organization. But other non-trade issues, often involving concessions by developing countries, will continue to form a part of the WTO agenda put forward by developed countries. One way to defuse this agenda is to re-focus attention on the conventional border-trade measures from whose liberalization all parties concerned can gain.

Second, in recent years, the impression has been conveyed that with developed-countries' post-UR Agreement average tariff rates coming down to 3 to 4 per cent, these countries have virtually reached a state of free trade with respect to border measures. Yet, from the viewpoint of developing countries, nothing could be farther from the truth. Thus, despite an end to the MFA, slated for 1 January 2005, tariffs in the US, the EU and Japan on textiles and clothing will remain very high. According to the calculations done by the United Nations Conference on Trade and Development (UNCTAD), the average tariff rates on products in this category are 14.6 per cent in the US, 9.1 per cent in the EU and 7.6 per cent in Japan. Within this category, many products have much higher rates. In the US, post-UR Agreement, rates on 52 per cent of textiles and clothing imports are between 15 to 35 per cent. Other categories of interest to Asian developing countries with high post-UR tariffs are leather, rubber and footwear, and fish and fish products.

Third, despite much liberalization in recent years, developing countries continue to have sufficiently high tariffs on industrial products to engage the developed countries in a bargain. In the countries in South Asia, with the possible exception of Sri Lanka, tariffs are extremely high. In East and Southeast Asia, they are lower but still high by developed-country standards. Thus, room for the first and perhaps a last major North–South bargain exists.

Fourth, on the surface, it may seem that trade barriers in developing countries are higher than in developed countries so that in a negotiation leading to more or less free trade across the board, the former will end up giving more concessions than they will receive and the ensuing bargain will be uneven.

There are two arguments against this line of reasoning, however. First, developed-country markets are much larger than developing-country markets. Therefore, a 1 per cent tariff reduction by the former, especially in products of interest to developing countries, is worth more than a similar reduction by the latter. Even if the extent of additional liberalization by developed countries is smaller, the gains to the developing countries may be larger. Second, developing countries being individually small, if a further round of MTNs is delayed, many of them are likely to carry out a substantial liberalization on a unilateral basis anyway. Therefore, it may be in their self-interest to push for such a negotiation.

Finally, some may argue that with the Information Technology Agreement, and the agreements on basic telecommunications and financial services successfully concluded, there is no need for a comprehensive round. Negotiations can proceed along sectoral lines on a piecemeal basis. In my judgment, this is an inefficient way to conduct negotiations and it does not serve the developing countries well.

First, to the extent that developed countries set negotiating agendas, those sectors of interest to developed countries will be liberalized first. The Information Technology Agreement was clearly pushed by developed countries with developing countries accepting it as fait accompli at the Singapore Ministerial. An extension of this approach is sure to place the sectors of interest to developing countries—for example, textiles and clothing—at the bottom of the liberalization timetable.

Second, a comprehensive negotiation offers a much greater scope for bargains than sectoral negotiations. For instance, concessions in industrial products can be exchanged against those in agriculture or services.

Finally, from the viewpoint of economic adjustment, simultaneous liberalization in several sectors is superior to sector-by-sector liberalization. The former offers opportunities for resource allocation across sectors while the latter limits them to a single sector. Indeed, in a subtle way, liberalization, which is limited to a few sectors that already have very low tariffs, despite its MFN nature, leads to a 'diversion' of trade from sectors with high protection and is likely to be harmful according to the standard economic analysis.

Some may argue that with the UR still under implementation, the time for initiating talks for another comprehensive round is not ripe yet. But it must be recalled that the preparations today will lead to the launching of a round no sooner than the year 2002. And if the UR Agreement is any guide, the negotiations will take another ten years, yielding an agreement sometime in the year 2012. Thus, the time for a consideration of the next round is now.

40

NARROWING DOWN THE SEATTLE ROUND AGENDA

22 September 1999

FROM 30 NOVEMBER TO 3 December 1999, representatives of the 134 member countries of the WTO will meet in Seattle for the Third WTO Ministerial Conference. Unlike its predecessor, this is not a routine conference: it will define the agenda for a new round of MTNs and, thus, influence the future course of the global trading system.

Defining the agenda is the first stage of a negotiating game, which every player must take with utmost seriousness. Seasoned players such as the US carefully choose their opening moves to ascertain that the outcome is the one desired by them. In the same vein, it is crucial for developing countries to arrive at an agenda that will serve their interests and forcefully push for it at Seattle.

Under the current circumstances, it is best to limit the Seattle Round agenda to liberalization in industrial products plus the UR Agreement built-in agenda. Since the latter already requires negotiations in agriculture and services, the inclusion of industrial goods will bring all sectors into the negotiating net. In addition, the UR built-in agenda requires reviews of certain aspects of the Dispute Settlement Understanding (DSU), and Agreements on TRIPS, TRIMs, Subsidies and Countervailing Measures, and Antidumping Measures.

I have offered the arguments in favour of the inclusion of industrial goods into the agenda in a previous column (*The Economic Times*, 14 December 1998) and will not repeat them here. Therefore, let me focus here on why developing countries should limit the Seattle Round agenda in the manner just described. There are at least three reasons.

First, to my knowledge, none of the developing countries have studied systematically either the desirable contents or the implications of likely multilateral agreements in areas other than traditional trade liberalization. Multilateral institutions and developed country think tanks have done some work on the inclusion of investment and competition policies, but the message of this work is equivocal, and, in any case, remains to be carefully studied and scrutinized by developing countries themselves. It is a mistake to enter into negotiations without some prior idea of the endgame. Indeed, precisely for this reason, the Antitrust Division of the United States Department of Justice chose to oppose the inclusion of competition policy in the Seattle agenda.

Second, at present, virtually all the major proposals that go beyond trade liberalization and the UR built-in agenda have been put on the table by developed countries. Not surprisingly, prima facie, they promise to serve the interests of developed countries. There is little doubt that the proposals for a link between market access, and labour and environmental standards, if accepted, will hurt developing countries outright. In the area of competition policy, developing countries have traditionally asked for a multilateral code. But the provisions desired by them in this code are not what developed countries have in mind when they seek the inclusion of competition policy into the WTO. In the area of investment, even if we accept the questionable proposition that a multilateral agreement will benefit developing countries, the distribution of benefits from it will be disproportionately in favour of developed countries. It is not immediately obvious that in a bargaining context, developing countries should accept such a deal without asking for a parallel agreement on the movement of natural persons which will give them the larger share in benefits.

The final argument for a minimalist agenda for the Seattle Round is that developing countries lack negotiating capacity for a round with an extended agenda. Even large developing countries have few experts who understand the game of negotiations as well as their developed country counterparts. An extended agenda spreads thinly whatever experts these countries do have, giving big, developed country players, such as the US and the EU, considerable extra advantage. The developing country experts also lack the experience of their developed country counterparts. The UR Agreement was the first time the former participated in a negotiation of this kind whereas the latter have been at this game for half a century.

In case developing countries fail to limit the Seattle Round agenda as above, a second line of defence is necessary. Under such circumstances, they should resist the *single undertaking* approach of the UR Agreement that committed members to accept or reject the entire negotiated package. Instead, they should insist that negotiations be carried out on two separate tracks. Trade liberalization and the built-in agenda should then be placed on one track and all other issues on a second track.

From the viewpoint of developing countries, the two-track approach has two important advantages. First, it allows an agreement on the trade-liberalization package without requiring an agreement on other issues simultaneously. It even leaves the door open to plurilateral agreements among a subset of countries on subjects relegated to the second track. Second, it makes bargains more transparent by ensuring that concessions are balanced within broad areas without undue pressure for cross-sectoral demands.

In this latter respect, the single undertaking approach served developing countries poorly in the UR negotiations. It effectively forced them to accept the Agreement on TRIPS in return for the removal of the MFA. The removal of the MFA promises to improve global efficiency and benefit developing as well as developed countries. In contrast, the Agreement on TRIPS is expected to reduce global efficiency and redistribute income from developing to developed countries. Thus, while developed countries benefit from the bargain on both counts, developing countries benefit on one count but lose on the other. The bargain has been uneven.

A final point to note is that even under the two-track approach, developing countries must seek a clear statement at Seattle that labour standards will not be a part of any future WTO negotiation. As already agreed in the Singapore Declaration, this subject should be delegated to the International Labour Organization (ILO).

41

WTO NEGOTIATIONS: INVEST IN RESEARCH

20 October 1999

LOCATED IN GENEVA, WTO is far and away from most developing-country capitals. Immediate, day-to-day domestic concerns in these capitals leave little room for long-term thinking on issues that continuously simmer at the WTO. Even large developing countries such as India seem to lack the capacity for systematic research on how best to promote their interests in trade negotiations. As a result, while developed countries gear up to launch yet another round of negotiations, our reaction is to oppose it entirely rather than shape its agenda according to our interests.

Given the far-reaching implications of the decisions made under the auspices of the WTO, the need for conducting research on a continuous basis and developing long-term strategies cannot be overemphasized. Developed-country members of WTO such as the US and the EU take this research very seriously. By the time they are ready to place a subject on the WTO agenda, they have conducted numerous studies on it.

But this is not all. To draw developing countries into the negotiations, developed countries promote research at multilateral institutions on the impact the negotiations would have on developing countries. Thus, soon after the European communities put forward the proposals for the Millennium Round, the UK went on to establish a $5 million trust fund at the World Bank. The principal objective of the fund was to do research on the implications of the round for developing countries and to help them prepare for the negotiations.

To date, developing countries have relied heavily on multilateral institutions, principally the World Bank, for research on WTO matters. This dependence is laden with risks. Being dominated by developed countries and yet having broad acceptance as developmental institutions, at crucial moments during the negotiations, these institutions successfully promote the ethos that the interests of developed and developing countries are in harmony. While this may be true to some extent in matters such as trade liberalization, when it comes to issues such as the Agreement on TRIPS, and the social and environmental clauses in the WTO, the interests of the two sets of countries are in direct conflict.

The danger of reliance on multilateral institutions and developed-country think tanks for conducting research is amply illustrated by the experience during the UR Agreement negotiations. Researchers at these institutions emphasized to developing countries only the benefits of the UR Agreement, often exaggerating them. In the quantitative estimates of the round they produced, the costs associated with the Agreement on TRIPS were systematically excluded. In qualitative discussions, repeated claims got made that the Agreement on TRIPS was in the long-run interest of developing countries. Public relations officers of the respective institutions further magnified the upward bias. When presented by their researchers with multiple estimates, they frequently chose the largest ones to give to the press.

The ethos created by the studies that systematically overstate the net benefits of an agreement to developing countries is likely to have an adverse effect on their bargaining power. It is for this reason that developing countries need to build their own research base on the short- and long-term WTO issues, devoting substantial human and financial resources to them. Developing countries not only need to be able to assess critically the research done by the institutions that may have a vested interest in promoting the interests of developed countries but must also offer and disseminate their own research to influence international public opinion.

Thus, it is not sufficient, as is the practice currently, for developing country researchers and policy specialists to travel abroad to attend conferences in developed countries to understand the latter's viewpoint. It is equally important for developing countries to conduct their own conferences and disseminate their findings to developed country researchers and policy analysts. This means for developing countries to host seminars and conferences not just in their own countries but also in Geneva and Washington, and to invite developed country researchers and policymakers to participate.

Building research capacity and disseminating findings in international forums are costly activities and raise the obvious issue of resources. Given the financial constraints developing countries face, it is tempting to fall back on the funds provided by developed countries either directly or through multilateral agencies as a part of their 'capacity-building' initiatives.

While recognizing that foreign funds do have a positive role to play in many research activities, in matters relating to WTO negotiations, it makes more sense to rely on domestic funds. Leaving aside some foreign agencies that are genuinely motivated by the desire to promote developing country interests, most agencies are likely to exact a price for the funds they give. This price will come in the form of the influence they exert on the outcome of the research.

One way this influence is exerted is by offering funds to researchers who are favourably disposed to the view espoused by the funding agency in the first place. Alternatively, given their dependence on the funding agency, the researchers themselves are vulnerable to endorsing the agency's view. Yet another instrument the funding agency has at its disposal is the selection of research topics that are funded. For instance, to my knowledge, no multilateral agency has funded research on the benefits of promoting labour mobility from developing to developed countries, even though, prima facie, such mobility is enormously beneficial to them and the world. Funding for research on capital mobility, on the other hand, has been plentiful.

The bottom line is that, in the long run, large developing countries such as India must make a substantial commitment of human and financial resources to promote research of their own in the area of WTO issues. With the WTO agenda rapidly moving into areas where the interests of developing and developed countries are in conflict with each other, developing countries need to be able to influence the ethos that governs the negotiations.

42

LAUNCHING THE QATAR ROUND

25 August 2001

INDIA HAS EXPRESSED ITS clear opposition to the launch of a new round of multilateral negotiations at the forthcoming WTO ministerial conference in Qatar.

India's position is not without justification. Yet, unless intended to be an interim, tactical move, it can hurt our ultimate interests. We have much to gain from a new round provided we actively engage in shaping its agenda.

But consider first the reasons why the hardline position taken by India is not without justification.

First, the origins of the scepticism on the part of India and several other developing countries can be traced back to the UR Agreement. Few developing countries had anticipated that the Punta del Este Mandate, which launched the UR, would turn into a gigantic negotiation, leading to the establishment of the WTO with its complex and elaborate rules. Many developing countries are still struggling to implement the unanticipated changes necessitated by the round.

Second, even more surprising to many developing countries was the UR Agreement on TRIPS. From the brief statement on IPR negotiations in the Punta del Este Mandate, few developing countries foresaw a comprehensive global IPR regime as the outcome. Countries such as India were taken by surprise by the reach of the TRIPS Agreement.

Moreover, unlike trade liberalization, which is a 'win-win' negotiation, many developing countries view the enhanced IP protection as redistributing income from the users of patented technology to the holders of patents, located principally in developed countries. The severe limit placed on the access of African countries to AIDS medicines by the TRIPS Agreement has magnified this anxiety.

Third, the slow pace with which developed countries, principally the US and the EU, have implemented the UR Agreement on Textiles and Clothing (ATC) has added to the disappointment of developing countries with multilateral negotiations. Under the agreement, developed countries had agreed to dismantle the Multi-fibre Arrangement by 1 January 2005, but have chosen the slowest possible route to it. The big gains to developing countries, widely advertised by researchers and the press at the time of negotiations, have so far failed to materialize.

Finally, in the aftermath of the UR Agreement, a link between labour standards and trade, which developing countries view as eroding their current trading rights without conferring any benefits, has become a central element of the negotiating agendas proposed by some developed countries. This fact has made developing countries further doubtful that a (new) round is in their interest.

Thus, the events of the recent past provide India and other developing countries ample reasons to view a new round with scepticism, even suspicion. Yet, it may be short-sighted to reject the round outright.

If the Quad countries, the US, EU, Japan and Canada, agree to a round, and offer enough incentives to other major developing countries to join hands, we may simply not be able to stop it. Our experience with the UR negotiations is a sobering reminder in this context. We opposed the conclusion of this round until almost the end. But by then we were left alone and without any option other than to accept the deal on the table. An alternative approach would have been to deploy our energies and negotiating capital into shaping the agreement itself.

An even more important reason why we must support a new round is that it is in our own best interest. The thrust of our efforts should be on shaping the agenda of the round rather than blocking it. The lesson of the past experience is not that we refrain from negotiations but that we negotiate hard, paying careful attention to every detail.

Two years ago, prior to the WTO ministerial conference in Seattle, I had argued that developing countries should support a minimalist negotiating agenda that includes the UR built-in agenda plus trade liberalization in industrial goods. The built-in agenda requires negotiations in agriculture and services, and reviews of certain aspects of the DSU and Agreement on TRIPS. This agenda still makes sense for India.

As a part of its economic reforms, India is likely to continue liberalizing its trade in industrial goods, agriculture and services. The benefit from this liberalization can be greatly leveraged by pursuing it in the context of a multilateral negotiation. This way, we will benefit not only from our own liberalization but from the liberalization of our trading partners as well. The dividend on the latter is double nowadays since it helps dilute trade preferences which have proliferated lately and discriminate against our exports in North America, Europe and other parts of the world.

We can also make speedier dismantling of the MFA or larger MFA quotas for India a pre-condition for launching the next round. Even this objective has a better chance of being addressed if pursued in the context of a negotiation than used as a reason for non-negotiation.

It is also important to recognize that most developing countries do not want a round that includes labour standards in any form whatsoever. Prospects for a round consistent with this goal have never been better. As a part of the mandate for the next round, developing countries may be able to assign this subject to the ILO once and for all.

This leaves principally the subjects of investment, competition policy, and environment and trade on which the EU is insistent. Even here, compromise may be possible. One option is to place these latter subjects on a second track and make participation in negotiations on issues on the second track optional. Alternatively, sufficiently tight wording could be chosen to limit the scope of negotiations in these areas.

The key element of our strategy must be to identify attainable objectives that best serve our interests. The negotiating strategy should be then targeted to achieve these objectives.

43

INDIA ARRIVES AT THE WTO

21 November 2001

'THE ONLY REAL LOSER in Doha was India,' writes Guy de Jonquieres in an editorial comment in the *Financial Times* (November 2001). 'It achieved no obvious gains except for the dubious pleasure of delaying the close of the meeting.'

If you were at the summit, and heard the frequent assertions in the corridors and the press room that India was hell-bent on bringing down the launch of the new round, you would likely believe the harsh assessment by de Jonquieres. But did India truly fare so poorly?

Consider first the outcome of the summit. I have consistently argued (*The Economic Times*, 25 August 2001) that the launch of a new round with a minimalist agenda that focuses on trade liberalization is in India's own best interest. The Doha agenda readily satisfies this criterion. It calls for negotiations in four areas: trade liberalization, trade and environment, WTO rules in certain areas and the DSU. The mandate on trade and environment and

WTO rules is truly narrow, and DSU negotiations are a part of the UR built-in agenda. This leaves trade liberalization as the main negotiating item on the agenda.

The Doha agenda calls for trade liberalization in all sectors: industry, agriculture and services. Given the urgent need to jump-start India's trade reform, the expected benefits to its farmers from increased access to the European market and the need to eliminate tariff peaks in developed countries in products such as textiles and clothing, footwear and fisheries, India stands to benefit big from the proposed liberalization agenda.

For the first time, the Doha Declaration places trade and environment on the negotiating agenda of the WTO. Most developing countries including India had vehemently opposed this. Yet, in my judgment, the principal negotiating item in this area promises to promote rather than hurt the interests of developing countries. This item requires the members to negotiate on 'the relationship between existing WTO rules and specific trade obligations set out in multilateral environmental agreements (MEAs)'. Currently, this relationship remains ill-defined, giving the so-called 'faceless bureaucrats' at the WTO a free hand in not just interpreting but also formulating policy. To safeguard against any protectionist outcome, the declaration explicitly states that the 'negotiations shall not prejudice the WTO rights of any Member that is not a party to the MEA in question'.

The third item on the Doha agenda requires clarification and improvement of disciplines on AD, subsidies and countervailing duties, fisheries subsidies, and the existing WTO provisions on regional trade agreements. Virtually all subjects under this item had been either pushed or backed by developing countries including India. Therefore, its inclusion is prima facie consistent with their interests.

The Doha Declaration represents a significant victory for India not just in terms of the items it includes but also the items it excludes. Thus, India has successfully kept the issue of labour standards off the agenda. Also excluded from negotiations are the so-called Singapore issues spanning investment, competition policy, transparency in government procurement and trade facilitation. A positive decision on the inclusion of these latter issues into the negotiating agenda can only be made by a consensus among members two years from now. The benefits from multilateral agreements in these areas having not been fully established, India had firmly opposed their inclusion.

India can also take pride in two other achievements at Doha. First, a separate declaration on the TRIPS Agreement has clarified that members have the right to grant compulsory licence in the area of pharmaceuticals and that they have the freedom to determine the grounds upon which such licences are granted. This and other provisions in the declaration remove several ambiguities with respect to flexibilities available in the TRIPS Agreement.

Second, India got concessions on a number of 'implementation' issues it had aggressively pushed, first at Seattle and then at Doha. While the benefits from these concessions are tiny in relation to the energy and negotiating capital expended on them, they had been sought with zeal by India.

Commerce Minister (Murasoli) Maran is, thus, to be congratulated for the victory he has scored in Doha. He was not only personally present at the summit from beginning to end, but also had a presence there. Though many developed country delegates, observers and journalists were irked by his aggressive negotiating style, he gave effective expression to the interests of India as well as many other developing countries, which had difficulty in having their voices heard. Had he not been true to his promise—'I will go down fighting'—and personally negotiated non-stop for the last thirty-six hours of the summit with the EU and the US, the Doha agenda would have surely included the Singapore issues as sought by the EU.

There are, nevertheless, lessons to be learned from the Doha experience. Ever since the UR, India has uniformly suffered from a negative image among negotiators. To some degree, this is the outcome of an old tactic whereby negotiators try to tilt the outcome in their favour by painting a particularly vocal rival as 'obstructionist'. But India also bears some responsibility for making the task of these negotiators easy. By opposing the very launch of the new round, India made itself an easy target of criticism by them. It could have instead taken the high road by supporting the trade liberalization agenda unequivocally and positioning itself in favour of a round that focused on this central function of the WTO.

In negotiations, it is common for participants to demand more than what they are willing to accept at the end. Yet, the initial position of India was so extreme as to effectively rob it of any room to claim an unqualified victory at the end of the day. Given the fact that Maran had publicly opposed the launch of the round altogether, his critics can now point to the newly agreed round as evidence of his defeat. They cannot be more wrong; yet, they will be technically right.

44

DOHA: WINNERS AND LOSERS
27 November 2001

IF VICTORY AND DEFEAT were judged by juxtaposing the initial objective and final outcome, India suffered an unequivocal defeat in Doha. But by that count, Doha produced no winners. The US wanted to include labour standards in the agenda, exclude AD and peak tariffs from it, and retain the existing IPR regime. The EU was vehemently opposed to the 'phasing out of subsidies' in agriculture as a negotiating goal and desperately wanted the Singapore issues to be included in the negotiating agenda. Both failed to achieve their respective goals.

But victory and defeat in negotiations must be judged differently. The questions we must ask are whether the outcome was in the negotiating party's interest and whether it had a significant impact on the negotiations. Regarding the first question, I have already argued (*The Economic Times*, 21 November 2001) that the Doha outcome squarely promotes India's interest. Therefore, I focus here on the second question.

India played a key role in influencing the Doha outcome on three fronts.

First, it pushed for and got concessions on several implementation issues. This is not a major achievement but worth acknowledgement.

Second, along with Brazil and South Africa, India led the effort for the Declaration on the TRIPS Agreement aimed at weakening the IPR regime. Though the legal standing of WTO declarations as opposed to 'agreements' is tenuous, this is a potentially major accomplishment.

Finally, and most significantly, India played a crucial role in keeping investment, competition policy, trade facilitation and transparency in government procurement—the so-called Singapore issues—out of the negotiating agenda.

India had to put up a fight on the last issue until the very end. The initial draft declaration admitted the inclusion of all Singapore issues into the negotiating agenda as a possibility. This was revised on 27 October to state that the Fifth Ministerial Conference in 2003 would decide the modalities of negotiations on the issues, assuming an implicit agreement on the launch of the negotiations.

After much haggling in Doha, the 13 November draft backtracked considerably. It stated that the decision on whether to launch negotiations on these issues would be made in 2003. On the surface, this would seem consistent with India's position. But there was a catch. India had consistently argued that as per the Singapore Declaration, the decision to launch negotiations on the Singapore issues required 'explicit consensus'. The draft did not acknowledge this and India remained firm in its opposition.

In the end, the impasse was broken by the creative ambiguity of language. The final declaration introduced the requirement of explicit consensus but was vague about whether it applied to the decision to launch negotiations or modalities. India insisted on clarification, which was provided by the Qatar trade minister

(Yousef Hussain) Kamal (Al Emadi) in his concluding statement. Though this statement carries no legal standing, it sufficed to bring India on board.

While India's fingerprints on the final document can, thus, be hardly denied, given its insignificant role in world trade, how was it able to exert any influence? Two factors, both unique to Doha, aided India.

First, given its political stakes, the US had no intentions of returning home without an agreement. Therefore, even though it was opposed to the EU expansionist agenda, it would have gone along with the language in the 13 November draft had it been acceptable to all other countries. The US knew it would have a veto in 2003 with or without the requirement of a consensus in the Doha declaration. This is where India's opposition became important.

Second, repeated claims that the round was a development round left developed countries boxed in their own rhetoric. They would not look good launching a development round without the endorsement of a poor country accounting for one-fifth of the world's population. Bringing India on board was essential.

Looking ahead, India needs to shed its persistent negative image among negotiators. Our negotiating position must be defined by what we want, not by what we do not want. With the entry of China, larger than us in population and much larger in the world market, the risk of our isolation is greater than ever.

45

DEFENSIVE PLAY SIMPLY WON'T WORK

(With Jagdish Bhagwati)

29 August 2003

OUR DEFENSIVE POSTURE IN the Doha negotiations, displayed in our negativism in almost all our positions, reflects a lack of clear vision of the end result we seek. The evidence of our negativism is pervasive.

Our proposals in the important area of agriculture seek significant reductions in tariffs, export subsidies and domestic support measures from developed countries. But they preclude virtually any liberalization on our part. Instead, they seek a new safeguard provision that will allow us to resurrect quantitative restrictions and a food security box that will legitimize almost any domestic intervention by us.

In the area of industrial products, we have proposed that developing countries be asked to roll back their bound tariffs only two-thirds as much as developed countries and that they be allowed to bind their currently unbound tariffs at the highest prevailing rate among the bound tariffs. We have chosen not to specify precisely how far we are willing to roll back our bound tariffs even within the context of our own proposals. Moreover, since our applied tariffs are already well below our bound tariffs and many of our tariff lines are not even bound, the proposal applies with potency only to developed countries and offers negligible real concessions on our part.

On the so-called Singapore issues—investment, competition policy, transparency in government procurement and trade facilitation (meaning cutting red tape at the point where goods enter a country and providing information on import and export regulations)—until early this week, we had been opposed to any negotiations. On 27 August, Commerce Minister Arun Jaitley seemed to soften just a little on the last three issues but not investment. Our folly in taking these positions follows from our failure to appreciate three key facts:

The massive proliferation of preferential trade arrangements (PTAs) around the world is steadily eroding our current and future market access in all the major markets. A successful completion of the Doha Round that liberalizes the markets of our partners as well as our own is essential to preserve and advance our markets abroad.

Our liberalization is in our own interests. How well we are able to exploit the markets of our partners depends not just on how open those markets are but also on how open our own markets are. This is amply illustrated by our own success in the last decade under the progressive opening of our markets. With the economic reforms taking root, our ability to benefit from increased openness at home and abroad is likely to be that much greater in the future.

Thanks to the excellent leadership provided by the prime minister and a succession of able foreign ministers, we are now much closer to the centre of the global political stage than we were five years ago. Yet, despite the succession of equally able commerce ministers, due to our refusal to negotiate in earnest, we face the prospect of being pushed to the periphery of the trade negotiations stage.

Proliferation of PTAs

The key development that ought to seriously concern—indeed, terrify—us today is the proliferation of preferential PTAs around the world. The new wave of PTAs, following the negotiations for and, successful conclusion of the NAFTA among the US, Canada and Mexico in the early 1990s, has now claimed all the major markets in Europe and the Americas, with East Asia about to take the plunge. By obstructing the liberalization process in the multilateral negotiations, we are unwittingly contributing to the further fragmentation of the global economy into trade blocs that limit market access for our exports, while also (in ways described below) discarding the one surefire recipe for eliminating the pernicious exclusionary effects on us of the many PTAs to which we do not belong.

Preferential trade areas, of which FTAs such as NAFTA are examples, liberalize trade among the member countries but leave the trade barriers against outside countries intact. As such, they place the outside countries at a competitive disadvantage, diverting trade from them towards member countries. For example, when the US eliminates its tariff on the imports of footwear from Mexico as a part of NAFTA, Mexican shoes, which could not previously compete against Indian shoes in the US market, are now able to outcompete them. Being free from the custom duty that must be paid on Indian shoes, Mexican shoes become competitive even though they cost more to produce.

Today, this displacement of our exports by FTA partners of the US, Europe and even many Latin American countries is taking place on a massive scale. The WTO had been officially notified of as many as 250 PTAs by the end of 2002. Of these, as many as 130 had been notified after January 1995. The proposed Free Trade Area of the Americas (FTAA), and emerging arrangements in East and Southeast Asia, will add to the economic exclusion we already suffer.

EU has been by far the most active in signing free trade agreements. Its agreements include the Europe Agreements with the eastern and central European countries of Bulgaria, Czech Republic, Slovak Republic, Poland, Hungary, Romania, Slovenia, Estonia, Latvia and Lithuania; Euro-Mediterranean Association Agreements with Tunisia, Israel, Morocco and Jordan; and FTAs with Switzerland, Denmark, Iceland, Mexico and Chile. Under the Barcelona Process, launched in 1995, the EU plans to have FTAs with all of its twelve Mediterranean partners and establish a WTO-consistent Euro-Mediterranean FTA by 2010. Likewise, under the Cotonou Agreement, which recently replaced Lomé IV, it plans to establish FTA agreements with a large number of countries in Africa, the Caribbean and the Pacific (ACP) that are not the least developed countries (LDCs).

The US moved slowly after the conclusion of NAFTA, but it too has intensified the process under the Bush administration. It now has FTAs with Jordan, Chile and Singapore, with negotiations under way with Australia, Morocco, five members of the Southern African Customs Union (Botswana, Lesotho, Namibia, South Africa and Swaziland), and five nations of the Central American Common Market (Costa Rica, El Salvador, Guatemala, Honduras and Nicaragua). Future plans include the FTAA, which will encompass the western hemisphere except Cuba, Enterprise for the ASEAN Initiative announced in October 2002 and a number of additional bilateral FTAs.

Within the developing world, Latin America has been the most aggressive in forging new FTAs. Mexico alone has signed a total of fifteen FTAs. Chile follows with eight agreements. Asia has been slow to react. But China has now made a decision to negotiate FTAs with the member countries of the Association of Southeast Asian Nations (ASEAN). Japan recently signed an FTA with Singapore and may gradually move to forge an arrangement with South Korea.

Numerous suggestions have been made to contain the harmful effects of PTAs. These include dismantling existing PTAs, prohibiting new ones and asking the current PTAs to eliminate preferences on a target date. While these are excellent suggestions, unfortunately, there are no takers for these suggestions. For India, there are only two ways of overcoming the discrimination facing its exports in the world markets: supporting the elimination of tariffs in the rich countries wholeheartedly so that preferences are killed at the source or joining each of the existing and future major trade blocs. We argue below in favour of the first option.

Both the US and the EU have put forward proposals for far-reaching cuts in tariffs on industrial products. The former has proposed to eliminate the tariffs entirely, offering that all countries bring their tariffs down to 8 per cent or below by 2010 and eliminate them by 2015. There are three compelling reasons why countries such as India must push for a modified version of this proposal that gives developing countries a longer phase-out period—say, until 2015 to lower the tariffs to 8 per cent and until 2025 to eliminate them—under the Doha provision of the special and differential treatment for developing countries.

First, India has long sought the elimination of tariff peaks against labour-intensive products in developed countries. The experience of the last forty years demonstrates persuasively that the removal of these peaks requires tough bargaining and reciprocal concessions by developing countries. For decades, trade economists, developing country leaders and the UNCTAD have condemned the tariff peaks against developing country products in the rich countries but without results. On the contrary, textiles and apparel imports into developed countries have been subject to severe restrictions through 3,000 bilateral treaties under the rubric of the MFA. The only substantive break developing countries got in achieving improved market access in labour-intensive products in the last forty years was the end of the MFA by 1 January 2005 under the UR ATC. And that break came through reciprocal bargaining. India will be deluding itself if it were to hang on to the notion, fed by World Bank officials and some NGOs in recent years, that hard-core developed country barriers against poor country products can be eliminated by exhortations and moral suasion without reciprocity on our part.

Second, such reciprocal bargaining offers an opportunity for the orderly elimination of our own protection, which hurts our consumers and acts as a deterrent to our exports. Simultaneous liberalization by our partners will allow export industries to rapidly expand to absorb the resources released by import-competing and non-traded sectors.

Finally, for a country like India, which almost uniquely does not belong to any PTA of substance, the zero-tariff proposal offers a golden opportunity to end all discrimination against its exports.

Seeking Trade Preferences

Because FTAs introduce discrimination in tariff policy across trading partners and, thus, fragment the global trading system, the present authors have taken a critical view of them. Yet, an individual country must base its decision on national rather than global welfare considerations.

The FTA route may make sense for India if it could forge FTAs with all its major trading partners within a short period of time. But this is not a feasible option. For instance, the current trade legislation in the US requires it to make labour and environmental standards an integral part of its FTAs. The Indian position is rightly opposed to this requirement, ruling out an FTA with the US.

Though Japan does not have a non-trade agenda, chances that it will enter into an FTA with India prior to entering similar agreements with its immediate, regional neighbours are negligible, especially when India is itself not seeking such an agreement aggressively. Indeed, given the pace at which Japan moves, even an aggressive pursuit of an FTA by India is unlikely to bear fruit in the near future.

Our best prospects of an FTA in the near term are with the EU. But given our very high tariffs, an FTA with just one large trading partner carries the major risk of what economists call trade diversion. The tariff preference to the EU will simply allow its inefficient exporters to out-compete the more efficient suppliers from Asia and the US. The cost of this inefficiency will fall on us.

Agriculture

Our proposals in agriculture consist of long lists of demands for liberalization from developed countries and even longer lists of exemptions for developing countries. They are divided into four areas: food security, market access, export competition and domestic support. Under the 'food security box' proposals, we seek a hike in some of our previously negotiated tariff bindings, exemption from previously negotiated minimum market access commitments, exemption from reduction commitments on all measures taken for poverty alleviation, rural development, rural employment and diversification of agriculture, and a new safeguard provision that will allow us to impose quantitative import restrictions under specified conditions. Our 'market access' proposals state that developed countries roll back their tariffs by at least 50 per cent as a 'down payment' by 2001 and commit to larger reductions eventually. They further seek substantial immediate expansion and eventual abolition of the tariff rate quota from developed countries with no liberalization commitments whatsoever on our part. Our proposals in the area of 'export competition' and 'domestic support' make similar one-way demands with respect to export subsidies and domestic support measures.

Frankly, why India has chosen to expend its very limited negotiating capital on these unrealistic proposals that fail to promote its own interest is a mystery to us. According to most calculations, in a world in which developed as well as developing countries give up agricultural subsidies and protection, Indian agriculture will be highly competitive. Even today, our share in the world agricultural exports is larger than that of industrial products. Despite all the protection and subsidies in the rich countries, our own liberalization has led agricultural exports to grow annually at nearly 9 per cent during the 1990s compared to the less than 2.5 per cent during the 1980s. So, it makes little sense for us not to offer to liberalize agriculture if this helps to push the cause of global liberalization. The objective of food security can be met by simply maintaining 10 per cent of the annual food grain consumption in buffer stocks at the Centre and an equivalent amount at the state level.

As regards the new safeguard provision, the existing WTO rules already offer two avenues to protecting farmers from import surges: AD and the GATT Article XIX safeguard. These provisions can be rapidly invoked to deal with import surges that may undermine the interests of our farmers, small or large. India has also acquired substantial experience in using them since the UR Agreement.

To assist the small and marginal farmers, we need income support programmes regardless of import surges. For example, in case of a drought, we will actually want to import more, not less, food grains. And to protect the small and marginal farmers, we will need income support programmes. The problem of small and marginal farmers is not that they do not get sufficiently high prices for their grain but that they do not have enough of it to sell.

Against this background, it is difficult to see how our immediate, unequivocal and very vocal rejection of the recent EU–US compromise plan on agriculture serves our own interests. Apart from significant concessions by developed countries in areas of market access, export subsidies and domestic support measures, the EU–US proposal on agriculture includes the special safeguard for sensitive products sought by India, and provides for lower tariff cuts and longer implementation periods for developing countries. This may not be enough but it is a step in the right direction. Members of the Cairns Group, who have spearheaded the effort to put an end to agricultural protectionism in rich countries, could see this far more clearly than us. They also criticized the plan but for falling short of expectations with respect to liberalization by developed countries rather than for making excessive demands on developing countries. We were alone in viewing the plan as an attempt to pry open developing country markets without significant commitments on the part of the US and the EU.

Singapore Issues

At the Montreal mini-ministerial of the WTO, the last such meeting prior to the full WTO ministerial conference in Cancun, the leader of the Indian delegation, Arun Shourie, flatly and wholly opposed the negotiations on the Singapore issues: investment, competition policy, transparency in government procurement and trade facilitation. This week, according to a report in the London *Financial Times*, Commerce Minister Arun Jaitley seems to have given a slight opening on the first three of these issues, but ruled out negotiations on investment in any form.

Again, such wholesale negativism hardly serves India's interest. As we have noted above, even China, which recently made significant market-opening commitments as a part of its WTO entry conditions, has quickly identified its self-interest and taken a more flexible position on issues such as competition and investment policies.

It is in our interest to participate in negotiations and shape the international regime in investment so as to maximize the autonomy of recipient countries. We may also want to limit the negotiations on investment to direct foreign investment and exclude portfolio investment from them. Unless we actively participate in shaping the modalities of negotiations on the Singapore issues, these objectives can hardly be fulfilled.

Marginalization on the WTO Stage

The name of the negotiating game is compromise. Even if some specific measures are harmful to our interests, we should accept them in return for bigger gains elsewhere. If we exhibit flexibility, our negotiating partners will take us seriously. But by being totally inflexible in offering concessions in any area—including even trade liberalization, which is entirely in our interest and an explicit item on our economic reforms agenda—we continue to be marginalized on the global trade negotiations stage. Small countries such as New Zealand and Thailand have walked away with the director generalship of the WTO, while India has stood on the sidelines. Minor players—Uruguay and Qatar—have hosted the WTO ministerial conference while New Delhi has been left out. Today, we chair hardly any major WTO committees.

In the misguided belief that we could stop the conclusion of the UR, we refused to negotiate in earnest until the very end. When the time came, large developing countries such as Brazil and many smaller African countries, which had promised to support our position, left us holding the bags. Entirely isolated, we were left with no option but to accept the deal we had helped shape only half-heartedly. We repeated this history in Doha, earning once again the distinction of being the last WTO member to sign the Doha Declaration. Unless we show more flexibility in Cancun, we run the risk of repeating this sad history yet again.

46

MAKING SENSE OF THE COLLAPSE IN CANCUN

24 September 2003

THE OUTCOME OF THE Cancun Ministerial Conference has been the one that India's former commerce minister Murasoli Maran had sought for the Doha Ministerial. The current commerce minister Arun Jaitley did not seek to bring the Cancun Ministerial down, but such has been the case.

Thankfully, Cancun is not Doha: whereas a collapse at Doha would have cost the member nations the new round itself, with some luck, the damage from the collapse at Cancun will be limited to a delay in the conclusion of the ongoing round. In view of the fact that the current date of 1 January 2005 for the conclusion is overly ambitious—each of the two previous rounds took substantially longer than the three-year target set for this one—the delay is not entirely surprising either.

Virtually all WTO members, including India, bear responsibility for the failure. That said, Jaitley must be given his due: He demonstrated more flexibility than his predecessors. He offered to undertake modest liberalization in industrial products. He also agreed to negotiate on two of the four so-called Singapore issues: transparency in government procurement and trade facilitation. But this was far short of what was needed to move the round forward.

Jaitley also abandoned the past practice of declaring India the leader of a disparate group of small developing countries with whom we have little in common in terms of negotiating interests except wholesale opposition to the negotiations. Instead, he joined a group of more influential, larger developing countries—the so-called G-21—that included Brazil and China. Whether or not this alliance will survive in the future remains to be seen, however.

Indeed, two factors make the alliance fragile.

First, neither China nor Brazil shares our intense opposition to negotiations on investment. Only Malaysia stood with us in opposing negotiations in this area at Cancun. As such, if a compromise is reached in other areas on a future date, G-21 is unlikely to support us in this area.

Second, the basis of the alliance between India and China on the one hand and agricultural-exporting countries, especially developing country members of the Cairns Group, on the other is rather fragile. With some exceptions, these latter countries have already substantially liberalized their markets and have at most limited concessions to offer. Therefore, in seeking agricultural liberalization from the US and the EU, they needed support from large developing countries such as India and China, which have substantial concessions to offer. But if India and China are unwilling to offer substantial concessions, the alliance cannot produce the desired liberalization in the US and EU.

While virtually all parties concerned share the responsibility for the collapse in Cancun, the first finger must be pointed at the misguided leadership at some of the international institutions. Joined by many Western NGOs, these leaders have recently bombarded the media airwaves with the assertions that the current trading system is unfair to poor countries, that rich country protection now exceeds poor country protection and that it is unfair to ask poor countries to liberalize when rich countries remain protected.

Not only is the factual basis of these feel-good assertions fragile, but their constant repetition has duped many developing country leaders into thinking that 'fairness' can be brought to bear heavily on the outcome of the negotiations. But as the distinguished economist Robert Baldwin of the University of Wisconsin explains, fairness can play at most a tiny role in negotiations. 'When it comes to hard bargaining,' says Baldwin, 'notions of fairness do not get you very far ... There is clearly a role for notions of fairness in any negotiation but, when they begin to dominate, the outcome is usually failure, since countries differ so much on what is "fair".'

Many self-declared well-wishers of developing countries among the Western NGOs and international institutions have gone on to celebrate the collapse of the talks, announcing that concerns of developing countries have at last been heard. It seems not to concern them that none of the objectives they had sought to advance—agricultural liberalization and end to tariff peaks against labour-intensive imports in the rich countries—have made any progress. They are content that fairness has been preserved by temporarily freeing developing countries of the pressure to liberalize their own markets.

Of course, developed countries cannot escape from the responsibility for the collapse. The US approach to negotiations in agriculture is especially puzzling. At Doha, the US had forged an alliance with the Cairns Group, consisting of seventeen agriculture-exporting countries, to push the EU into agreeing to the language in the Doha Declaration that aimed to eliminate agricultural export subsidies. Just prior to Cancun, it abandoned that alliance, however, joining hands with the EU, thereby essentially embracing and blessing its cautious approach in this sector. Had the US stayed with the Cairns Group and kept the pressure on the EU in this important area, a different dynamic, more conducive to success, could have been unleashed.

Likewise, the EU must share the blame for pushing an overly ambitious agenda. There is little pressure from domestic corporations for a multilateral agreement on investment or competition. Yet, pushed by the Brussels bureaucracy, EU Commissioner Pascal Lamy has pushed these contentious issues on the agenda, alienating many developing countries.

From India's perspective, the bottom line is that it has most to gain from a successful completion of the Doha Round. Its goods already suffer hugely from the discrimination resulting from trade preferences to most of its competitors in the EU and North American markets. In the aftermath of the Cancun failure, this is likely to get worse with further acceleration of bilateral arrangements. Maybe that is what it will take to convince our commerce ministry officials that liberalizing our own markets in return for liberalization by our partners, thus, putting an end to the preferences is not such a bad idea after all.

47

THE WORLD TERRORIST ORGANIZATION OR A GODSEND?

22 October 2003

IMMEDIATELY PRECEDING THE CANCUN conference, three former prime ministers—H.D. Deve Gowda, I.K. Gujral and V.P. Singh—lent their support to a rally decrying WTO as the 'World Terrorist Organization'. Deve Gowda and Gujral had served as prime ministers *after* the birth of the WTO on 1 January 1995 and therefore had the opportunity to withdraw from it. They did no such thing perhaps because they knew that India benefited hugely from the membership. But now that they are in the Opposition, they must not feel the same responsibility any longer.

That the WTO is beneficial should be obvious from the fact that as many as 148 countries are its members today. China made very substantial concessions to join it two years ago and Russia is waiting in the queue. While new members have steadily been added, few have exited the institution.

Why member governments nearly universally view the WTO as beneficial can be best appreciated by understanding what it does. In its current form, the WTO has three major functions: administering the trade agreements negotiated by its members in the past, settling trade disputes and acting as a forum for negotiations for further trade agreements. All of these functions contribute to the smooth flow of trade within a rules-based trading system.

The existing agreements require the WTO administers span three areas: trade in goods, trade in services and IPR. The agreements in the last two areas were concluded relatively recently, as a part of the UR Agreement that established the WTO, while those relating to goods have had a much longer history. The GATT, the principal agreement governing trade in goods, had come into force as early as 1 January 1948. Initially, only twenty-three nations including India had signed it, but the membership expanded steadily over time.

Though GATT has now been in existence for more than five decades, it never became controversial in the way WTO has become controversial today. For decades, it has provided a set of rules within which world trade has grown rapidly. The cornerstone of this agreement is the so-called MFN principle, which says that member nations are not to discriminate among GATT signatories in their trade policy. This means that if the US lowers its tariff on Japanese automobiles in return for a tariff reduction by Japan on the imports of US steel, the two nations must automatically extend these tariff reductions to all other GATT signatories to rule out discrimination.

A key function of GATT (like that of the WTO now) was to serve as a forum for negotiations of new agreements among member nations. This mandate translated into the conclusion of seven negotiating rounds by 1979, principally aimed at tariff reductions among the signatories. A key feature of these negotiations was that until the seventh round, known as the Tokyo Round and concluded in 1979, developing countries were allowed to stay out of the active negotiations if they so chose. The result was that even though developing countries undertook no liberalization commitments whatsoever, under the MFN rule of GATT, they became the beneficiaries of the massive liberalization commitments made by developed countries.

Developing countries such as South Korea, Taiwan, Hong Kong and Singapore, which nevertheless chose to adopt outward-oriented policies themselves, were able to take advantage of this progressive opening of the developed country markets and rapidly transformed themselves into semi-industrialized economies. Countries such as China and India that chose to be inward, oriented, on the other hand, missed the boat until they too began to open up their economies in the 1980s.

It was in launching the UR Agreement in the 1980s that the US and other developed countries insisted that developing countries actively join the negotiations and undertake liberalizing commitments of their own. Moreover, they also insisted on bringing trade in services and IPR within the ambit of international rules. The round became contentious with a key source of controversy being IPR that the US insisted on and developing countries vehemently opposed. In the end, the US prevailed and the round concluded in 1993 with the signatory countries agreeing to establish the WTO as a permanent institution, and trade in services and IPR brought under its purview along with trade in goods.

Reflecting their greater bargaining power due to a very large share in world trade and income, developed countries benefited more from the UR Agreement than developing countries. Developing countries benefited from their own liberalization, the liberalization by developed countries, especially the agreement to end the MFA that restricts their exports of textiles and apparel to developed countries through a web of bilateral quotas, and a strong dispute-settlement system that protects their trading rights on equal footing with developed countries. But they lost on account of the agreement on IPR, which allows developed countries to collect large rents from them on innovations and is expected to put an end to the availability of inexpensive copies of patented medicines.

Unfortunately, in the post-WTO era, international institutions and civil society groups have failed to emphasize sufficiently the benefits of the WTO to developing countries and have chosen, instead, to focus exclusively on the protection that remains in developed countries. Worse yet, the proposition that the UR Agreement benefited developed countries more has been translated by many into the proposition that developing countries were actually hurt by it. Such focus has contributed to the demonization of an institution that has been a godsend for developing countries.

Those who view the WTO as an evil organization need only contemplate the counterfactual. Suppose there was no WTO. Will developed countries then need to *negotiate* a link between trade and labour standards or trade and environmental standards with developing countries? No. In the absence of a rules-based system offered by the WTO, these countries would simply impose trade sanctions unilaterally against countries that do not adhere to their desired standards.

48

THE CHALLENGE BEFORE PASCAL LAMY

21 September 2005

PASCAL LAMY, THE NEW director-general of the WTO, has begun to set the agenda for the Doha Round negotiations at the Hong Kong Ministerial Conference during 13–18 December 2005. Recognizing the vast differences that remain among participants, he has publicly stated what has been known for some time: contrary to the original deadline, the round will not be concluded by 31 December 2005.

Instead, Lamy has urged the member countries to forge an agreement at Hong Kong that would bring them two-thirds way to the final agreement. He has proposed the members complete the remaining one-third of the task by the end of 2006. That would still close the round two years faster than the preceding UR Agreement and is therefore an ambitious undertaking.

Lamy faces a truly uphill task. A relatively recent development that adds to the challenge he faces is the sophistication, organization and coherence that developing countries have achieved in articulating their demands in the negotiations. In the UR Agreement negotiations, only agricultural-exporting developing countries were successful in effectively voicing their demands through the so-called Cairns Group.

And even then, they had to align themselves with a subset of agricultural-exporting developed countries whose interests outside of agriculture were in conflict with theirs. The remaining developing countries were at best loosely organized and eventually became the victims of the 'divide and rule' strategy of developed countries.

In contrast, virtually all of the major developing countries from Asia, Africa and Latin America—Brazil, China, Egypt, India, Indonesia, Pakistan, Mexico, South Africa and Tanzania—are today members of the developing country grouping known as G-20. At the same time, when compared with the total number of developing countries, G-20 is small and therefore less unwieldy than the past developing country groups such as G-77.

The benefit of these two key attributes was illustrated soon after the group's inception during the preparations for the Cancun Ministerial meeting two years ago: it successfully led the effort to persuade the EU to drop three out of the four Singapore issues from the Doha negotiating agenda.

Another factor strengthening the negotiating power of developing countries is their increased share in world trade. They now account for more than 30 per cent of the world merchandise trade. Add to this fact the vast population in these countries and you know that the Quad countries—the US, the EU, Canada and Japan—can no longer determine the outcome of the round by themselves as they did in the past.

The task faced by Lamy is further complicated by the fact that liberalizing the agenda itself is politically more challenging in developed countries than in the past. The UR liberalization focused principally on industrial goods and services, and essentially sidestepped agriculture. Neither the liberalization of industrial goods nor services posed serious political hurdles. The main controversial proposal concerned the removal of the quotas on textiles and clothing, but it was handsomely compensated by the introduction of very high standards of IP worldwide.

In contrast, the key sector the Doha Round aims to liberalize is agriculture. Farm lobbies are powerful and interventions include subsidies on output and exports whose removal is highly contentious. Even in industrial goods, developed countries must now deal with peak tariffs that apply virtually exclusively to labour-intensive products that employ unskilled or low-skilled workers.

Developed countries also see the already large developing country market turn even larger over the course of the implementation period of the Doha Round if it is successfully completed. Therefore, they are reluctant to proceed with liberalization unless the major developing countries such as Brazil, China, India and other developing countries in Asia and Latin America reciprocate. Because China has gone a long way towards opening its markets as a result of its WTO entry conditions, the burden is greatest on Brazil and India. It is here that Lamy faces his greatest challenge.

Encouraged by the heads of multilateral institutions such as the World Bank and IMF, influential NGOs such as Oxfam and the vast majority of well-intentioned but ill-informed press, developing countries have come to believe that protection is principally a developed country problem and it is these countries that must undertake the liberalization they have been preaching for the last five decades.

Unsurprisingly, in the 'Bhurban Declaration' issued by G-20 following the 9–10 September 2005 summit in Bhurban, Pakistan, the member countries demand many concessions including the elimination of export subsidies within five years from developed countries but offer few concessions of their own.

Lamy himself accords a high priority to ending export subsidies in agriculture by a certain date and to substantial reductions in domestic support measures. Nonetheless, his success in moving the Doha Round forward at Hong Kong will very much depend on his ability to persuade developing countries to undertake liberalization commitments commensurate with those they seek from developed countries.

The pressure on India to undertake liberalization commitments at Hong Kong will be immense. The massive liberalization undertaken during the last fifteen years notwithstanding, India remains among the most protected markets. Moreover, even though it currently accounts for less than 1 per cent of the world's imports, it promises to be a vast market in the forthcoming decades. Therefore, developed countries see liberalization by India as perhaps the most important key to the successful completion of the Doha Round.

India's own experience, and that of all its neighbours, shows that liberalization brings benefits. These benefits are multiplied if the country's trading partners liberalize along with it. Therefore, while India must drive a hard bargain at Hong Kong, it would be tragic if it allowed the negotiations to fall on its unwillingness to liberalize.

49

SALVAGING THE DOHA AGRICULTURAL TALKS

30 November 2005

AS THE SIXTH WTO Ministerial Conference to be held in Hong Kong during 13–17 December 2005 approaches, the EU, the US and the group of twenty mainly larger developing countries are deadlocked over the Doha negotiations on agriculture. Breaking the deadlock requires dispelling several myths spread by the press, international institutions and non-governmental organizations. Among the myths are: rich countries annually spend hundreds of billions of dollars on trade-distorting subsidies, agricultural protectionism is largely a rich country phenomenon, and the LDCs are the worst victims of these subsidies and protection.

Twice recently the *New York Times* has editorialized that the 'developed world funnels nearly $1 billion a day in subsidies', which 'encourages overproduction' and drives down prices.

The World Bank president Paul Wolfowitz similarly referred to developed countries expending '$280 billion on support to agricultural producers' in a recent op-ed in the *Financial Times*. the NGO Oxfam routinely accuses rich countries of giving more than $300 billion annually in subsidies to agribusinesses.

Astonishingly, these estimates bear no relationship to the subsidies subject to the Doha negotiations. Instead, they have originated in the Producer Support Estimate (PSE) devised and published by the Organization for Economic Co-operation and Development (OECD). The PSE includes all measures that raise the producer price above the world price including border measures such as tariffs and quotas. Most economists would find the idea of identifying such a measure with subsidies laughable.

The economically correct measure of subsidies that drive down world prices must be confined to the subsidies contingent on exports or output. When this is done, the extent of subsidies turns out to be considerably smaller than $1 billion per day. Thus, rich country export subsidies that have been so much in the news currently amount to less than $5 billion, perhaps as little as $3 billion.

Subsidies contingent on output (identified as 'amber box' subsidies by the WTO) are larger but not enough to add up to $1 billion per day. Based on the latest data available from the WTO, these subsidies amounted to $44 billion in 2000 in the EU, $21 billion in 2001 in the US, and less than $15 billion in 1998 in Japan, Switzerland, Norway and Canada combined.

Recognizing that there have been no major cases of backsliding and the EU has made further progress in decoupling its subsidies from output, we can comfortably conclude that rich country domestic subsidies that encourage production and lower world prices currently are substantially below $100 billion.

By focusing exclusively on subsidies, the media has distracted attention from the critical fact that the most important obstacle to agricultural trade comes from border barriers, also called market access measures by the WTO.

And since the developing countries are not big offenders on the subsidy front, this focus has promoted the false impression that agricultural protection is an exclusively rich country problem. In reality, when it comes to border barriers, the developing countries more than match the developed countries.

Among the latter, in 2001, the trade-weighted average tariff was 36 per cent in Japan, 29 per cent in the European Free Trade Area, 12 per cent in the EU and 3 per cent in the US. Among the former, the rate was 94 per cent in South Korea, 44 per cent in India, 39 per cent in China and 30 per cent in Pakistan.

Interestingly, protection in the developing country members of the Cairns Group, which contains countries with the greatest comparative advantage in agriculture, is not low: in 2001, trade-weighted average tariff was 13 per cent in Argentina and Brazil, and 11 per cent in Malaysia, Thailand and Indonesia.

Rich-country subsidies and protection drive down the world prices. To the extent that LDCs import agricultural products, especially cereals, they benefit from these low prices. Rich country protection also raises their internal prices. Under its Everything But Arms initiative, the EU grants the LDCs duty-free access to its market. This means the LDCs also benefit from the high internal EU prices they receive on their exports.

The widely cited contrary case of cotton exporters is an exception rather than the rule. The EU does not have any cotton producers to protect so that it has a zero tariff on cotton. The US subsidies drive down the world cotton prices as well as the EU internal price. Therefore, LDC cotton exporters receive the same low price whether they export to the EU or another country. Beyond cotton, the assertion that the removal of agricultural subsidies and protection by rich countries would benefit the LDCs is false. Even if it were true, telling rich countries that their trade policies hurt the LDCs would not produce the desired outcome. History offers few examples whereby countries choose trade policies to promote the interests of other countries rather than their own citizenry.

Therefore, dismantling protection would require reciprocal concessions from partner countries rather than exhortations.

The US has a comparative advantage in agriculture. It therefore insists on within-agriculture reciprocity. To persuade its farmers to accept deep cuts in subsidies, it would need deep cuts in agricultural tariffs by the EU and G-20, including the Cairns Group of countries.

The EU, on the other hand, lacks a comparative advantage in agriculture. To mobilize support for deep cuts in its agricultural interventions, it would require cross-sector reciprocity. Offers in industrial goods and services will have to be put on the table.

As for the G-20, benefits to them will come from agricultural liberalization, the end to tariff peaks on clothing and footwear by the rich countries, and improved access to each other's markets. In return, they will have to offer access to their own goods and services markets. A bargain that benefits all those negotiating actively, thus, exists and can be forged.

50

HAILING HONG KONG, COMPLETING DOHA

28 December 2005

CONTRARY TO THE DOOM and gloom scenarios advanced by many, the WTO ministerial conference at Hong Kong concluded successfully on 18 December 2005, making significant progress towards completing the Doha Round. True, the conference did not produce dramatic results.

But that was just as some among us had predicted: with the final round of negotiations still a year away, few accomplished negotiators could be expected to put their best offers on the table.

Two key factors explain the failure to achieve progress in agriculture at Cancun turned into success at Hong Kong. First, having learned from its mistake at Cancun, where it had made common cause with the EU, the US chose to forge partnerships with developing countries at Hong Kong.

Because the US has a strong comparative advantage in agriculture while the EU lacks it, developing countries with a comparative advantage in agriculture were its natural allies. On one hand, the tactic helped persuade developing countries that the US was genuinely interested in agricultural liberalization and on the other hand it intensified pressure on the EU to liberalize.

Second, the grouping of twenty larger developing countries known as G-20, initially formed at Cancun to counter the US–EU alliance, came of age at Hong Kong. While the G-20 naturally used its leverage to promote the interests of its membership, it also worked constructively to advance the negotiations.

Thus, early during the conference, led by ministers Kamal Nath of India and Celso Amorim of Brazil, the G-20 joined hands with the grouping of ninety smaller developing countries known as G-90, and successfully negotiated duty- and quota-free access for the products of the fifty LDCs into developed country markets.

Later, in an important act of leadership, minister Nath broke ranks with Brazil and with China on his side, went on to support the reasonable EU demand that the date for the end to agricultural export subsidies be set at 2013 instead of 2010. That support provided the necessary balance to clinch the deal on export subsidies.

The Hong Kong conference has moved the WTO members significantly closer to a final Doha agreement. In addition to agreeing to end agricultural export subsidies by 2013, the member countries have made progress on tackling domestic agricultural subsidies.

They have agreed to create three tiers of countries whereby the EU, which is by far the biggest user of such subsidies, will be required to make the deepest cuts; the US and Japan, the next largest users of the subsidies, will be subject to the next deepest cuts; and the remaining countries will be subject to the smallest cuts. While the final agreement is to be reached on 30 April 2006, under the current proposals, the cuts for the EU are expected to be in the 70–80 per cent range, and for the US and Japan in the 53–75 per cent range.

On market access in agriculture, the member countries have agreed to base tariff cuts on four bands defined according to the existing level of tariffs with deeper cuts applied to higher tariffs. The precise modalities, meaning threshold levels of these bands and the extent of the cuts, are to be negotiated by 30 April 2006.

On market access in non-agricultural products, the member countries have explicitly adopted the Swiss formula that would cut higher tariffs more and lower tariffs less. Again, the modalities, meaning the precise levels of cuts, are to be negotiated by 30 April 2006. There has been less progress in services, but even here deadlines have been set for the submission of the offers.

A key achievement of the conference has been to address several demands of the LDCs. For example, developed countries have agreed to open their markets for 97 per cent or more products on a duty-free basis to them. The LDCs will also not be required to undertake reciprocal tariff cuts on any products. While trade economists question the advisability of both these measures as ways to assist the LDCs, they remain intensely popular with the latter. The conference also made significant progress towards 'aid for trade' for the LDCs.

These achievements notwithstanding, hard bargaining at Hong Kong has left developed country leaders uniformly sceptical that the Doha Round can be brought to a successful conclusion. The risk is that this scepticism can become self-fulfilling. That will be sad for developing countries, including India, which have fought hard to give the negotiations their current shape.

Thus, at Doha, late Commerce Minister Murasoli Maran had valiantly fought against the inclusion of the Singapore issues—investment, competition policy, government procurement and trade facilitation—into the negotiating agenda. With that objective achieved except for the innocuous trade facilitation issue, the round

Hailing Hong Kong, Completing Doha

is now squarely focused on trade liberalization that produces win-win bargains.

Considerable progress has also been made on the trade liberalization front along the lines sought by India and other developing countries. A failure at this juncture will not only wipe out these gains, but also strengthen the hands of the US and EU labour lobby that may then return with vengeance with their self-serving and damaging demand for the inclusion of labour standards in the WTO.

With LDC demands effectively addressed or on the way to being addressed, the larger developed and developing countries, such as the US, EU, Japan, Brazil, China, India and South Africa, must now focus efforts on completing the modalities of the negotiations. They must quickly get down to the business of putting precise numbers on the agreed-upon bands and the associated magnitude of liberalization of domestic subsidies and market access.

Given the progress already made as summarized in the annexes of the Hong Kong declaration, this is a task well within reach. Minister Nath may even wish to take the lead and call a mini-ministerial conference in New Delhi to complete this crucial step in the negotiations.

51

A HISTORIC OPPORTUNITY FOR INDIA

(With Jagdish Bhagwati)

1 July 2006

WITH THE DOHA ROUND at a critical juncture, India has the historic opportunity to seize the leadership role in bringing the Round closer to a successful conclusion. Such an initiative promises to place India among key players on the world stage as it seeks the Indo-US nuclear deal and a permanent seat on the Security Council.

The challenge and the opportunity for India are best understood against the progress that has been made in the Doha Round. For, progress there has been, despite the cacophony of condemnation, now mostly from financially flush NGOs such as Oxfam and a handful of anti-globalization economists.

The 2003 WTO meeting in Cancun, following the launch of the Doha negotiations in 2001, was regarded as a failure simply

A Historic Opportunity for India 231

because, after two years, it failed to conclude. But the earlier UR took over eight years, and the Tokyo Round before that took over five years! As it happens, Cancun produced some progress.

The EU had insisted on an agreement on the four 'Singapore issues', opposed by many developing countries including India, before it reduced its agricultural subsidies and trade barriers. Pascal Lamy abandoned three of these at Cancun: investment, competition policy and government procurement.

Cancun also gave the developing countries a place at the table. The developing country group, G-20, emerged as a serious force for the first time in the history of multilateral negotiations. It is equally significant that after Cancun we have witnessed the death of the traditional quartet of developed countries, the so-called Quad, consisting of the US, Canada, the EU and Japan, which had made many of the key decisions in the past.

Today, we have a different Quad—the US, EU, India and Brazil—that, with greater sensitivity to other negotiating countries and with a significant role for Japan (which is a major power and must also make significant agricultural concessions), effectively takes major initiatives.

The 2003 Hong Kong Ministerial Conference also registered progress on several fronts. The LDCs were promised quota- and duty-free access to at least 97 per cent of the goods in rich country markets.

Thanks to Indian leadership, when Brazil was dragging its feet, a compromise was also worked out whereby rich countries would eliminate agricultural export subsidies by 2013 instead of 2010. On domestic subsidies, and agricultural and non-agricultural tariffs, progress was more limited but real: agreements were reached on the formulas that would cut higher barriers more and lower barriers less, with precise levels of the cuts to be decided later by 30 April 2006.

We can therefore see Cancun and Hong Kong as having effectively cleared the way, leaving the negotiations now focused on the major players, the new Quad, who must make mutually acceptable concessions to close the Round. The negotiations are nevertheless truly deadlocked. With the crucial 30 April 2006 deadline having been missed, we run the risk of losing the Doha Round altogether. How do the key players stack up in this final game? The US, which has a strong comparative advantage in agriculture, wants substantial cuts in both domestic subsidies and tariffs in agriculture in the EU in particular before cutting its own agricultural support. Its lobbies in manufactures and services are also seeking concessions, especially from India and Brazil, in manufactures and services.

The EU has already agreed to eliminate export subsidies and also to some cuts in the trade-distorting production subsidies. With no comparative advantage in agriculture, it argues that any further cuts in agricultural protectionism must be matched by significant reciprocal cuts in manufactures and services abroad.

Developing countries—read Brazil and India—have so far taken the view that unless the EU moves further on agriculture, they are not willing to move on non-agricultural market access (NAMA) and in services. Japan has suggested it will cut rice protection, but it is not identified with any impassioned demands for reciprocal concessions. The talks are deadlocked as everyone waits for others to move.

Now, consider that President Bush is a sure-fire friend of India as also of free trade. The president would like to close the Doha Round before his Trade Promotion Authority (TPA) expires. He has already made a journey to Europe two weeks ago to press the case for Doha. But to date, the EU has remained a reluctant player beyond its current offer.

This is where India can seize the initiative. By moving ahead of the curve and offering real concessions in manufactures (meaning cuts in the applied tariffs) and services in return for concessions for its own exports, it can take credit for moving the Round forward and also advance its friendship with the US. But, aside from the kudos we would get for breaking the logjam, it is important to appreciate that our lowering of our own trade barriers is in our own interest.

There are now few who doubt that opening up to trade has been good for India. It was the reforms of the mid- to late 1980s that helped place India on the higher growth trajectory starting in the late 1980s while the more systematic reforms of the 1990s helped sustain that growth over the long haul.

The major advantage of moving aggressively within the Doha framework, however, is that it will also earn us the trade concessions by others, 'doubling' the benefits to us. Five years from now, we will be bringing down our industrial tariffs to the 5 to 7 per cent range with or without Doha.

But with Doha, whose full implementation would take five or more years, we can simultaneously bring down the peak tariffs on our labour-intensive exports, such as apparel, in the rich countries, and extract assured and expanded market access for our IT and other service exports. On top of that, we are bound to make gains in agricultural markets and become substantial agricultural exporters with suitable internal reforms.

The determination of President Bush to win the Doha trophy is manifest and there is much sentiment for moving the Round forward worldwide among the political leaders. So the likely scenario today is that President Bush will succeed in striking a deal with the EU and moving the negotiations forward. If he succeeds, is it not better that we would have taken the lead instead of having waited to become a reluctant follower? So, Dr Manmohan Singh and Kamal Nath, go right ahead and win this one for India!

52

CLOSING THE DOHA ROUND

12 August 2008

PASCAL LAMY, THE TIRELESS director general of the WTO, will be in New Delhi this week trying to break the impasse in the Doha negotiations. New Delhi should oblige the visiting dignitary, not because its current negotiating position is without merit but because it can bring the negotiation to a conclusion without either diluting the overall benefits to India or compromising the interests of its farmers.

The latest round of negotiations ending 29 July 2008 has brought the Doha agreement well within our grasp. So much progress was made during the first six days that by 27 July only three key issues remained to be resolved: the Special Safeguard Mechanism (SSM) in agriculture, special treatment for cotton and sector-specific liberalization initiatives in manufactures. Unfortunately, no further progress could be made in the following two days.

Of the three unresolved issues, the SSM is the most complex and therefore in need of careful explanation.

The operating principle of the WTO is that democratic governments will not commit to liberalization unless they are assured that they will have the flexibility to temporarily re-erect trade barriers in case of an import surge that may cause injury to domestic producers. Therefore, 'safeguard' measures that allow temporary increases in tariffs in response to import surges are an integral part of the existing WTO agreements.

Under Article XIX of the GATT, a member country is allowed to temporarily raise protection in response to an import surge provided the country can demonstrate injury or threat of injury to domestic producers. Alternatively, under GATT Article VI, the WTO allows a country to impose temporary AD duties on a firm that injures the country's producers by selling its product below cost.

WTO members have found these safeguard measures adequate to deal with import surges in industrial products. But when liberalizing agriculture—a process that got under way only in 1995 with the conclusion of the UR Agreement—they have insisted on additional safeguard measures they can invoke speedily without demonstration of injury. Thus, under the UR Agreement on Agriculture, a temporary Special Agricultural Safeguard (SSG) was introduced.

Countries that chose to replace all border measures with an equivalent tariff—mainly developed and a handful of developing countries—got the right to use this safeguard. Under it, the countries are given the right to raise the tariff on a product whose imports account for 30 per cent or more of the total consumption by one third in response to a 5 per cent increase in imports. Higher triggers are applied to products whose imports are smaller than 30 per cent of total consumption. An eventual Doha agreement is expected to either eliminate or considerably restrict the scope of the SSG.

Under the UR Agreement, most developing countries bound their agricultural tariffs at levels vastly higher than their actual applied tariffs. For example, India bound 98 per cent of its agricultural tariffs at 100, 150 or 300 per cent. Given that the vast majority of India's applied tariffs are 30 per cent or less, these bindings give it the flexibility to raise the latter manifold.

Under an eventual Doha agreement, developing countries would be required to reciprocate agricultural liberalization by the developed countries. Therefore, many developing countries have insisted that they be permitted a new, relatively generous SSM to combat import surges. The rest of the membership has accepted this demand in principle but disagrees on its form proposed by the advocates.

During the latest negotiations, approximately seventy-five developing countries tabled a proposal under which larger developing countries will have the authority to raise tariffs on 7 per cent of agricultural products by 30 per cent of the UR bound rates or 30 percentage points, whichever is larger, in response to a 10 per cent expansion of imports. For a product with UR binding of 150 per cent, this will mean an addition of 45 percentage points to the applied tariff rate. For a product with 60 per cent UR binding, the applied tariff would rise by 30 percentage points. For the remaining 93 per cent of the tariff lines, the tariff increase would be applied on the basis of post-Doha bound rates. The US categorically opposes this and other similar proposals. It is particularly insistent that the trigger point be set at a 40 per cent expansion in imports.

There are at least three reasons why the developing countries have a strong case for a generous SSM. First, when the Doha Round was launched, agricultural liberalization was principally a developed country issue. The US has now changed the terms by insisting on a significant expansion of market access in agricultural markets in the developing countries. Second, the US itself has not been a shining example of liberalization: its offer to bind agricultural subsidies at $14.5 billion remains vastly higher than even its current applied level of $9 billion. If a rich country cannot sell genuine liberalization to just 1 million well-to-do farmers, a poor and noisy democracy sure cannot do it to its 250 million mostly poor farmers. Finally, the trigger under the SSG at the 5 per cent that developed countries got is even more generous than the one sought by the developing countries.

Nevertheless, it is a serious mistake for India to walk away from almost a done deal. Given the vast gap between likely post-Doha bindings and applied tariffs, provision of minimal or no liberalization in sensitive products, and 9 per cent annual growth that promises a rapidly expanding domestic market for farm products, India can accept a higher trigger and less generous SSM tariffs without compromising the interests of its farmers. In return, it can insist on a genuine liberalization by the US that binds its farm subsidies to no more than their current applied level of $9 billion. In addition, the US must drop its insistence on mandatory sectoral negotiations.

Perhaps this time around, the emerging giant can accomplish something the diminishing giant couldn't!

53

HOW THE US HAS WEAKENED THE WTO: THE MULTILATERAL TRADING SYSTEM IS UNDER STRESS, MEMBER COUNTRIES MUST REPAIR IT

27 May 2021

AS WE PREPARE TO enter the post-COVID-19 era, an important question concerns the future of the global trading system, which has been under stress since well before the onset of the dreadful pandemic.

Though the global merchandise trade took a significant hit in the first half of 2020 and fell as much as 15 per cent in the second quarter, it exhibited an astonishing recovery in the second half of the year. According to a 31 March 2021 press release by the WTO, merchandise exports fell by only 5.3 per cent over the full year. This compares with a whopping 12 per cent fall in 2009 following the global financial crisis. WTO predicts that the merchandise export volume will rise by 8 per cent in 2021.

Global merchandise exports have thus well survived the onslaught of COVID-19. With vaccine supplies expected to rise at an accelerated pace globally, prospects for the WTO forecast coming true are excellent. While this fact removes a weak global market as a source of worry in the immediate aftermath of the COVID-19 crisis, we would still face challenges posed by the fissures and fractures in the WTO system.

Central to the enforcement of multilaterally agreed-upon rules under the auspices of WTO is its DSB, which does for international trade disputes what domestic courts do for civil disputes. If a WTO member feels that another WTO member has violated its trading rights enshrined in WTO rules, it can bring a case against the latter in DSB. If the initial efforts to settle the dispute through intermediation fail, the DSB appoints a panel to investigate and hear the case and give a ruling. If either party is dissatisfied with the ruling by the panel, it can take the matter to the Appellate Body (AB). Ruling by the AB is final and binding.

Judges to the AB are appointed for a four-year term (renewable for at the most another term) by consensus among the WTO members. At any time, the AB can have up to seven members of which three make the quorum for hearing a dispute.

For more than a decade, the US has been unhappy with the rulings by the AB in the cases brought against it. As a result, beginning in 2011, it has been vetoing the renewal of the AB members completing their first term as well as the appointment of others to succeed them. The cumulative effect of the vetoes has been that the total number of AB members fell to two on 11 December 2019, one short of the quorum for a hearing.

Consequently, the WTO is no longer able to enforce its rules. If this emboldens one or more members to begin exploiting the system by violating the rules, members whose rights are violated and are unable to seek a remedy via the DSB are bound to respond in kind. That is what has happened in cases of steel and aluminium tariffs, and the US–China trade conflict.

While the US has expressed its displeasure with a number of features of how the DSB has operated, so far, it has not placed a proposal to reform it to the WTO membership. Therefore, the path to bringing the DSB process back on track is simply not clear.

In part, the US' reluctance to offer a reform proposal may be rooted in its dissatisfaction with the WTO on other counts, many of them centred on China. It contends that under the existing WTO rules, it is not possible to satisfactorily deal with China's State-Owned Enterprises, industrial policy, subsidies and IPR violations. China for its part resents the US for not making good on its promise to give it market-economy status.

The US also remains unhappy with the developing-country status (which qualifies them for Special and Differential treatment under WTO rules) to countries such as China, India and Brazil. Additionally, it wants greater transparency and better enforcement of WTO notification obligations.

Most of these issues cannot be resolved without renegotiation of many of the current WTO rules. Unfortunately, rule-making negotiations are currently stalled and may take some years to return on track. In the meantime, one can only hope that the member countries will recognize the value of trade benefits they have enjoyed within a rules-based multilateral trading system since the Second World War, and adhere to their commitments and obligations.

As far as India is concerned, with global merchandise exports holding up at $18–19 trillion and commercial services exports at another $6–7 trillion, it has much to gain from the current system even if it is somewhat broken. To return the country quickly to a 7–8 per cent growth path in the post-COVID-19 era, it must unwind its higher tariffs rather than continue with the losing strategy of import substitution.

For geopolitical reasons, India aims to distance itself from China. To achieve this objective while simultaneously improving its access to foreign markets, its recent decision to pursue FTAs with the United Kingdom and European Union is a very welcome development. India has much to gain from duty-free access to these large markets. The issue of protecting the interests of sensitive import-competing products should be handled via a ten- to fifteen-year phase of tariffs on them rather than protection in perpetuity.

PART IX
PREFERENTIAL TRADE LIBERALIZATION

54

SAARC: FOLLOW APEC, NOT NAFTA

29 July 1998

AT THE END OF this month, the heads of state of the member nations of the South Asian Association of Regional Cooperation (SAARC) will get together in Colombo to discuss the future agenda of the Association. Should the countries follow the lead of the NAFTA and limit liberalization to member countries, or should they emulate the Asia Pacific Economic Cooperation (APEC) forum and thus adopt a non-discriminatory approach to trade liberalization?

Despite much enthusiasm on the part of some regional leaders and policy analysts, the creation of a discriminatory trade bloc in the region, dubbed the South Asian Free Trade Area (SAFTA), along the lines of the NAFTA, will be a mistake. The region's interests will be served by following the APEC model which calls for full adherence to the MFN principle and, hence, non-discrimination in trade policy.

It may be recalled that at their celebrated summit in Bogor, Indonesia, in 1994, the APEC members had agreed to free up all trade by the year 2010 in developed member countries and 2020 in developing member countries. At the time, the agreement neglected to specify whether such liberalization was to be discriminatory as in NAFTA or non-discriminatory as pursued by the Asian countries. Despite some sentiment in favour of the discriminatory approach on the part of the US, the Asian members prevailed at later summits and the APEC is now fully committed to the MFN principle.

The original inspiration for the SAARC had come from the ASEAN, founded in 1967 by Brunei, Indonesia, Malaysia, the Philippines, Singapore and Thailand. Often viewed as a preferential trading agreement, the ASEAN actually began as a cultural organization and, until as late as 1997, had no economic component.

Though the ASEAN Preferential Trading Area (APTA) was introduced in 1977, it led to little action. In January 1992, the ASEAN members did sign a framework agreement to form the ASEAN Free Trade Area (AFTA) by the year 2007 (later revised to 2003), but they wisely included a provision, which permits member countries to fulfil their obligations by liberalizing trade on a non-discriminatory basis.

One may argue that preferential trade agreements may still be good if trade creation dominates trade diversion. In recent years, economists have gathered sufficient empirical evidence to suggest that trade diversion can be a serious problem, however. Especially in the context of South Asia, this is a major worry. Trade diversion would be minimal if, for most products, the world's most efficient suppliers were located within the region.

There is no doubt that some countries in the South Asia region do not trade nearly as much with each other as will be justified by their location and other factors. But that is principally due to high barriers to trade in general rather than a lack of trade preferences.

In particular, India and Pakistan, who are both among the twenty-three original signatories to the GATT, effectively do not extend even the MFN status to each other.

Some analysts argue that despite trade diversion, SAFTA may be a desirable instrument for keeping the process of trade liberalization moving ahead. This is also a misguided argument since such liberalization is likely to become a binding constraint on true, non-discriminatory liberalization. Countries such as Mexico and Brazil have virtually abandoned their programmes of non-discriminatory liberalization since entering preferential trade agreements. Indeed, following such arrangements, they have raised external tariffs.

In the wake of the peso crisis, Mexico raised its external tariffs on non-NAFTA countries from less than 20 per cent to 35 per cent in the case of 503 items. Likewise, after the Asian currency crisis, the members of the Southern American Common Market, including Brazil, raised their average external tariff from 9 per cent to 12 per cent.

In my judgment, we should leave to SAARC precisely the task suggested by its title: the promotion of cooperation among member countries. There may be road, water, electricity or other projects that are justified if undertaken jointly by two or more members. SAARC can help advance such projects. The APEC agenda may offer an insight into further areas of fruitful cooperation.

55

A MISGUIDED IDEA

10 July 2000

THE IDEA OF A FTA between India and the US was floated in the Indian press at the time of the US President Bill Clinton's highly successful visit. Subsequently, steered by Rahul Bajaj, the Confederation of Indian Industry has supported the idea.

There are many reasons why an FTA between the US and India is a bad idea. To begin with, it is likely to give rise to what economists call trade diversion. In an FTA, as opposed to the WTO-style non-discriminatory liberalization, India and the US will eliminate tariffs on each other, but not on outside countries. In turn, the two countries will expand their exports to each other, displacing cheaper imports from outside countries. This trade diversion will lower economic efficiency and thus the real incomes of the member countries as a whole.

But more to the point, an FTA with the US is overwhelmingly against India's economic interests. When we remove tariffs on a non-discriminatory basis as is done in the WTO-style liberalization, much of the lost tariff revenue will pass on to our own consumers in the form of lower prices. The removal of the tariffs will induce exporters from different countries to compete against one another, leading to lower prices. But when the tariffs are removed on a preferential basis, as will be the case under the proposed FTA, the tariff revenue lost on the imports from the US will turn into extra profits for the exporters. The American firms will have no incentive to lower their prices when similar goods from the outside countries continue to pay the duty and, therefore, are sold at approximately their pre-FTA prices.

Of course, by symmetry, our exporters will receive a preferential access to the US market, thereby capturing the tariff revenue the US custom authorities would have collected in the absence of the preference. The catch, however, is that on average India's tariffs are much higher than those of the US. This asymmetry implies that the exchange of tariff preferences with the US will be highly lopsided. India will give a much greater margin of preference than what it receives. Correspondingly, it will lose much more tariff revenue to the US exporters than what its exporters gain by the preference in the US market. Thus, while the Indian industry might benefit from increased profits on exports, explaining the CII support for the FTA, the country as a whole will lose. According to my calculations, based on the 1996 trade data, the net annual losses to Mexico from a similar asymmetric exchange of preferences with the US under the NAFTA amount to as much as $3.25 billion.

Some may argue that the US tariffs on many products in textiles and clothing are 15 per cent or higher so that India could benefit from duty-free access in this important sector. Given that India stands to lose from the FTA on a net basis, the gains to the textiles and clothing industry alone can hardly justify the arrangement from the country's viewpoint.

Even leaving this objection aside, the potential benefits to the textiles and clothing industry can easily be overstated. For, the FTA will be subject to the rules of origin that could greatly undermine our access to the US market. These rules will require, for example, that in order to qualify for duty-free access, Indian shirts use fabric and yarn made in the US or India. But to the extent that these countries are costly suppliers of high-quality yarn and fabric compared to China, Korea and Taiwan, the benefit from the duty-free treatment of shirts will be greatly diluted. Even if that does not happen, the US will readily invoke AD action should our exports pose a major threat to the local industry.

Yet another argument given in support of the FTA with the US is that it can lead to more liberalization. But this is a spurious plea as much of the evidence suggests that FTAs lead to a slowdown of liberalization programmes.

For example, during the 1980s, Mexico undertook massive trade liberalization. But since it entered the NAFTA, its external trade liberalization has come to a complete halt. On the contrary, many of the Mexican tariffs have actually gone up. The experience of other preferential arrangements has been similar.

It has also been suggested that the FTA with the US will boost direct foreign investment in India. This is a claim grounded in very little empirical evidence or theoretical analysis. To date, much of the evidence points to domestic economic reforms and the general openness of a country being the key to attracting investment. India's own experience in recent years stands out, especially when contrasted with the pre-reforms period. But more dramatically, China is by far the largest recipient of foreign investment among developing countries, but it has no PTA with any country.

The Mexican experience is often invoked to bolster support for the thesis that an FTA may lead to increased foreign investment. Yet, it is rarely mentioned that a key element in Mexico's economic reforms was a massive liberalization of its investment regime in 1989. Moreover, anecdotal evidence suggests that the bulk of the post-NAFTA foreign investment in the country has taken place in response to the rules of origin which economists regard as being inefficient.

The greatest threat from the FTA with the US, however, lies in the demands it is bound to make on India in terms of higher labour and environmental standards as a side condition. It is naïve for New Delhi to enter into negotiations thinking that the US will be 'pragmatic' and drop such demands to obtain preferential access to India's large market. For, all available evidence points to the contrary. The very first trade policy action Mr Clinton took as president was to attach environmental and labour side agreements to the NAFTA. Last December, he readily sacrificed the launching of a new round of MTNs to appease the labour lobbies, insisting that labour standards be brought into the WTO.

Most recently, the African Growth and Opportunity Act, signed by him into law on 18 May, has offered the countries in Africa trade preferences in the US markets provided they satisfy many conditions, most notably, upgrading of labour standards. The specific standards in the Act include the right of association, the right to organize and bargain collectively, a prohibition on the use of any form of forced or compulsory labour, a minimum age for the employment of children, and acceptable conditions of work with respect to minimum wages, hours of work, and occupational safety and health.

This latest initiative is a direct assault by the US on the virtually united opposition to the link between trade and labour standards by the developing countries. The US is attempting to achieve through the bilateral route what it has failed to accomplish by the multilateral route. We must stay clear of falling prey to such a strategy.

Thus, no matter how we look at it, an FTA with the US is a bad idea. It may benefit some of our export lobbies by buying them preferential access to the US market. But the price we will pay is extremely high. Since the beginning of reforms in 1991, our liberalization strategy has been highly successful. There is little reason to change course. Or, to paraphrase Prof. Jagdish Bhagwati, why take the dirt road of preferential liberalization when the turnpike of non-discriminatory liberalization is available?

56

IS THIS FREE MEAL WORTH HAVING?

19 June 2002

THE GATT LARGELY GOVERNS the global trade in goods. GATT itself is an integral part of the WTO. At the heart of this agreement is the MFN principle, which requires each WTO member to treat all other members as favourably as its MFN. If a member lowers a tariff against one member nation, it must do so against all other member nations. In effect, the principle prohibits discrimination in trade policy.

Over time, the WTO members have accommodated several exceptions to this principle, however. One such exception is the so-called GSP under which developed countries are encouraged to discriminate in favour of developing countries by granting them one-way tariff reductions not applicable to developed countries. The exception was introduced through a ten-year waiver in 1971 and given legal status through the so-called 'Enabling Clause' in 1979.

Developing countries originally pushed for GSP during the 1960s as a part of their overall quest for the Special and Differential treatment within the multilateral trading system. Since then, they have viewed the provision as an important instrument for seeking improved access to developed country markets. On the surface, this seems a sensible strategy: other things being the same, the ability of developing countries to compete in a developed country market is enhanced if they face lower custom duties than developed-country exporters.

Nonetheless, upon closer examination, the experience with trade preferences appears no more encouraging than that with aid. Under the original conception, GSP preferences were to cover all products ('generalized'), be non-discriminatory across developing countries, except if the discrimination was in favour of the LDCs, and preclude reciprocal concessions by developing countries. But given the 'permissive' rather than 'mandatory' nature of the Enabling Clause, developed countries have often been able to violate this conception along all three dimensions without risk of a challenge in the WTO DSB. Thus, they frequently exclude precisely those products in which developing countries have a comparative advantage, 'graduate' a country out of the preference for a product just as it begins to achieve significant success as an exporter, and attach side conditions that amount to reciprocal concessions from developing countries.

Not only does the US exclude such critical items as textiles and clothing and footwear from its GSP programme, but it also subjects them to very high MFN trade barriers. In addition, it imposes a $100 million limit on exports per tariff line, per year, per country. Exceeding this limit results in the loss of the preference, discouraging countries from export expansion in the first place.

In addition, the exporting countries are required to satisfy certain 'rules of origin' to substantiate the claim that they indeed produced the goods rather than import them from a country excluded from GSP privileges. The commonest such rule makes the preference contingent on a minimum valued addition to the product within the exporting country. This requirement can be a major deterrent since many small and poor countries are able to perform only simple assembly operations. And even if the requirement is not prohibitive initially, developed countries have been known to raise it after a country successfully penetrates their markets.

The rules of origin often require beneficiaries to use inputs produced in the preference-granting country in their exports. For example, under the recent Africa Growth and Opportunity Act (AGOA), introduced by the US, shirts assembled by the more successful African exporters must be made from fabrics formed and cut in the US. In addition, the fabric must be made from US yarns. Given that the US is unlikely to be the cheapest source of these inputs, this raises the production costs of exporters with the preference for shirts effectively protecting the US producers of fabric and yarn.

Often the preferences also end up benefiting one set of developing countries at the expense of others. The US preferences under AGOA apply only to the countries in Africa and, thus, carry the potential to displace exporters in other parts of the world. More subtly, to the extent that more advanced and larger developing countries are more likely to be able to satisfy the minimum value-added requirements, perversely, the preferences may divert exports from smaller, poorer countries from among the beneficiary nations.

The worst aspect of the preferences, however, is their use by developed countries as instruments for extracting concessions from developing countries in non-trade areas. After a point, the EU explicitly links the grant of its GSP preferences to meeting labour and environmental standards. Likewise, the US trade laws allow the president to use GSP to promote labour standards and IPR. In April

1992, the US terminated India's GSP privileges on $60 million worth of exports of pharmaceuticals and chemicals on the pretext that the country did not have adequate IP protection.

At Doha, the preferences also became an instrument of breaking the united front presented by a group of developing countries against the Singapore issues. The US decision to go along with the waiver sought by the African countries to preserve their preferences in the EU market substantially muted their opposition to the Singapore issues. In the future, preferences can also become the instruments of breaking the generally unified position of a large majority of developing countries against the inclusion of labour standards into WTO agreements.

Therefore, on balance, GSP may have done more harm than good. According to empirical studies, they had at most a marginal impact on a country's economic performance. Above all, they have given developed countries an easy escape from genuine liberalization in products of interest to developing countries.

Developing countries must rethink their negotiating strategy. As with aid, the experience with GSP points to the conclusion that free meals, which are also worth having, are rare. Genuine expansion of market access will come only through reciprocal bargains.

57

AN INDIA–CHINA FREE TRADE AREA?

20 April 2005

INDIA–CHINA TRADE IS AMONG the fastest growing bilateral trade relationships in the world currently. According to the Indian commerce ministry data, India's exports to China rose from a paltry $18 million in 1990–91 to approximately $3 billion in 2003–04. India's imports from China expanded equally rapidly, from $35 million to $4 billion over the same period.

So rapid has this expansion been that from an insignificant supplier until the beginning of the 1990s, China has now come to replace the US as India's top source of imports. During April–December 2004, the latest period for which the commerce ministry data are available, imports from China grew a phenomenal 70 per cent over those during April–December 2003. That effectively overwhelmed the hefty 25 per cent growth in imports from the US during the same period.

Of course, this expansion is a healthy development since it represents a shift from costlier domestic or other foreign sources of supply. Nevertheless, the domestic import-competing firms (as opposed to the buyers of cheaper Chinese goods that include both the consumers and firms) may be inclined to appeal to the import surge to demand increased barriers against Chinese goods. But that will be absurd for many reasons, including the fact that the competitive Indian firms have been equally successful in penetrating the Chinese market: India's exports to China during April–December 2004 grew 61 per cent over those during April–December 2003. True, the bilateral balance is in favour of China (though the reverse is true according to the Chinese data), but no economist worth his salt would suggest that bilateral trade flows must be balanced—after all, India too runs a huge trade surplus vis-à-vis the US.

Indeed, rather than fear the Chinese imports, we must use the occasion to address a more provocative question that figured prominently during the recent visit by the Chinese prime minister Wen Jiabao: is there a case for an India–China FTA?

I have generally been critical of the discriminatory trade blocs not just because such arrangements fragment the global trading system but also because they often hurt economic efficiency within the countries forging the arrangements. This is particularly true of the arrangements such as the India–Sri Lanka and SAFTA that exclude and therefore discriminate against countries accounting for nearly 99 per cent of the world trade. The discrimination works particularly to the disadvantage of India since it has relatively high trade barriers. For example, when India gives tariff-free access to Sri Lanka, tariff revenue previously collected on the imports from Sri Lanka turns into export revenues for the exporting firms of Sri Lanka. Since tariffs in Sri Lanka are low, Indian exporting firms have less to gain from tariff-free access there.

Of course, this argument would apply to the India–China FTA as well—though with less potency, since China is a large player in the world market and a super-efficient producer of many goods. The latter fact means that the tariff-revenue loss on the imports from China might translate at least partially into a reduction in the consumer prices. Nonetheless, as long as India continues to have substantially higher tariffs than China, the danger of potential losses from the transfer of tariff revenue to the Chinese firms in the form of higher profits remains. As such, in thinking of such an FTA, one must assume that India would remain committed to its current non-discriminatory liberalization and bring the external tariffs down to the Chinese levels in two or three years' time.

The case for an India–China FTA is based principally on its strategic value. During the last decade, with the creation of the NAFTA, several expansions of the EU and a host of smaller FTAs in Latin America, Asia has suffered from a diversion of these regions' trade away from it. One response to this trade diversion for Asia would be to move towards a bloc of its own. Such a bloc may give Asia the necessary leverage to pry open the NAFTA and EU blocs to outsiders through multilateral liberalization.

If one accepts this argument, an India–China FTA is probably the best starting point for such an Asian bloc. For example, as an alternative, even if India and China both make good on their respective framework agreements with the members of the ASEAN to forge FTAs with them, an effective Asian bloc will not form without these two countries signing an FTA agreement with each other. On the other hand, if India and China signed an agreement, chances are much higher that the remaining countries in Asia will rush to sign agreements with them. Presently, the ASEAN is driving the integration process in Asia but with the emergence of India and China as major economic powerhouses and the relative stagnation faced by the most populous ASEAN country, Indonesia, its ability to serve as the engine of Asian integration has substantially diminished.

An India–China FTA also has the advantage that it will help promote an alternative FTA template that focuses on trade integration rather than non-trade subjects including labour standards, IPR and even restrictions on the use of capital controls. These subjects are integral parts of the US FTA template that the US may eventually want to turn into the WTO template. An Asian bloc that relies on a 'trade only' template will be an effective instrument for countering the US template in future WTO negotiations.

Internally, India can surely benefit from cooperation with China in shaping its labour-intensive industry. In particular, direct competition with China may help push some of the key reforms necessary to stimulate the expansion of the labour-intensive industry. With the wages in China now rising, the time for India could not be more opportune for moving in a big way into such labour-intensive sectors as apparel, footwear and toys. Likewise, China could gain from increased interaction with India in the information technology sector.

58

RCEP AS WINNING STRATEGY

19 September 2018

THE MULTILATERAL TRADE REGIME, which saw trade flourish for seventy years following the Second World War, faces an existential threat today. A trade war has broken out between the two largest economies, the US and China. From being the principal architect of the system, the US has come to view itself as a victim of it.

Therefore, in the medium run, we are likely to be left with regional trade agreements as the only game in town. This fact makes a successful conclusion of the RCEP agreement among its sixteen partner countries critically important. For reasons I explain below, India has much to gain from the agreement.

India is often criticized, even vilified, for its tough stance in trade negotiations. But all major nations with bargaining power negotiate hard to maximize access for their exports in return for the access they give to imports in their markets. The criticisms must therefore be heavily discounted.

This being said, India must not fear imports that would flow as a result of its reciprocal trade liberalization. Conventionally, negotiators view imports as a cost and exports as a benefit. But in economic terms, true gains come from imports while exports represent the cost of obtaining those imports.

No nation would export its products to another nation if it did not allow it to import something more valuable in return. As Nobel laureate Milton Friedman once said, we can eat imports but not exports. Once shipped out, exports are no longer available to us.

One particular import-related fear that has shaped the actions of our RCEP negotiators is the prospect of an already large trade deficit with China turning yet larger. To be sure, it is a good negotiating tactic to use this bilateral trade deficit as a bargaining chip to maximize access for our exports to the Chinese market. But it is not good economics to let this fear determine the fate of the negotiations.

While there are good reasons for a country to care about its overall balance of trade in goods and services, the same is not true of a bilateral trade deficit. A country must sell its exports to trading partners that offer it the highest prices for those exports. And it should buy its imports from partners that charge the lowest prices for them. When this is done, except by sheer coincidence, the resulting trade flows would fail to balance bilaterally.

For instance, the US pays high prices for many products that India exports but it also charges high prices for many products that India imports. This leads India to sell a large volume of its exports to the US and avoid buying an equally large volume of imports from it. Consequently, India runs a bilateral trade surplus with the US.

The situation with China is the reverse, leading India to run a bilateral trade deficit with it. But India maintains a healthy trade balance overall and thus avoids accumulating unduly large foreign currency debt.

In its negotiations, India must also pay particular attention to the benefits it can reap from membership in the RCEP through a large-scale movement of multinational enterprises. It is a reasonable expectation that its large domestic market, large pool of labour and relatively low wages would combine to make India a progressively attractive production base for multinational enterprises. Membership in the large RCEP market would multiply this attractiveness manifold for two reasons.

First, the membership will give multinationals located in India tariff-free access to the vast RCEP market. And second, the movement of inputs without tariffs and other frictions across borders of the sixteen member countries would make the multinationals doubly competitive.

Such movement is especially important in modern times because supply chain management requires inputs to cross international borders multiple times before being assembled into the final product. If tariff and friction characterize each crossing, costs multiply.

In the negotiations, India has made services liberalization and freer movement of information technology workers a make-or-break issue. While India has strength in these areas, it must take two qualifications into consideration. One, our success in services exports to RCEP markets is likely to be limited due to language and cultural barriers that a free trade agreement cannot overcome. And second, preoccupation with services and freer movement of workers can result in an underestimation of the benefits India stands to reap in manufactures.

Given where India stands today in terms of its large pool of labour, low wages and reformed policy regime, past history is a poor guide to its future success in employment-intensive manufactures. With half of India's farms less than half a hectare in size, many of its farmers need decent jobs to escape poverty. Historically, labour-intensive manufactures have been the principal engine of growth in such jobs in every successful country. The RCEP offers India the same opportunity.

With a population of 3.5 billion, the volume of shirts, blouses, trousers, accessories, towels, bed sheets and pillowcases an RCEP membership would buy in the next several decades is beyond measure. Think of India as the dominant supplier of these labour-intensive products and you have an irrefutable case for the RCEP as a winning strategy.

59

STAYING OUT OF RCEP IS NOT IN INDIA'S ECONOMIC INTEREST

(With Pravin Krishna)

8 November 2019

EARLIER THIS WEEK, INDIA announced that it was dropping out of the RCEP—a trade agreement that had been under negotiation for over seven years between sixteen countries, namely, China, Japan, Korea, India, New Zealand, Australia and ten countries from the Association of South East Asian Nations (ASEAN).

India's exit came amidst a wide array of assertions from commentators—with some claiming that India's past trade agreements had harmed its economy and that the RCEP would do worse, others going further to demand a return to the inglorious days of 'self-sufficiency' and yet others insisting that the withdrawal reflected the weakness of the government against the efforts of protectionist lobbies.

What were the actual outcomes of India's past trade agreements? Did they hurt the Indian economy? What lessons do they hold for India with respect to the RCEP or other future trade deals?

Between the years 2000–2011, India signed a total of fourteen preferential trade agreements, ten of which were bilateral agreements with individual countries (including with Japan, Korea, Malaysia and Singapore) and four were plurilateral agreements (including with ASEAN and the Southern Common Market [MERCOSUR] in Latin America). What will likely come as a surprise to most is the fact that the effects of these agreements on trade have been modest. Thus, while India's imports from its ten bilateral partners added up to 13.3 per cent of its overall imports in 2007, that number actually fell slightly to 11.8 per cent in 2017. Similarly, exports to these ten partners added up to 13.7 per cent in 2007 and stayed nearly the same at 14 per cent in 2017. India's imports under ASEAN, its most significant plurilateral agreement inched up from 9.6 per cent in 2017 to 10.2 per cent in 2017, while exports expanded modestly faster from 9.5 per cent to 12 per cent.

What about the trade deficit? Many analysts have erroneously derided India's trade agreements by pointing to an increased bilateral trade deficit in dollar terms. They miss the obvious point that a significant rise in all nominal magnitudes must accompany the approximate doubling of India's economy over the relevant years. When we examine the size-corrected appropriate measure— the share of the trade deficit contributed by India's agreements—it turns out that India actually improved its bilateral position vis-à-vis its FTA partners during 2007–2017.

Furthermore, it is not the case that large parts of the Indian economy have come under stress because of intensified import competition under these agreements. Between 2007–2017, the sectors in which imports under trade agreements had grown faster than overall imports from all trading partners by even just 25 per cent accounted for only 6–7 per cent of overall imports. Admittedly, liberalization under many of these agreements was 'phased in' and, in some cases, is yet to be completed. But the argument that India's agreements have already strained India's economy and that they offer a cautionary tale against future agreements finds no support whatsoever in data.

What about the RCEP? First the positives: the RCEP covers over 3 billion people and over 20 per cent of the global GDP. Access to this market on a 'frictionless' duty-free basis would have provided tremendous advantages to India's exports. In the absence of trade barriers on its imports (imposed by itself) and its exports (imposed by partner countries), India would have had an excellent opportunity to integrate itself into regional and global value-chains, where India's participation has been low. India would have been more easily able to attract FDI and to also take over production in sectors that China is now vacating.

Finally, the RCEP would have been an easier agreement for India to sign as compared to any potential agreements with the US or the EU, because its focus was on trade liberalization. In contrast, agreements such as the TPP pose a greater challenge since they require concessions over a range of contentious non-trade issues such as environmental and labour regulations, IP protection and the operations of state-owned enterprises.

On the flip side: India's trade deficit with China is large. It accounts for about 40 per cent of our overall deficit. Signing the RCEP would have exposed India to the risk of surging imports from China and an even wider deficit. However, if these were India's primary concerns, it could have negotiated hard for the expansion of market access in the Chinese market in areas of its comparative strength, such as pharmaceuticals and IT services. On the import side, it could have sought exclusions of especially sensitive sectors and a more gradual liberalization schedule. This would have allowed

India to simultaneously exploit greater market integration with Asia, while giving itself time and economic space to adjust.

Where do we go from here? Statements by the commerce minister that he now proposes to turn West to the US and the EU may be read to imply that he plans to abandon the RCEP permanently. As eternal optimists, we do not believe this interpretation and view India's current decision as a bargaining tactic aimed at extracting further concessions from other RCEP members and cutting a more favourable deal for India. It is unlikely that Prime Minister Narendra Modi would walk away from his 'Act East' and leave India at a disadvantage.

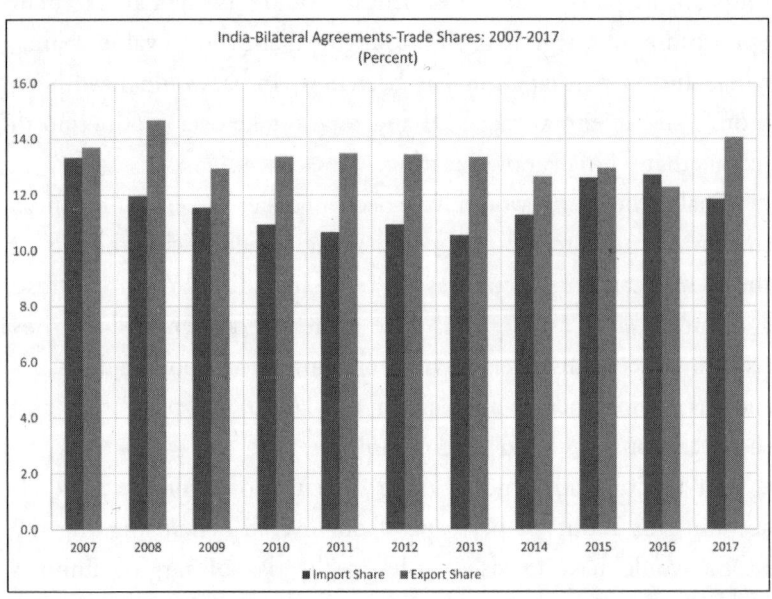

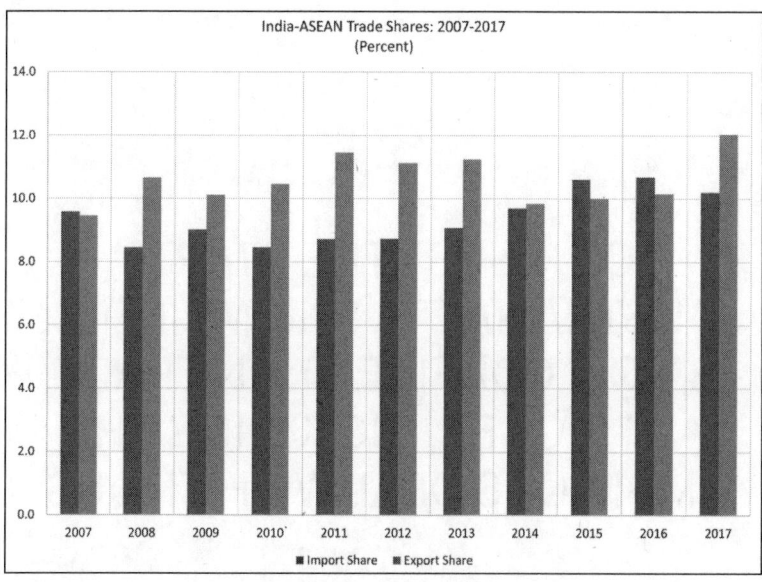

60

OZ IS JUST THE START: AUSTRALIA FTA SHOWS INDIA IS NOW CONFIDENT ON TRADE. AIM BIGGER, INCLUDING THE AMBITIOUS DEAL WITH THE US

6 April 2022

THE ECONOMIC COOPERATION AND Trade Agreement (ECTA), signed by India and Australia on 2 April, establishes a FTA in both goods and services between the two nations. From the viewpoint of India, this is a landmark development.

The WTO rules on FTAs in goods require that whenever an FTA includes one or more developed countries as members, all member countries must *eliminate* duties and other trade restrictions on *substantially all products* traded among them. That is, whenever one or more developed countries are members, an exchange of partial trade preferences in FTAs is prohibited. Nearly all trade must be covered and trade barriers must be eliminated rather than just lowered.

FTA rules are significantly looser, however, when FTA members happen to *all* be developing countries. In this case, the member countries may choose to simply reduce, rather than entirely eliminate, trade barriers and apply the reductions to as few or as many products as they choose. In other words, in arrangements involving only developing countries, the exchange of trade preferences can be as selective as the members want.

To date, with the exception of the India–Japan FTA, all FTAs India has signed have been with other developing countries (Singapore in 2005, South Korea in 2010, ASEAN in 2010, Malaysia in 2011 and the United Arab Emirates in 2022). As a result, they have all involved partial trade preferences with a large proportion of products excluded altogether from liberalization. FTA with Japan does eliminate trade barriers on substantially all products, but India–Japan trade being historically insignificant (in 2010, India sent only 2.2 per cent of its exports to Japan while Japan sent 1.2 per cent of its exports to India), it has not amounted to much.

Therefore, Australia is the first significant trading partner with which India has entered into a genuine free trade relationship. The fact that the current bilateral trade balance is in favour of Australia by a wide margin also represents the restoration of confidence on the part of India in the benefits of enhanced competition. Recall that in recent years India has viewed competition from foreign goods with a sense of scepticism, raising external tariffs on a large proportion of imported items.

In 2021, Australia exported goods worth $13.6 billion to India and imported goods worth $6.4 billion from it. In addition, the two countries trade approximately $7 billion in services with each other. By far the largest export item from Australia to India is coal, with pearls, gold, copper ore, aluminium, wine, fruits and nuts, and cotton and wool representing its other exports. In the reverse direction, Australia's leading imports from India are petroleum products, pharmaceuticals, gems and jewellery, electrical machinery, articles made of iron and steel, and textiles and apparel.

The FTA provides for immediate tariff cuts on the vast majority of imports by each country and their eventual elimination. Once fully implemented, 96 per cent of India's exports to Australia and 85 per cent of Australia's exports to India will acquire duty-free status. To speed up the approval of Indian medicines, Australian regulators would now use inspection reports and approvals from Canada and the EU in the evaluation process for Indian pharmaceuticals and manufacturing facilities.

With India's GDP close to $3 trillion and predicted to grow 7 to 8 per cent annually in the coming years and Australia's GDP at $1.3 trillion, there remains considerable scope for further expansion of bilateral trade between them. Given that countries such as China and Vietnam have existing FTA agreements with Australia, Indian exporters to the latter have been at a disadvantage in the past. The FTA promises to give India a level playing field vis-à-vis its competitors, especially in labour-intensive products such as apparel and other light manufactures.

Equally, buyers of Australian goods in India stand to benefit from the duty-free entry of imports from that country. In the case of the consumers, lower prices would translate to direct gains to them. In the case of producers who use Australian imports as inputs into their products, such access would translate to lower costs and hence improved competitiveness. Enhanced competition with Australian goods would also force better cost discipline on our producers of similar goods in India and lead to enhanced productivity.

FTA in services covers such areas as financial services, telecommunications and professional services. A separate chapter in the agreement also covers the movement of natural persons. In an important concession for Indian students, Australia has agreed to grant extended post-study work visas to graduates in science, technology, engineering and mathematics.

There is little doubt that the FTA is part of a larger strategy on the part of India to decouple its economy from that of China. With an FTA with Japan already in existence, India now has FTAs with two of its three partners in the Quadrilateral Security Dialogue, or Quad. It can therefore be hoped that the India–Australia ECTA will not be a one-off event and that it will serve as the stepping stone to similar agreements with India's larger trading partners, notably, the UK and the EU. Once these agreements are under its belt, India must turn to the most ambitious free trade relationship of all: an India–US FTA.

PART X

NON-TRADE ISSUES IN MULTILATERAL TRADE NEGOTIATIONS

61

PATENT RIGHTS: TRIPPING ON FACTS AND FALSEHOODS

16 January 1996

TRIPS AGREEMENT OF THE Dunkel Draft—now the UR Agreement—has been the source of abounding controversies. Recently, a challenge to a neem-based patent held by W.R. Grace & Co. has returned many of these controversies to centre stage. Backed by the signatures of more than 1,00,000 Indians and 225 agricultural, scientific and trade groups in forty-five countries, Jeremy Rifkin, president, Foundation on Economic Trends, has petitioned the US patent and trademark office to review Grace's patent, issued in 1992, for 'storage-stable azadirachtin formulations'. Azadirachtin is a natural substance extracted from neem.

The first controversy, in its extreme form, has centred on the possibility that TRIPS will lead to the patenting of the entire neem tree and that Indian citizens may lose free access to even neem branches used as toothbrushes. In a less extreme form, the controversy has manifested itself in claims that foreign companies could, and indeed, have, patent natural substances obtainable from neem.

Claims False

Any claims that natural substances such as azadirachtin can be patented are utterly false; only products made from natural substances (for example, a neem cream or an azadirachtin-based pesticide) can be patented. As Grace notes in its response to the Rifkin petition, its patent 'narrowly focuses on a formula which extends the shelf life and effectiveness of the neem-based pesticide'. At present, according to Grace, there are forty different patents on products or processes related to azadirachtin. Twenty-two different companies or groups of which three are Indian own these.

The second controversy, not altogether without merit, rests on the argument that Grace has essentially acquired exclusive rights to the use of a process and product that Indian farmers have been using for decades. This is the main thrust of the petition filed by Mr Rifkin and his allies. They argue that the patent gives Grace exclusive rights to formulations which have been developed and used by Indian farmers for centuries. Typically, the farmers break the seeds and soak them overnight in water, alcohol or other solvents. The emulsions float to the surface, and can be placed directly on crops as a pesticide and insect-repellent. According to Mr Rifkin, Grace modified this process in minor technical ways that are not truly innovative. Under present patent laws and those envisaged in the TRIPS Agreement, an invention is not patentable if the difference between it and the prior art is obvious.

Grace argues, however, that its process and product represent a substantial innovation over the traditional practice; in particular, its formulations extend the shelf life of the pesticide from a few days or weeks to two years. Traditional methods used by Indian farmers yield pesticide emulsions, which deteriorate within a matter of days. Mr Rifkin's petition counters, 'Several Indian scientists had developed stabilization techniques prior to W.R. Grace's patent application. Stabilization research occurred within India in the 1960s and 1970s.'

From the available information, it is difficult to judge whether Grace's formulations were the outcome of non-obvious advances over the existing knowledge at the time it applied for the patent. Conversely, Mr Rifkin's petition does not pinpoint which existing processes yielded stable azadirachtin-based formulations and for how long were they stable. This is the central issue the US patent and trademark office will have to resolve in the next few months. If it rules in Grace's favour, the patent can still be challenged in the US courts.

Thorny Issues

The third controversy raises a much more fundamental but thorny issue: how should the benefits deriving from the world's biological resources be shared? This issue was on the agenda of the 1992 Earth Summit. The Biodiversity Convention adopted at the Summit declared that countries have a sovereign right to their resources and that benefits resulting from them should be shared fairly. Though the Bush administration refused to sign the Convention, the Clinton administration has done so. The Convention now awaits ratification by the US Congress. It is not clear what immediate impact the Convention will have on the division of benefits deriving from biological resources. But because such resources are located predominantly in developing countries, it is in their interest to keep pressuring the international community to devise mechanisms for ensuring them a fair share of the benefits.

A final set of controversies relates to the impact of the Grace patent on India. To the extent that Mr Rifkin and his allies are pushing for a larger share of benefits from biological resources for developing countries, they are to be commended. But in the process, they also seem to contend that the patent has been harmful to India. This is incorrect. The main argument offered to support this contention is that the purchases of neem seeds by Grace have made the seeds more expensive for Indian farmers.

Grace has been quick to point out that its purchases amount to only 3 per cent of the seeds collected which account for 16 per cent of the total seeds growth. The reliability of such figures notwithstanding, this defence is flawed: if the elasticity of the supply of neem seeds is low, even small purchases can have a large effect on the price. More importantly, the demand for neem seeds could grow substantially in the future.

Good Increases

The difficulty with Mr Rifkin's argument is not that Grace's purchases cannot raise neem-seed prices perceptibly, but it is that these price increases are good, and not bad, for India as a whole. When oil prices rose, countries exporting oil profited from this. Closer home, though tea exports hurt tea drinkers in India by raising tea prices, such exports are beneficial overall: the losses of the tea drinkers are more than offset by the profits earned on tea exports. As net sellers of neem seeds, Indian farmers will benefit from a rise in their prices even though they are adversely affected as their users. Indeed, Indian fears ought to be the reverse: that foreign companies might buy seeds at throwaway prices and, thus, reap virtually all benefits from them. Fortunately, even here, GATI permits export taxes, which can be used to favourably change the distribution of the benefits from neem seeds.

It has also been suggested that Indian farmers will now have to pay royalty on products based on processes they themselves helped devise. As noted above, the issue of whether Grace's and other similar inventions were non-obvious is as yet unresolved. But even if it is accepted that it was non-obvious, for the existing patents, Indian farmers will not have to pay any royalty. Agricultural products are, as yet, not patentable in India; none of the neem-based products are patented in India. Thus, it is perfectly legal for an Indian farmer to market a product identical to Grace's in India. What he cannot do is call it Neemix—a registered trademark of Grace—or sell it in the US where Grace holds a patent on the product.

62

YES TO IPRS, BUT NOT UNDER THE WTO

26 January 2000

IN A PROVOCATIVE COLUMN last week, Swaminathan Aiyar (*The Economic Times*, 19 January 2000) took the view that the inclusion of IPRs in the WTO was a good idea after all. He argued that IPRs have now become central to the evolution of world trade and as such belong to the Geneva-based institution. The veteran columnist has such good instincts that only rarely can one disagree with him. This is one of those occasions.

At the outset, let me state that the opposition to the inclusion of IPRs in the WTO does not imply opposition to IPRs. Though India opposed the Agreement on TRIPS, which will eventually bring IPRs under the purview of the WTO, it has long had world-class legislation in copyrights. This legislation meets or exceeds the standards required by the TRIPS Agreement and even protects computer programmes on a par with artistic and literary works.

India has also had a patent regime, though our standards in this area have been substantially weaker than those required by the TRIPS Agreement. In particular, it allows the patenting of only processes (and not products) in pharmaceuticals, chemicals and food. But this has been a deliberate choice to limit the monopoly power of the patent holder, thereby making newly discovered medicines rapidly accessible to the poor. It is not an accident that a sizable low-cost medicine industry has evolved around reverse engineering in India.

It is tempting to argue that in the absence of the TRIPS Agreement, *nationally* chosen intellectual property rights regimes will hamper trade in an age when products are increasingly technology-intensive. Yet, there is little evidence to support this view. All the existing division of labour between 'brain intensive' and 'material intensive' goods that Swaminathan Aiyar describes in his column and ascribes to the TRIPS Agreement has, in fact, taken place under the *nationally* chosen IPRs. Even the recent, much-publicized innovation of a drug by the Indian pharmaceutical firm Ranbaxy, sold for $60 million to AG Bayer, has taken place under the nationally chosen IPRs. For the implementation of the TRIPS Agreement did not begin until 1 January 2000. And full implementation will not be achieved until 1 January 2005.

The reason why innovations and trade have progressed smoothly even before the implementation of the TRIPS Agreement is that developed countries, where much of the demand for newly innovated products is concentrated, have had intellectual property rights regimes at par with the TRIPS Agreement for some time. This protection has been sufficient to make innovations profitable even in countries where intellectual property rights protection is lax.

Thus, there is nothing to prevent an Indian firm such as Ranbaxy from patenting the fruits of its innovation in developed countries. The popular argument that Indian firms do not innovate because India has a weak patent regime is patently false. What matters for the profitability of innovations is whether they enjoy sufficient protection in the markets where demand is concentrated. These are mainly developed country markets.

What the TRIPS Agreement accomplishes is to require all WTO members to adhere to the same intellectual property rights standards, which have been chosen to approximately equal those already achieved in developed countries. Therefore, the effective burden of adjustment falls virtually entirely on developing countries. Economists Michael Finger and Philip Schuler estimate that the cost of legislation required to implement the TRIPS Agreement alone will be a hefty $150 million per country. For many poor African countries, this is a substantial burden with no commensurate benefits.

But more importantly, under the TRIPS Agreement, all countries must provide both product and process protection to all innovations for twenty years. Under TRIPS, it will be illegal to reverse engineer the patented drugs, making India's low-cost medicine industry a thing of the past. To take just one dramatic example, if a cure for AIDS is found, millions of patients in poor countries will be unable to afford it.

The principal objective of the WTO is to remove trade barriers. But IPRs can hardly be construed as trade barriers and as such constitute what many of us call the 'non-trade agenda'. Countries choose intellectual property rights standards with a view to balance the rights of innovators against benefits from innovations in the light of the prevailing social and ethical norms rather than to acquire any 'unfair' advantage in international trade. Like other domestic policies such as excise tax, labour and land laws, and investment rules, intellectual property rights do have an effect on international trade. But this hardly justifies equating lower intellectual property rights to higher trade barriers.

There is yet another factor distinguishing trade barriers from IPRs and other non-trade issues including labour and environmental standards that are now creeping into the WTO agenda. The removal of trade barriers is an efficiency-enhancing activity that benefits all parties including the one undertaking liberalization. In contrast, non-trade agenda, as pursued so far, redistributes income from the developing to developed countries and may even lower world efficiency. For instance, by extending the monopoly right of innovators, the TRIPS Agreement is likely to lower efficiency.

Worst of all, the TRIPS Agreement has become an effective instrument for promoting more non-trade agenda by labour and environmental groups. They say the WTO must now do for workers and nature what it has already done for corporate interests. The following excerpt from an article in the *Washington Post* by Elaine Bernard on behalf of labour groups offers a dramatic illustration: 'For example, the WTO says its purview does not include social issues—only trade. So it claims to be powerless to do anything about a repressive regime selling the products of sweatshops that use child labour. Yet let the same regime use the same children to produce "pirated" CDs or fake designer T-shirts, and the WTO can spring into action with a series of powerful levers to protect corporate "intellectual property rights".'

63

HOW TO BREAK THE TRIPS IMPASSE

3 April 2003

THE DOHA NEGOTIATIONS ARE at an impasse partially due to a disagreement between the US and other WTO members on how to effectively extend the compulsory-licensing provision of the TRIPS Agreement to countries that lack manufacturing capacity in medicines. The impasse can be broken.

The TRIPS Agreement gives all WTO members the right to issue a compulsory licence on a patented product to a third party without prior authorization of the patent holder in the case of health emergencies or other circumstances of extreme urgency. The Doha Declaration on the TRIPS Agreement and Public Health reaffirms this right: 'Each Member has the right to determine what constitutes a national emergency or other circumstances of extreme urgency, it being understood that public health crises, including those relating to HIV/AIDS, tuberculosis, malaria and other epidemics, can represent a national emergency or other circumstances of extreme urgency.'

For the WTO members such as India and Brazil, who have manufacturing capacity in pharmaceuticals, this provision ensures access to patented medicines at low costs in health emergencies. But many of the poorest countries lack this capacity. The only potential course available to them is to issue the compulsory licence to a manufacturer in a third country. But the current rules rule out this option.

During negotiations for the Doha Declaration on the TRIPS Agreement and Public Health, developing countries had insisted on finding a solution that would allow the WTO members with insufficient or no manufacturing capacity to take advantage of the compulsory licensing provisions. But no agreement could be reached so the Declaration instructed the WTO Council on TRIPS to 'find an expeditious solution to this problem' and to report to the General Council before the end of 2002. Due to disagreements between the US and other members, the TRIPS Council missed the deadline. The last two attempts to break the impasse by mini-ministerial conferences at Sydney and Tokyo respectively ended in failure.

The WTO members must resolve three issues to bring the negotiations on this subject to a close: which countries would have the right to issue compulsory licences to manufacturers in third countries, which countries would qualify as third countries for the issuance of such licences, and for which diseases?

The resolution of the first question is most critical to breaking the current impasse. In principle, it may be argued that all the WTO members must have the right to issue a compulsory licence to manufacturers in third countries. Otherwise, we create a dual regime in which some countries are able to take advantage of the compulsory licensing provision while others are not, even though it was intended for all of them. An exclusionary list means that countries such as Singapore and Norway, which lack a domestic pharmaceutical industry, could be effectively denied the right to issue the compulsory licence in emergencies, while larger countries such as Canada and Germany, which have a pharmaceutical industry, will be able to take advantage of it.

The fear expressed by the US pharmaceutical industry is that leaving all the WTO members free to issue compulsory licences to third countries can potentially move a significant proportion of the production and sales of patented drugs outside the purview of the patent holder. It also contends that the mandate in the Doha Declaration on the TRIPS Agreement and Public Health for devising ways to give effective access to compulsory licensing to countries without manufacturing capacity was intended for poor countries even though it is worded more generally.

Regardless of which view is right, progress can be made only through a compromise. The best course for developing countries would be to insist on a per capita income or other similar criterion. For example, all countries that qualify as Low or Lower Middle Income Countries according to the World Bank definition could be conferred the right to issue a compulsory licence to a manufacturer in a third country. A more generous criterion would confer the right on all developing countries other than those in the OECD.

This approach has several advantages. First, it offers an objective criterion, which has a precedent in the WTO, as, for example, in the case of the export-subsidy exemption in the Agreement on Subsidies and Countervailing Measures. Second, it eliminates the need for an outside institution such as the WHO or WTO to determine which countries do or do not have 'sufficient' domestic manufacturing capacity. Third, it allows countries to acquire manufacturing capacity in a subset of patented medicines without the threat of being eliminated from the eligibility list. Finally, it maximizes the potential benefits to the poor. Even countries such as India and Brazil, which have manufacturing capacity, may find it necessary to go to third countries in certain emergencies.

As regards who qualifies as a third country, no restrictions other than the WTO membership should be imposed. To maximize benefits to the importing country, which would be faced with a health emergency, that country should be free to choose the manufacturer from an unrestricted set. A compromise position, likely to be more acceptable to the US pharmaceutical industry, would be to restrict the list to developing country members of the WTO. Potential exporters such as India will evidently benefit from such a restriction on potential competitors.

On the third and last question, there have been demands from the US pharmaceutical industry to limit the diseases for which the compulsory licence can be issued. This is an unjustifiable demand. The limitations on the countries with manufacturing capacity have already been defined in the TRIPS Agreement and the Doha Declaration on the TRIPS Agreement and Public Health. There is no rationale for subjecting the countries without domestic manufacturing capacity to additional or different limitations.

64

CURBING CHILD LABOUR: RUGMARK LABEL ON THE MAT

14 November 1996

AN IMPORTANT BATTLE WHICH India and many other developing countries will have to fight at the first WTO ministerial conference in Singapore in December 1996 and its aftermath is against the introduction of a social clause in the WTO charter. If the US and the EU succeed in their demands for such a clause, WTO members will acquire the right to impose trade sanctions on other members judged to have low labour standards in certain areas. The principal labour practice under attack by the US and the EU is the use of child labour. With an estimated 40 million children participating in the workforce—some sources place the number at as much as 115 million—the potential damage to India's exports from such a clause could be very substantial.

As the leading international economist Jagdish Bhagwati has argued, the case for a social clause in the WTO charter is indefensible. His arguments, detailed in the Prebisch Lecture, leave little doubt that the demands for the social clause are yet another manifestation of the growing protectionism in the US and the EU.

Case Rejected

While rejecting the case for a social clause, however, many developing-country critics of child labour have suggested that alternative strategies be adopted to combat the practice. Among these is the use of 'social labelling', which effectively gives the consumers the option to refuse to buy goods produced by child labour.

Thus, in 1994, the Indo-German Export Promotion Programme, the South Asian Coalition on Child Servitude, which claims to be a conglomeration of 200 NGOs, UNICEF and a few carpet exporters came together to form the Rugmark Foundation. The Foundation, in turn, took it upon itself to certify through the Rugmark logo that the carpet in question is 'not made by child labour'. Under current procedures, carpet exporters must apply for the logo. If, upon inspection, the Foundation finds that the exporter does not employ child labour, it gives the latter the logo.

But even this strategy has serious problems: it could well be ineffective or even counter-productive. Let me explain why.

First, the practice of child labour is widespread: Children are employed in virtually all industries in India. Zeroing in on a single industry such as carpets can simply push children from that industry into others like textiles and clothing, household services or construction with virtually no impact on the total number of child workers.

Second, the effect of introducing Rugmark on the carpet industry itself could be ambiguous. The separation of carpets by the label need not move children out of the carpet industry in significant numbers. It could simply create dual markets: a low-price market for carpets made by children and a high-price market for carpets made by adults. Thus, the production and marketing of carpets made with child labour could continue, only the wages paid to children would decline due to the decrease in the price of carpets made by them.

Adverse Effects

Third, if 'social labelling' in the carpet industry or on a wider scale is successful in moving children out of employment, it can very well lead to adverse social effects. On the one hand, it could lead to increased juvenile delinquency and, on the other, to destitution and prostitution among children. Lest this seems pure speculation, consider a recent experience in Bangladesh. The proposed Harkin Bill in the US Congress against imports from countries using child labour and threats by the US child labour coalition, an NGO, to campaign against garments from Bangladesh led to fears in Bangladesh that it might soon lose access to the lucrative US garments market. The Bangladesh Garment Manufacturers' and Exporters' Association (BGMEA) responded on an emergency basis and induced garment factories to lay off thousands of young workers. The result was more, not less, distress for children. With no place to go—UNICEF later found—some of the children ended up becoming prostitutes and welders. The BGMEA had to reverse its decision. Later, a tripartite agreement was worked out between BGMEA, ILO and UNICEF. Taking recourse to constructive ambiguity, the agreement stipulated that child labour would be phased out of the garment industry 'at an early date', but no children would be retrenched without being rehabilitated.

Fourth, entrusting an agency such as the Rugmark Foundation, whose resources are limited, with the authority to certify whether or not an exporter uses child labour is likely to result in an abuse of the authority. The Foundation was created in October 1994 with five full-time inspectors, and the plan was to raise the number of inspectors to eight by the end of April 1995. Given that the carpet industry is mostly rural in character and is spread over a vast area of 1,00,000 square miles, it is simply not possible for a handful of inspectors to verify the absence of child labour even once, let alone repeatedly, in a significant proportion of the industry. The inability to monitor could result in charges of fraud. This could then hurt even 'good' firms, which could become unwitting victims of the problem: Rugmark will survive, but not the firms.

Inevitable Bias

Fifth, the existence of Rugmark introduces an inevitable bias in favour of large factories. Regular inspections required for effective enforcement are feasible only when production is concentrated in large establishments. It is unlikely that tiny operations located in remote villages will be able to obtain the Rugmark logo even if they've never used child labour. Thus, the essentially rural, cottage-industry organization of carpet manufacturing will have to give way to large factories. This is not necessarily a change for the better.

Finally, labelling such as 'no child labour' is prejudicial, given the indiscriminate agitation against it, which does not distinguish in the political domain between exploitative and other uses of child labour. How are labels designed and by whom does matter. 'Eco-labelling', aimed at distinguishing 'environment-friendly' products from other products has been a contentious issue. Even the involvement of the International Standards Organization (ISO) in developing guidelines for eco-labels has been a matter of debate in the WTO committee on trade and environment.

These arguments lead to the conclusion that though developing countries share the developed countries' goal of ending child labour, there are few sensible paths to achieve it in a short period of time.

Ultimately, the main vehicles for achieving the goal are rapid economic growth, and the expansion of primary and secondary education. The former will raise adult incomes and eliminate the families' dependence on child labour for survival. The latter will offer a natural alternative to children as they are moved out of the labour force.

65

THE RETURN OF LABOUR STANDARDS INTO THE WTO?

17 November 1999

WITH THE SEATTLE MINISTERIAL Conference right around the corner, the US has tabled a proposal for a working group on labour standards at the WTO. The US wants the working group to prepare a report in two years on the relationship between international trade and employment, social protection and the so-called core labour standards that include child labour. It also wants the proposed working group to study the impact of derogations from national labour standards in export processing zones.

Three years ago, at the conclusion of the Singapore Ministerial Conference, developing countries had taken a sigh of relief that the issue of labour standards had at last been delegated to the ILO. The Singapore Declaration, signed by all the WTO members, including the US, provided ample grounds for this sense of relief. The sole paragraph dealing with labour standards in the Declaration, reproduced below in its entirety, states:

We renew our commitment to the observance of internationally recognized core labour standards. The International Labour Organization (ILO) is the competent body to set and deal with these standards, and we affirm our support for its work in promoting them. We believe that economic growth and development fostered by increased trade and further trade liberalization contribute to the promotion of these standards. We reject the use of labour standards for protectionist purposes, and agree that the comparative advantage of countries, particularly low-wage developing countries, must in no way be put into question. In this regard, we note that the WTO and ILO Secretariats will continue their existing collaboration.

Only the most credulous readers will argue that this paragraph leaves the door open to setting up a working group on labour standards at the WTO. Indeed, in his concluding speech, Singapore's Trade and Industry Minister Mr Yeo Cheow Tong, who also chaired the ministerial conference, had explicitly noted, 'Some delegations had expressed the concern that this text may lead the WTO to acquire a competence to undertake further work in the relationship between trade and core labour standards. I want to assure these delegations that this text will not permit such a development.' Yet, in a move that is reminiscent of its heavy-handed tactics in the UR negotiations on IPR, the US has reinterpreted the Singapore mandate and put forward the proposal for a WTO working group on labour standards.

The renewed effort by the US raises once again the issue of how developing countries should respond to developed country demands for the linkage between trade and labour standards. This was one of the several important questions debated on 5–6 November by academics and developing-country policymakers at a conference at Harvard University. The principal panellist on the subject, Professor Devesh Kapur of Harvard University, noted that the available options ranged from refusing any discussion of the subject even at the cost of a total breakdown of the Seattle discussions to a 'grand bargain' in which developing countries could agree to negotiate labour standards in return for more liberal rules of migration for labour in developed countries and considerable weakening of the agreement on IP. He felt it was critical for developing countries to turn the terms of the debate from standards to the core issue of poverty. He concluded, however, that the best course would be to insist on compliance with the spirit of the Singapore mandate for the delegation of the subject to the ILO.

Professor Dani Rodrik, also of Harvard University, argued that by refusing to discuss labour standards in the WTO, developing countries would be missing the opportunity to take the high moral ground since, to date, the US had itself refused to sign the ILO conventions on core labour standards. They would also be depriving themselves of the possibility of negotiating reciprocal concessions from developed countries. For instance, they could ask for tighter rules on AD and increased immigration into developed countries in return for enforcing core labour standards, which is a desirable goal in any case.

Disagreeing with Rodrik, the present author argued that the *discussions* should be in the ILO and that developing countries should eschew *negotiations* in the WTO. Once negotiations begin, rich countries are in a position to threaten the rival nations with retaliation or offer them side deals on an individual basis until the remaining countries are too few and powerless to resist. This strategy was successfully employed by the US in the TRIPS negotiations and may be repeated in the event of a negotiation on labour standards.

A recent statement entitled 'Third World Intellectuals and NGOs: Statement Against Linkage' (TWIN-SAL), circulated by Professor Jagdish Bhagwati of Columbia University and others, argues that achieving freer trade and improving labour standards are both desirable goals. But assigning them to a single institution, namely the WTO, is like trying to kill two birds with one stone. Such a strategy is bound to miss both birds except by fluke.

Therefore, it is best to let the WTO promote free trade and delegate the responsibility to promote labour standards to the ILO. TWIN-SAL suggests that the ILO could be asked to do periodic reviews of objectionable labour practices in both developed and developing countries along the lines of TPR, done by the WTO. Such reviews can be then used to put moral pressure on the offending countries to improve upon their standards. This approach has the advantage that it maintains symmetry across rich and poor countries. By contrast, under the US approach, only the objectionable labour practices in developing countries are being addressed. Moreover, in the WTO, only bigger, richer countries can credibly wield the instrument of trade sanctions.

66

SEATTLE: FAILURE WITHOUT LOSERS

13 December 1999

TALKING TO THE SEATTLE Post-Intelligencer during his visit to Seattle, Bill Clinton decided to take a long leap from his original demand for a WTO working group on labour standards and proceeded to tell the newspaper that the working group should define core standards, which should then be part of every trade agreement. 'And ultimately,' he continued, 'I would favour a system in which sanctions would come for violating any provision of a trade agreement.' According to many, this statement was the last straw that broke the camel's back and sealed the fate of the negotiations.

The truth of the matter is that neither Clinton's statement nor the (un)civil society groups to which it catered did any such thing. The camel had arrived in Seattle with an already broken back. It was only the USTR, Charlene Barshefsky, who refused to confront the looming failure, painting an overly optimistic picture prior to the conference. But within a week, as the conference prepared to fold without an agreement, dropping all pretences, she admitted, 'We could have stayed all night. We could have stayed for five days. It wouldn't matter: governments weren't ready to take the lead.'

It may be surmised that Clinton had already sown the seed of the failure in early November when he put on the table the proposal for a WTO working group on labour standards. One cannot rule out the possibility that this was a calculated move on his part to assist Vice President Al Gore in the forthcoming presidential elections. If developing countries capitulated and agreed to a WTO working group, he would have positioned Gore favourably in the elections, especially with respect to labour interests. If not, no WTO round will be launched but he will, nevertheless, still win kudos from the labour lobbies and successfully relegate the contentious trade issues to the background. After he arrived in Seattle, the insurmountable resistance to the working group from developing countries must have reinforced this view, leading him opportunistically to go a step further and call for eventual WTO provisions for trade sanctions for violations of agreed labour standards.

The Government of India, like almost all other WTO members, is likely to take a sigh of relief at the outcome. Frankly, given where the round was heading, even pro-free trade economists such as myself are relieved for the moment: it was better not to kick off negotiations at all than to launch a round that piles up non-trade agendas on to an institution that is specifically designed to address trade issues and, ironically, threatens to reverse the trade liberalization that was achieved in the previous rounds.

The Seattle episode brings both good news and bad news for developing countries. The bad news is that developing countries can ill-afford to be complacent about their access to developed-country markets. The increasing willingness of the US government to lend its ear to civil society groups opens the door wider to interventions by it on behalf of protectionist interests that increasingly disguise themselves as groups pursuing genuine social goals. The good news, however, is that developing countries are not powerless: They have arrived on the global negotiating scene. With these countries standing united in opposition, even the mighty US failed to launch a round that would have moved the system closer to bringing labour standards into the WTO.

But we are hardly off the hook and there is little time to be lost rejoicing in having dodged the bullet. The next two years promise to be especially crucial when fresh attempts will be made to launch the new round, with the US returning with its labour and environmental agenda. Developing countries will need to fight the ensuing battle on many fronts. And India, the key developing country that is also likely to bear the brunt of labour and environmental clauses if they are incorporated into the WTO, bears special responsibility in leading the charge.

At the governmental level, it is essential to strengthen the bridges that got spontaneously built across developing country delegations in Seattle in response to one-sided demonstrations and their mindless endorsement by the US' government. Rather than limit ourselves to the G-15, we must take the lead in forging a wider coalition. In particular, *Prime Minister Vajpayee must initiate immediately an effort to get as many developing country governments as possible to sign a joint statement opposing unequivocally any inclusion of labour standards from future WTO rounds.*

We must also actively seek media opportunities to take our message directly to the American and European public. In this respect, the former commerce secretary, A.V. Ganesan, is to be applauded for his excellent defence of the developing country position in a recent article in the *Washington Post*. Also laudable are the efforts of Pradeep Mehta of CUTS, an NGO, for informing the readers of the London *Financial Times* that, contrary to the impression conveyed in the Western media, as many as 120 million workers around the world actually oppose bringing labour standards into the WTO.

By the same token, it was disappointing to learn that during the Seattle conference, the Indian delegation passed the opportunity to appear on the influential television programme *PBS Newshour*, hosted by Jim Lehrer. The *Newshour* then invited its Pakistani counterpart to join the European Commissioner Pascal Lamy and Brazilian Foreign Minister Luiz Felipe Lampreia. It is unlikely, however, that the Pakistani representative carried the same credibility with the American public on issues such as child labour that a representative of the largest democracy in the world would have.

Finally, our own civil society groups bear a special responsibility in this fight. The ethos being promoted by the US civil society groups is that NGOs around the world speak with one voice: *their* voice. Our NGOs need to articulate the message to the industrial world that even as they support higher labour and environmental standards, they carry a *different* message.

67

THE SHOE IS ON THE OTHER FOOT

20 December 2000

IN A RECENT REPORT entitled *Unfair Advantage: Workers' Freedom of Association in the United States under International Human Rights Standards* (31 August 2000), Human Rights Watch offers a stunning indictment of the laws governing worker rights and their enforcement in the US. Based on systematic field research in California, Florida, Michigan, New York and numerous other states, the report offers an unusual window into the violations of worker rights that happen routinely in the country.

The report also reveals a danger underlying the proposed link between trade and labour rights that has not been recognized to date: the link may lead to trade wars between developing and developed countries in which each accuses the other of violations of labour rights.

But consider first the assessment of the laws themselves as presented in the report. Addressing the US laws on the rights of workers, the report states:

Millions of workers are expressly barred from the law's protection of the right to organize. The U.S. legal doctrine allowing employers to permanently replace workers who exercise the right to strike effectively nullifies the right. Mutual support among workers and unions recognized in most of the world as legitimate expressions of solidarity is harshly proscribed under the U.S. law as illegal secondary boycotts.

The report is even harsher when it comes to the protection of worker rights actually conferred by the existing laws. Based on the first-hand evidence gathered from field studies in a large number of states, it concludes, 'Many workers who try to form and join trade unions to bargain with their employers are spied on, harassed, pressured, threatened, suspended, fired, deported or otherwise victimized in reprisal for their exercise of the right to freedom of association.' The report goes on, 'The cases studied in this report are not isolated exceptions in an otherwise benign environment for workers' freedom of association.'

Led by Jagdish Bhagwati, many of us have argued for the past several years that the US agenda on the proposed social clause in the WTO charter is one, sided. Issues such as child labour, minimum wage, freedom of association and rights to bargain collectively figure prominently on its list. But because of the deficiency of its own laws, the rights of workers to strike without the fear of retrenchment and to organize secondary boycotts are conspicuously missing from it. The Human Rights Watch report echoes and effectively validates this argument.

But more importantly, the report brings to light an aspect of the proposed trade-labour link that has not been recognized to date. The inability to enforce labour laws satisfactorily even by the greatest power on earth suggests that delegating to the WTO the power to enforce higher labour standards runs the risk of wrecking the trading system.

Thus, suppose that a consensus can be forged among nations on the desirable minimum labour standards. As a concrete example, take the recent ILO Convention on the Worst Forms of Child Labour, 1999 (C182). This convention has been signed by all 175 members of the ILO with a promise to rapidly ratify it. What will happen if this set of standards is enforced through the WTO instrumentality? We can be sure that either we will achieve no progress in the standards or end up in a trade war.

To invoke trade sanctions against a country, we must first determine whether it is effectively enforcing the standards. But how is this determination to be made? Should we simply accept the government's word for it or ask an independent agency such as the Human Rights Watch? In the former, no country is likely to be found in violation and little progress on the standard will be made. And in the latter, every country is likely to be found in violation and a trade war can scarcely be avoided.

To date, while assessing the role of trade sanctions in enforcing labour standards, proponents of these sanctions have focused exclusively on the possibility of their use by developed against developing countries. But in view of the lax enforcement of labour laws in developed countries themselves, we must worry equally about sanctions by developing on developed countries. And, indeed, there is much danger of developing countries imposing sanctions on one another. Thus, a disaster is likely to visit the trading system if labour standards are enforced through trade sanctions.

Some may argue that since trade sanctions by developing countries on developed ones will hurt their own national interests, they are unlikely to target the latter. This is a naïve argument. Trade policy in developing countries is driven as much by producer interests as in developed countries. Anyone who doubts this fact need look only at the large number of AD actions India has taken recently against both developed and developing countries.

A sad dimension of the debate on trade-labour link has been the failure of our leaders to inform the American public why India opposes such a link. Last year, just prior to the Seattle conference, the London *Financial Times* noted in an editorial (3 November 1999) that most Western governments 'admit privately that they lack a persuasive intellectual case' for linking trade and labour. It is a pity that despite this, our leaders have not made enough of an effort to counter the public opinion in the US.

With the election of George Bush as the president, we may think that the pressure for a trade-labour link will now disappear. But there is no room for such complacency. The House and Senate are evenly divided between the Democrats and Republicans. But more importantly, in four years' time, a Democrat is likely to be back in the White House. None of the past three presidents who failed to win the popular vote, as Bush has, got a second term. Our best bet remains convincing the American public of the futility of the link sought by their government.

68

PROTECTIONISM'S OTHER NAMES: TRAPS INDIA SHOULD AVOID AT G-20

(With Jagdish Bhagwati)

23 February 2010

LAGGING EMPLOYMENT RECOVERY AND continuing high levels of unemployment have marked the macroeconomic recovery in the US. So, it is natural that the US, which chaired the G-20 meeting in Pittsburgh, would use its privileged position as the host to invite the US Secretary of Labor, a well-known union activist, to convene a meeting of the employment and labour ministers on the jobs situation prior to the next G-20 heads of state meeting in Canada.

The macroeconomic aspects of the labour situation are indeed a proper focus of such a meeting. But the Pittsburgh declaration goes further and urges the G-20 countries not to 'disregard or weaken internationally recognized labour standards' and to 'implement policies consistent with ILO fundamental principles and rights at work'.

Led by their federation, the AFL-CIO, the US labour unions have had a long history of pushing for a 'social clause' in trade treaties at every forum. For international economists familiar with this history, and the stranglehold the unions exercise on the Democratic Party and Congress today, the G-20 declaration constitutes a carefully designed trap. It is drafted in a way in which the US and the EU can get developing-country employment and labour ministers unfamiliar with the agenda and the influence of developed-country unions to endorse measures that have a 'feel-good' façade, but are in fact a protectionist dagger aimed at our jugulars. Indeed, the US Undersecretary of Labor Sandra Polanski, who has been put in charge of the meeting, is well known to us as a long-standing proponent of such measures and a relentless activist on their behalf.

When the unions in the US and the EU insist on a set of labour standards in the developing countries with which they compete for markets at home and abroad, they take an altruistic line: we are doing this out of solidarity, we are doing it for *your* workers. But when you push them hard, they always say: it is 'unfair' to have to compete with others who do not have our standards. Now, the latter is an argument about competition—it is about losing out in trade—so it is an argument motivated by self-interest, not altruism.

The traditional demand by the American unions has been that others should have the same standards as the US does. But this argument would be comic, were it not tragic. Is the US a paragon of virtue on labour standards? After all, less than 10 per cent of its private workforce is now unionized. And this is because the main weapon that unions have, the right to strike, has been crippled by the Taft-Hartley legislation of over fifty years ago. Even liberal universities have refused to let their administrative employees organize. In consequence, Human Rights Watch, which has investigated the right to unionize, a central feature of the ILO principles, has found that this is far from being guaranteed in the US.

So, the US unions have shifted to asking for IL0 'core standards' instead. But this will not wash either. The US has not even ratified many of these core conventions. So, in effect, this version is also to be aimed at others, not themselves.

The truth of the matter is that the name of the game here is that, frightened by the competition from our exports, the American and the European unions seek relief. This can be obtained by conventional import protectionism. But, if this is constrained by WTO obligations, then it can be obtained by raising the cost of production of the foreign rivals. Raising their labour obligations is one way of doing this. Therefore, we have called it a form of 'export protectionism', like the Voluntary Export Restraints where the exporting country restrains its exports.

An alert must therefore be sounded and the matter discussed at the highest levels of the Indian government, with the labour minister fully briefed by trade experts and officials on the traps that await him at the impending meeting.

We can also be sure that the US delegation will be assisted by Washington think-tank proponents of such protectionist proposals, many of them from the Carnegie Endowment (where Ms Polaski sat during the Bush years), the Petersen Institute for International Economics (which has had a history of advocating trade-labour link), and the Center for Global Development (which is captive to the protectionist notion of fair trade extending to labour standards in trade). Our best trade experts can effectively counter their arguments if only we use them.

But it is not enough to push back on proposals that will harm us, and the developing countries more generally. India needs to be proactive and offer its own resolution that explicitly discourages the insertion of labour clauses into trade treaties and institutions. The intellectual argument is on our side on this issue. We should not be content to act as if we can eat at the banquet, but have no say in the choice of the menu.

69

SAY 'NO' AT COPENHAGEN
23 July 2009

DURING HER RECENT VISIT, US Secretary of State Hillary Clinton forcefully urged India to contribute to carbon-emission reductions to combat global warming. India's Environment Minister Jairam Ramesh responded with equal force stating that emission caps would not cut ice in India. Widespread criticisms of this response in the Western press notwithstanding, Ramesh is on a strong wicket when refusing to accept mitigation obligations.

The push Secretary Clinton has made for emission reductions by India partially reflects a switch in the US' policy towards climate change under President Obama. The Congress, which has also come to be dominated by the Democratic Party following the November 2008 elections, reinforces this switch. Specifically, the House of Representatives recently passed the American Clean Energy and Security (ACES) Bill of 2009, which provides for a 'cap and trade' programme that would place an annual cap on the overall carbon emissions in the US. The cap would progressively tighten to 80 per cent of 2005 emissions in 2020, 58 per cent in 2030 and 17 per cent in 2050. Each year, the government would issue tradable permits matching the amount of the carbon cap. Companies would be required to acquire permits for every ton of carbon they emit either from the government or the marketplace. To become law, the Senate must also pass the ACES Bill.

While 'cap and trade' programmes have existed in Europe as a part of the Kyoto Protocol, an international treaty negotiated under the auspices of the United Nations Framework Convention on Climate Change (UNFCCC), the proposed US programme differs from them in one key respect: beginning in 2020, it requires the US President to impose tariffs on selected carbon-intensive goods from countries that do not introduce caps on carbon emissions. It specifically targets India and China by requiring the USTR to annually certify that these countries are adopting emission standards at least as vigorous as those prevailing in the US.

According to legal opinion, the import tariff is likely to violate some key WTO provisions. Even President Obama, who has actively sought the passage of the ACES Bill has expressed disappointment with the insertion of the import duty provision. Nevertheless, if the bill does become law, India will have to eventually challenge any carbon tariffs the US imposes on it in the WTO DSB and be willing to retaliate in a WTO-consistent manner.

But a more immediate and perhaps bigger battle on climate change looms in Copenhagen in December. According to the UNFCCC, which came into force in 1994 and is currently subscribed by 192 countries, developed countries must periodically negotiate mitigation commitments to avoid 'dangerous anthropogenic interference' with the climate system. The convention explicitly exempts developing countries from similar mitigation commitments. Consistent with this provision, the Kyoto Protocol, ratified in 2005, requires only developed countries to mitigate.

The US, which had refused to ratify the Kyoto Protocol but is now keen on a post-Kyoto climate change treaty, insists, however, that China and India undertake binding mitigation commitments. It reasons that these countries are among the world's four largest emitters in absolute terms.

But beyond this size-based argument, there is little else on which the US case can be pegged, especially against India. Given India has the second-largest population in the world with the US being a very distant third, it is hardly surprising that India is among the top four emitters in absolute terms. But in per capita terms, it ranks a low 137th. Forty per cent of the households in the country are even without an electricity connection. And there are 300 million people living in abject poverty. If India were to agree to even cap its emissions at current levels, let alone mitigate, its growth process will be crippled. And with it, the country would lose any hope of bringing electricity to all households or of eliminating poverty.

Therefore, from the viewpoint of its own citizenry, India has every reason to refuse mitigation commitments for some decades to come. It also has a good moral case. Rich countries have been responsible for more than 70 per cent of the emissions between 1850 and 2000. India's contribution to emissions during these same years was a paltry 2 per cent. Even setting aside this history, Canada, the US, Europe, Eurasia and Japan together account for more than 50 per cent of the current emissions and India only 4.4 per cent. If environment were to be viewed as a common resource, which it is, almost any principle of moral philosophy would say that developed countries must bring their emissions down very substantially before they demand similar reductions from the poor countries. The fact that they have emitted a lot in the past and they continue to do so today ought to give them rights to less, not more, future emissions than the poor countries.

The exemption to the developing countries from mitigation commitments unless they choose to voluntarily undertake them is also enshrined in the UNFCCC to which developed countries are signatories. In its preamble, the convention explicitly recognizes that 'the largest share of historical and current global emissions of greenhouse gases has originated in developed countries, that per-capita emissions in developing countries are still relatively low and that the share of global emissions originating in developing countries will grow to meet their social and development needs'. The UNFCCC requires mitigation commitments only from developed countries.

The US knows that it is on thin ice when it insists on mitigation commitments from India in the near future. The principal reason it targets India is that it is ill-at-ease targeting China alone. It can be scarcely unaware that mitigation by India from its current low emission levels would do little to alleviate the global warming problem.

At Copenhagen, India should clearly indicate to the US that it will not sign an unjust and inequitable treaty permitting trade sanctions against other countries, that it will challenge any attempt at enforcing such sanctions against non-signatories in the WTO DSB, and that if necessary it would exercise its right to retaliate in WTO-legal fashion.

70

A THOUGHTLESS TAX: CARBON-TAX-EQUALIZING TARIFFS ARE A BAD IDEA

(With Jagdish Bhagwati)

8 December 2009

THERE ARE SEVERAL SUBSTANTIVE issues dividing the developed and developing countries as we enter the Copenhagen conference on climate change. But none are more gratuitous than the threat posed by the US Congress—in its proposed legislation such as the Waxman-Markey Bill—and in the remarks by President Nicolas Sarkozy and the French proposals, that any carbon tax (or its equivalent 'cap premium' in national cap and trade schemes) in the developing countries which falls below the one in the developed countries would be 'equalized' or countervailed through border taxes or in other equivalent ways.

Such proposals are based on fears that have little grounding in economic analysis. They are also likely to be considered in violation of the WTO rights of the developing countries on whom such tariffs would be imposed and, even if WTO-legal found in a challenge at the WTO Dispute Settlement Mechanism, will certainly provoke WTO-legal retaliation in several ways by countries that are hit with such tariffs. Besides, the implementation of such tariffs raises impossible conceptual problems in implementation. In fact, the threat of such tariffs will certainly produce a 'local warming' at Copenhagen and undermine the progress to a satisfactory conclusion of a new climate change treaty. At the outset, the demands are driven by a misguided sense of 'fairness' and morality: that, unless others cut their emissions, we should not be asked to cut ours. If a pastor at one's church said to his flock, however, that it should be virtuous only if others are, that moral restraints by oneself in the presence of licentiousness by others should be rejected, his sermons would be popular but would draw the wrath of his superiors.

But there is also the fear of trade un-competitiveness of one's industries if other countries do not have an identical burden: virtue practised alone would have too high a cost. This sounds more reasonable, but the fear is not grounded in compelling economic analysis. Careful empirical analysis at the Brookings Institution by Warren McKibbin and Peter Wilcoxen, under the leadership of economist Lael Brainard, now with the US treasury, has demonstrated that un-competitiveness is a much-exaggerated fear.

Importantly, the Netherlands Bureau for Economic Policy Analysis concluded recently that raising import tariffs on imports from low carbon–tax countries would have little impact on total carbon emissions. For example, only 6 per cent of cement produced is traded internationally whereas only 8 per cent of China's steel, admittedly carbon-messy, is exported. In short, the most polluting industries serve the domestic, not the export, market. Then again, many fear that our industries will go abroad to exploit lower carbon tax burdens. But many studies show that the investment decision, as to where to locate, reflects several factors such as infrastructure, availability of raw materials and political stability.

The administration of carbon tariffs is also a complex task that will raise hackles. For example, in today's interdependent world economy, most production involves importation of components and raw materials from several sources. Calculating the carbon content of a product is therefore as arbitrary as calculating the 'local content' and source of origin in implementing preferential trade agreements and eligibility for cheaper market access. And, because it involves imposing tariffs rather than exemptions from tariffs, it will be more contentious and productive of disharmony. What are the better alternatives to carbon tax-equalizing tariffs? There are several.

First, the use of such carbon tariffs must be effectively ruled out. This cannot be done by mere advocacy and hoping that governments will become more enlightened. This is particularly so because, if there is ambiguity about the WTO-illegality of such tariffs, the temptation to go this route will be great. So, the Copenhagen accord, when concluded, must contain a moratorium under which no such tariffs would be levied, foregoing therefore the use of Articles II, III and XX at the WTO to do so.

Second, we need to shift to an incentive, rather than a punishment, mode. At the moment, there is ambiguity about our ability to use green subsidies. In fact, under the 1995 Subsidies and Countervailing Measures Code at the WTO, the use of green subsidies, unless they are strictly across the board, is actionable. Even the currently designed cap-and-trade regime in the US, with its many exemptions for different industries and hence differential sector-specific subsidies implicit in the scheme, is actionable. We need, therefore, to get a waiver from the SCM Code; or we need to amend it.

Finally, we can also unite behind the proposal to free trade in environmentally friendly products and services. This market has been variously estimated but is likely to be close to a turnover of half a trillion US dollars. Surely, this has to be a matter of high priority in any climate change treaty.

SOURCES

Part I: The Case for Free Trade

- Chapter 1 was previously published in *India Today*.
- Chapters 2, 5–7 were previously published in *The Economic Times*.
- Chapters 3–4 were previously published in *The Times of India*.

Part II: Recidivism in Trade Policy

- Chapters 8–12 were previously published in *The Economic Times*.
- Chapter 13 was previously published in *The Times of India*.

Part III: Pitfalls of Import Substitution

- Chapters 14 and 17 were previously published in *The Economic Times*.
- Chapters 15, 16 and 18 were previously published in *The Times of India*.

Part IV: Tariff Structure, Exchange Rate and Other Issues

- Chapter 19 was previously published in *The Economic Times*.
- Chapters 20–25 were previously published in *The Times of India*.

Part V: Lessons from History

- Chapters 26, 27 and 29 were previously published in *The Times of India*.
- Chapter 28 was previously published in *The Economic Times*.

Part VI: India–US Trade Relations

- Chapter 30 was previously published in *The Times of India*.
- Chapters 31 and 32 were previously published in *The Economic Times*.
- Chapter 33 was previously published in *Business Standard*.
- Chapter 34 was previously published in *Foreign Policy*.

Part VII: India–China Trade Relations

- Chapters 35 and 37 were previously published in *India Today*.
- Chapter 36 was previously published in *The Times of India*.

Chapter 38 was previously published in *The Economic Times*.

Part VIII: India and Multilateral Trade Negotiations

- Chapters 39–52 were previously published in *The Economic Times*.
- Chapter 53 was previously published in *The Times of India*.

Part IX: Preferential Trade Liberalization

- Chapters 54, 56, 57 and 59 were previously published in *The Economic Times*.
- Chapter 55 was previously published in *The Hindu*.
- Chapters 58 and 60 were previously published in *The Times of India*.

Part X: Non-trade Issues in Multilateral Trade Negotiations

- Chapters 61, 64, 68 and 70 were previously published in *The Times of India*.
- Chapters 62, 63, 65-67 and 69 were previously published in *The Economic Times*.

ACKNOWLEDGEMENTS

FOR THE CHAPTERS IN this book, my greatest debt is to my friend and mentor, Jagdish Bhagwati. I say this for two reasons. First, intellectually, he has been the greatest influence on me when it comes to economic policy, especially so in the area of international trade. Second, but no less important, in the early days when I had just begun writing in the media, I got excellent advice from him. He was quick to point out that I was making assertions that I did not support with arguments or evidence when I shared drafts of my work with him. He told me that my pieces would be rejected if I merely expressed an opinion without persuasive arguments and evidence. That piece of advice has guided my media writing over the last several decades.

I also take this opportunity to thank Inder Sawhney, who had served as the bureau chief of *The Times of India* in Jaipur in the late 1980s. He paved my entry into journalism in June 1989 during a visit to Jaipur, assuring me that he would get me a hearing at the newspaper in Delhi. He successfully did that. He later also introduced me to the late Gautam Adhikari, the then executive editor of *The Times of India*, who in turn introduced me to Sanjaya Baru, the erstwhile editor of the editorial page. This helped me as I published my next few op-ed articles in the 1990s in the newspaper.

My next major break was an invitation from Swaminathan Aiyar, whom I met at a conference in Washington D.C. in the late 1990s. He called and asked me if I would write a column once a week in *The Economic Times*. It was an exciting offer, but I lacked the confidence at that time—would I be able to write a regular column at that kind of frequency? However, I knew it was an opportunity I did not want to miss. So, after sleeping over the offer for a few days, I called Swami back and asked if I could write once a month instead. He readily agreed and, from then on, I became a regular contributor to *The Economic Times*. Though I subsequently moved to *The Times of India* for my regular once-a-month column, I have continued to write for *The Economic Times*.

Over the years, I have dealt with a number of editors and I am grateful to all of them. Mythili Bhusnurmath worked on the editorial page of *The Economic Times* when Swami first invited me to write for the newspaper and I had the pleasure of working with her for many years. Later, I got to work with T.K. Arun and Saubhik Chakrabarti, who succeeded Mythili in that order. I wish to thank them from the bottom of my heart.

With rare exceptions, I did not write in the media between 2015 and 2017 when I served in the NITI Aayog, the Government of India think tank. Since returning to Columbia University in September 2017, I resumed writing for *The Times of India* once a month. It has been a real pleasure working with Swagato Ganguly while contributing to this most widely read newspaper. Recently, Swagato has been succeeded by Saubhik Chakrabarti, which has given me another chance to work with him. In parallel, I have had the good fortune to get regular requests for articles on specific issues of economic policy from Indrajit Hazra at *The Economic Times*. Occasionally, I have also written for other outlets, including *India Today*, *Outlook*, *Business Standard*, *The Indian Express* and *The Hindu*. My gratitude to them all.

Last but not the least, my thanks to Amita, my wife, who has read nearly all the articles in this book as drafts and commented on the clarity of arguments in them. As a non-economist who reads widely, she represents my target readership well. Her comments have often led me to revise the articles, sometimes multiple times.

INDEX

Adhia, Hasmukh, 51
Africa Growth and Opportunity Act (AGOA), 251, 255
Africa trade preferences, US markets, 251
aggregate employment, 10
agricultural liberalization, 211, 212, 225, 227, 236
agriculture, 151, 199
    EU-US compromise plan, 207
    export, 163, 206, 211, 212, 219, 227, 231, 233
    export competition and domestic support, 205, 206
    export subsidies, 227, 231
    'food security box' proposals, 205
    income support programmes, 207
    protectionism, 222, 232
    subsidies and protection, 222–25
    workforce in, 122
    WTO rules, protecting farmers, 206–7
Aiyar, Swaminathan, 282, 283
Al Gore, 300
American Clean Energy and Security (ACES) Bill of 2009, 311, 312
Amorim, Celso, 227
Amsden, Alice, 22
Anand, Abhishek, 93
anti-dumping, 94, 95, 147, 206, 235
    definition, 45
    domestic firms, protection to, 41, 42, 45–46
    foreign firms, 42, 46
    GATT, 40–43, 45–46
    long-term solution, 43
    MFA quotas, 43
    monopoly price, 41
    UR Agreement, 43, 46

anti-export bias, 64
anti-trade, 19, 21, 22
APEC. *see* Asia Pacific Economic Cooperation
Appellate Body (AB), 239
appropriations bill, H-1B visa, 142–43
ASEAN Free Trade Area (AFTA), 246
ASEAN Preferential Trading Area (APTA), 246
Asian currency crisis, 247
Asian tigers, 17, 21
Asia Pacific Economic Cooperation (APEC), 245–47
Association of Southeast Asian Nations (ASEAN), 203, 246, 259–60, 265, 266
Australia, 42, 110, 112, 265
  ECTA, 270, 273
  FTA, 270–73
  work visas, 273
autarchic trade policy regime, 4
Autonomous Employment Zones, 108
Ayushman Bharat Yojana, 74

Bajaj, Rahul, 248
balance-of-payments (BoP) crisis
  1991, 62
  1957-58, 4, 124, 129
balance-of-payments (BoP) identity
  CAD, 97, 98
  capital inflows, 98, 99
  export expansion, 99, 100
  RBI foreign exchange reserves, 98
Balassa, Bela, 21

Baldwin, Robert, 212
Bangladesh garment manufacturers' and exporters' association (BGMEA), 292
Barshefsky, Charlene, 299
Bastiat, Frédéric, 52
Bernard, Elaine, 285
Bhagwati, Jagdish, 21, 252, 290, 298
Bhatt, Ajay, 139
Bhurban Declaration, 220
Big Pharma, 146, 147
bilateral trade, 153, 157, 158, 168
  agreements, India, 266–67
  deficit, 135, 158, 168, 262, 266
  India-China, 157–71, 257–60
  India-US, 133–54
bilateral US trade deficit, 135
BoP identity. *see* balance-of-payments
Brainard, Lael, 316
Brazil, 27, 64, 133, 136, 197, 209, 211, 219, 220, 227, 231, 232, 247, 287, 289
budget
  2018, 51–54
  1996-97, 35
  1997-98, 36
  2002-03, 85
  2003-04, 85
Bush, George W., 142, 145, 202, 232, 233, 279, 306

Cairns Group, 207, 211–13, 219, 224, 225
Cancun ministerial conference, 207, 219

INDEX

alliance, India and China, 211
failure, 210–11, 226, 230–31
G-20, 227, 231
misguided leadership, 211–12
Quad, death of, 231
US approach to negotiations, agriculture, 212–13
'cap and trade' programme, 311–12, 317
capital-intensive sectors, 117, 118
carbon-tax-equalizing tariffs, 312, 315–18
Carnegie Endowment, 309
cell phone revolution, 106
Chidambaram, P., 35, 36, 38
child labour, 290, 305
   adverse effects, 292–93
   case rejected, 291–92
   inevitable bias, 293–94
   Rugmark, carpet industry, 291, 293
China, 70, 111–12, 145, 211, 216. *see also* India-China trade relations
   competition and investment policies, 208
   employment-intensive sectors, 102
   FTAs, 203
   merchandise exports, 99, 105
   poverty reduction, 26
   sanctions, 109, 111, 160–63
   SEZs, 102–3
   US-China trade conflict, 240
Chinoy, Sajjid, 106
Chung-hee, Park, 57
Clinton, Bill, 248, 251, 299, 300

Clinton, Hillary, 140, 311
Coastal Economic Zones (CEZs), 103
compulsory licensing provisions, 148, 194, 286–89
consumer goods' imports
   ban on, 19
   and domestic consumer goods industry, 19
   liberalization, 17–18
   licensing, 20
   luxuries, 19
   SIL, 19–20
   tariff rates, 20
consumption tax, 19, 20
coordination failure problem, 22
Copenhagen convention, 311–14
core labour standards
   developing countries, refusal of discussions, 296–97
   Singapore Declaration, 295–96
   trade and, 296
   TWIN-SAL, 298
   WTO working group, 295, 296, 299
Cotonou Agreement, 202
cotton exporters, 224
Covid-19 crisis, 162, 166, 239
current account deficit (CAD), 68, 76, 97–99, 110, 158
customs-duty, 127–30
   on imports, 35, 36, 51
   on MMF fabrics, 94

de Jonquieres, Guy, 192
devaluation, rupee, 124
digital India, 53

direct benefit transfers (DBT), 74
Directorate General of Trade Remedies (DGTR), 95
Discovery of India, The (Nehru), 120
discrimination, trade policy, 253–56
dispute settlement body (DSB), 239, 240
Dispute Settlement Understanding (DSU), 190, 192–93
Doha Ministerial Declaration, 46
Doha Round, trade negotiations, 192, 218
    agricultural talks, 222–25
    challenges, agenda, 218–21
    closing of, 234–37
    defensive posture, India, 199–209
    India leadership role, opportunity for, 230–33
    launch of, 188–91
    liberalization commitments, 220–21
    multilateral agreements, 193, 194
    negotiating agenda, 194, 228
    SSG, 235
    SSM, 234, 236, 237
    trade and environment, 193
    trade liberalization, 193, 229
    TRIPS Agreement, 181, 183, 185, 189, 194, 197
    TRIPS Agreement and Public Health, 287–88
    unresolved issues, 234
    winners and losers, 196–98
dollar dominance, 109–12
Dunkel Draft, 277

Earth Summit, 1992, 279
eco-labelling, 293
Economic Cooperation and Trade Agreement (ECTA), 270, 273
Elliott, Larry, 29
'Enabling Clause,' 1979, 254
equity investments, 90
Euro-Mediterranean Association Agreements, 202
European Economic Community (EEC), 136–37
European Union (EU), 8, 79, 152, 159, 162, 167, 170, 182, 184, 189, 191, 195, 219, 222, 226, 241, 268, 273, 290, 308, 309
EU-US compromise plan, 207
EU-US proposal on agriculture, 207
EU-Vietnam FTA, 167
Everything But Arms initiative, 224
exchange rate
    adjustment process, 90
    capital inflows, 90–91
    foreign exchange budgeting, 89
    macroeconomic adjustment, 89, 90
    rupee depreciation, 90
excise duties, revenue from, 37, 38
export
    global merchandise, 105, 239, 240
    growth, India, 106
    imports, decline of, 107
    logistical process, 107
    subsidies, 21, 73, 199, 206, 207, 212, 221, 223, 227, 231, 232, 288
    trade-friendly ecosystem, 106–8

INDEX

export-oriented strategy, 57, 66
export protectionism, 309
external commercial borrowings (ECBs), 91, 98, 99

Fabian socialism, 120
faceless bureaucrats, 193
FDI. *see* foreign direct investment
Finger, Michael, 284
First Globalization, 3
flow of goods, 3–4, 32
foreign direct investment (FDI), 48, 90, 153, 267
foreign-exchange, 90, 91
    budgeting, 4, 89
    reserves, 12, 89, 91, 97, 98, 110, 111, 123, 125, 126
    shortages, 67
free trade, 4, 9–12
    arguments against, 11–12
    Korean growth, 21–24
    liberalization, consumer goods, 17–20
    openness, 25–28
    protectionist policy, India, 13–16
    sceptics, 29–32
free trade agreements (FTAs), 79, 241
    European Union, 202
    India-China, 162, 167
    Latin America, 203
    US, 202
Free Trade and Prosperity (Panagariya), 75
Free Trade Area (FTA), 201
    India-Australia ECTA, 270–73
    India-China, 257–60
    and liberalization programmes, 250
    US and India, 248–52
Free Trade Area of the Americas (FTAA), 202
Friedman, Milton, 262
friendshoring, 170

G-15, 301
G-20, 219, 220, 225, 227, 231, 307, 308
G-21, 211
G-77, 219
G-90, 227
Galwan valley brawl, 160, 165
Ganesan, A.V., 301
General Agreement on Tariffs and Trade (GATT), 247, 253
    anti-dumping, 40–43, 45
    Article VI, 235
    Article XIX, 42, 46, 206, 235
    function, 215
    MFA, 176
    MFN rule, 175, 215, 216
General Agreement on Trade in Services (GATS), 143
Generalized System of Preferences (GSP), 150, 152, 153, 253–56
George, Henry, 3–7
global financial crisis 2008, 90, 99, 166, 239
globalization, 25
global merchandise exports, 105, 239, 240
goods and services tax (GST), 74, 129

INDEX

Gowda, H.D. Deve, 214
Goyal, Arun, 85
green subsidies, 317
growth 'debacles,' 26, 27
growth 'miracles,' 26, 27
Guardian, 29
Gujral, I.K., 214

Hasan, Rana, 101, 159
H-1B visa, 142–44, 151
Headley, David, 140
heavy-industry development, India, 119–22
Hills, Carla, 134
Hong Kong Ministerial meeting, 218, 222
    agricultural export subsidies, 227
    G-20, 227
    LDCs, demands of, 228, 231
    partnerships, US, 226–27
Human Rights Watch, 303, 304, 309

imperialism, 120
import
    custom duty on, 35, 36
    liberalization, 56
    mobile phones, 67–68
    protection, 75
    protectionism, 309
    -related fear, 262
import licensing, 47, 53, 56, 117, 121
    consumer goods, 4–5
    removal of, 36–37
    stricter enforcement, 116, 124, 129

import-substitution, 26–27, 56, 105, 106
    domestic firms, 76
    domestic sourcing, 48–49
    GDP growth, 47
    India, 66–69
    investible resources, 76
    Latin America, 61–65
    manufacturing policy, 2011, 48
    mobile phone industry, 78
    open markets, 49–50
    small nations, 78–81
import substitution industrialization (ISI), 120
    Brazil, 64
    electronics industry, 71, 76
    failure, 71–72
    growth, developing countries, 62, 64
    Latin America, 61–65
    macroeconomic instability, 63, 64
    revival, 70–73
income-distribution argument, 11, 12
India
    bilateral agreement trade shares, 2007-17, 268
    CAD, 98-99
    Doha Declaration, 192–94, 196–98
    economic failure, 119–22
    export expansion, 100
    global merchandise exports, 240
    heavy industry, 119–22
    import substitution, 66–69

INDEX

leadership role, opportunity at Doha, 230–33
textiles and clothing industry, 93–96
at WTO, 192–95
India-ASEAN trade shares, 2007-17, 269
India-Australia ECTA, 270–73
India-China trade relations
  anti-dumping cases, 157, 158
  bilateral trade, 157, 158, 168
  border hostilities, 161
  colonial pattern, 158
  distancing, 164–67
  exports, 157, 159, 160
  FTAs, 162, 167, 257–60
  labour laws, 159
  national security, 165–66
  RCEP, 164–65
  trade sanctions, 160–63
  transgressions, border, 168
  yin-yang, 168–71
India-Japan FTA, 271, 273
Indian Fiscal Commission, 1921-22, 128
India-Sri Lanka trade, 258
India-US trade relations
  driver of, 138–41
  patents, 146–49
  strengthening, 142–45
  Super-301 actions, 133–37
  trade war, 150–54
Indo-German Export Promotion Programme, 291
Indo-US nuclear deal, 230
infant-industry protection, 5–6, 22–24

inflation, 10, 11, 36, 62, 90, 99, 106, 121, 124, 125
Information Technology Agreement, 178
Insolvency and Bankruptcy Act, 74
intellectual property rights (IPRs), 134, 147, 151, 189, 215, 216, 240, 256, 260. *see also* Trade-Related Intellectual Property Rights
  copyrights, 282
  inclusion into WTO, opposition to, 282
  trade barriers, 284–85
international banking, 110
International Labour Organization (ILO), 292, 295–98, 305, 308, 309
international trade, 68, 70, 74, 110, 120, 239, 284, 295, 319
international trade disputes, 239
iron and steel industries, 4

Jain, Toshi, 106
Jaitley, Arun, 200, 208, 210, 211
Jandoc, Karl, 159
Japan, 41, 45, 111, 134–36, 162, 203, 205, 227, 231, 232
Jiabao, Wen, 258

Kamal, Al Emadi, 198
Kapoor, Nidhi, 101
Kapur, Devesh, 297
Krishna, S.M., 140
Krueger, Anne, 21
Krugman, Paul, 14, 110

Kyoto Protocol, 312, 313

labour-intensive industry, 260
labour-intensive manufacturing, 15, 19, 23, 100, 117, 118, 164, 260
labour rights
   Human Rights Watch report, 303–4
   trade-labour link, 304, 306
   trade sanctions, role of, 305
   trade unions, 304
labour standards, 152, 183, 189, 191, 194, 196, 217, 229, 251, 256, 260, 290, 300–302, 308
   Singapore Declaration, 295–96
   trade sanctions in, 305
   working group, WTO, 295–99
Lampreia, Luiz Felipe, 302
Lamy, Pascal, 213, 218–21, 231, 234, 302
Land Acquisition Act, 108
large firms, 101–3, 107, 108, 159, 167
Latin America
   FTAs, 203
   and import substitution, 61–65
least developed countries (LDCs), 222, 225, 227
   aid for trade, 228
   duty-free access, 224
Lehrer, Jim, 302
liberalization. *see also* preferential trade liberalization
   agriculture, 205–6, 211, 212, 225, 227, 236
   of consumer goods, 17–20
   custom duty, 36

Doha agenda, 193, 220–21
economic adjustment, 178–79
of foreign investment, 31, 136
on imports, 56
industrial products, 180, 190, 220
non-discriminatory, 247, 248, 252, 259
tariff, 38, 52
Vietnam trade policies, 31
liberal trade policies, 3, 5, 25, 29–30, 129
licence-permit raj, 53, 54, 71, 115, 124
Little, Ian, 21, 23
luxury consumption, 18–20

macroeconomic instability, 63–65
macroeconomic stability, 24, 26, 32, 65, 68, 90, 158
Make in India, 55, 68
'Make in India for the World,' 79, 81
Making Openness Work (Rodrik), 62
man-made fibre (MMF) segment, 93–94
Maran, Murasoli, 194, 195, 210, 228
marginalization, WTO, 208–9
market access measures, 224
McKibbin, Warren, 316
Mehta, Pradeep, 301
merchandise exports, 99, 105, 159, 238–40
Mexico, 29, 32
   FTAs, 203
   NAFTA, 30, 201, 249–51

INDEX

trade liberalization, 250–51
micro and small enterprises, 105, 106
micro, small and medium enterprises (MSMEs), 51, 53
mitigation commitments, 312–14
mobile phone industry, 78
Modi, Narendra, 68, 105, 268
MODVAT system, 39
monopoly price, 41
Most Favoured Nation (MFN) principle, 42, 157, 175, 215, 245, 246, 247, 253
Multi-fibre Agreement (MFA), 43, 176, 217
Multi-fibre Arrangement (MFA), 189, 191
multilateral environmental agreements (MEAs), 193
multilateral trade negotiations (MTNs)
  Cancun ministerial conference, 210–13
  defensive play of India, Doha negotiations, 199–209
  Doha agricultural talks, 222–25
  Doha Round, 192–95, 234–37
  Hong Kong declaration, 226–29
  Qatar Round, 188–91
  research, 184–87
  Seattle Round Agenda, 180–83
  victory and defeat, Doha negotiations, 196–98
  WTO and developing countries, 175–79
multinational enterprises, 263

Nath, Kamal, 227, 229, 233
National Higher Education Commission Act, 74
National Medical Commission (NMC) Act, 74
Nehru, Jawaharlal, 115, 119–22
Nehruvian socialism, 119, 120
Netherlands Bureau for Economic Policy Analysis, 316
New Industrial Policy, 1991, 53
Newly Industrialized Economies (NIEs), 26
Newshour, 302
New Trade Theory, 14
NIEs. *see* Newly Industrialized Economies
NITI Aayog, 130
non-agricultural market access (NAMA), 232
non-discriminatory liberalization, 247, 248, 252, 259
non-trade issues
  child labour, 290–94
  IPRs, 282–85
  labour standards into WTO, 295–98
  labour rights, 303–6
  patent rights, 277–81
  protectionism, 307–10
  Seattle, 299–302
  TRIPS impasse, 286–89
North American Free Trade Agreement (NAFTA), 202, 245, 259
  environmental and labour side agreements, 251
  Mexico, 30, 201, 249–51

Obama, Barack, 50, 138, 140, 142, 144, 311, 312
Omnibus Trade Practices and Competitiveness Act, 134
openness, free trade, 13, 75
  growth 'miracles' and 'debacles,' 26, 27
  import-substitution, 26–27
  poverty reduction, 26
  rapid growth, 25–26
  reduction in trade barriers, 28
  South Korea, 23
open trade regime, 28, 75
Organization for Economic Co-operation and Development (OECD), 223, 288
Oxfam NGO, 220, 223, 230

Pack, Howard, 22
patent rights
  agricultural products, 281
  claims, 278–79
  price increases, 280–81
  thorny issues, 279–80
  TRIPS, 277
Patents (Amendment) Act, 2005, 148
patents, India-US trade relations, 146–49
peso crisis, 247
pharmaceutical industry, 146, 169, 288–89
phased manufacturing programme (PMP), 15, 51, 53, 71, 72, 80
plurilateral trade agreements, 266
Polanski, Sandra, 308
poverty, 264, 297

India, 313
  liberalization and, 12
  reduction, 26
  Vietnam, 30
preferential trade arrangements (PTAs)
  harmful effects of, 203
  NAFTA, 201, 202
  WTO, 202
preferential trade liberalization
  GSP, 253–56
  India-Australia ECTA, 270–73
  India-China free trade, 257–60
  RCEP, 261–69
  SAARC, 245–47
  US and India FTA, 248–52
'principle of comparative advantage,' 9
priority foreign country, Special 301 Report, 134, 147
Producer Support Estimate (PSE), 223
production-linked incentive (PLI) scheme, 72, 96
protectionism, 35–39, 49, 52, 307–10
  excise duties, revenue from, 37, 38
  return to, 51–54
  SAD, 35, 36
  'swadeshi' tax, 35, 36
  tariff and tax reforms, 38–39
Protection or Free Trade (George), 3
Punta del Este Mandate, 188, 189

Qatar Round, trade negotiations, 188–91

INDEX

Quadrilateral Security Dialogue (Quad), 190, 231, 273

Ramesh, Jairam, 311
Rao, P.V. Narasimha, 52, 68
Reason in Common Sense (Santayana), 53
recidivism
    anti-dumping, 40–46
    budget 2018, 51–54
    import substitution, 47–50
    protectionism, 35–39
    trade policy folly, 55–58
reciprocal bargaining, 204
Regional Comprehensive Economic Partnership (RCEP), 164–65
    benefits, India, 261–64
    India's exit, 265–69
regional trade agreements, 193, 261, 265
research, trade negotiations
    'capacity-building' initiatives, 186
    developed country members, WTO, 184–85
    developing countries, 185, 186
    funds, 186–87
    topics, selection of, 187
    TRIPS, 185
Reserve Bank of India (RBI), 18, 68, 76, 90, 91, 97–99, 123, 125
retaliatory tariffs, 7, 8
Rifkin, Jeremy, 277–79
Robinson, Joan, 7
Rodrik, Dani, 22, 23, 29, 30, 32, 61–64, 297
Rugmark, carpet industry, 291–93

rupee depreciation, 99. *see also* exchange rate
    foreign investors, exit of, 91
    macroeconomic adjustment, 89, 90
    oil price hike, 91–92
Russia, 109, 111, 112

Sagarmala project, 103
Samuelson, Paul, 9, 57
Santayana, George, 53
Sarkozy, Nicolas, 315
Schuler, Philip, 284
Schumer, Charles, 144
Seattle ministerial meeting, 295
    failure, 299–300
    India, 301
    labour standards, 299–301
    media opportunities, 301–2
    news, developing countries, 300–301
Seattle Round Agenda
    competition policy, inclusion of, 181, 182
    developing countries, 181–83
    liberalization, industrial products, 180–81
    two-track approach, 183
Second World War, 4
self-employment, 164, 167
self-sufficiency
    capital-intensive sectors, 117, 118
    and heavy industry, 119–22
    industry divisions, 117
    and productive efficiency, 115–16

skilled-labour-intensive sector, 118
SSI reservation, 115, 117
short-term capital mobility, 65
Shourie, Arun, 207
Singapore issues, WTO, 195, 196–97, 200, 207–8, 219, 228
Singapore Ministerial meeting, 295, 296
Singh, Manmohan, 35, 142, 145, 233
Singh, V.P., 214
single tariff rate, 85–88
    advantages, 87
    criticism, 87–88
    vs. two-part, 88
Sinha, Yashwant, 35, 36, 38
skilled-labour-intensive sector, 118
small-scale industries (SSI), 53, 115
socialism, 119, 120
social labelling, 291, 292
software industry, 104
South Asian Association of Regional Cooperation (SAARC), 245–47
South Asian Coalition on Child Servitude, 291
South Asian Free Trade Area (SAFTA), 245, 247
Southern American Common Market, 247
South Korea, 57, 66, 112, 118, 139, 167, 203, 216, 224, 271
    coordination failure problem, 22
    export expansion, 22
    infant-industry promotion, 22–24
    outward orientation, 21–22
    trade strategy, 22
Soviet Union, 24, 27
special additional duty (SAD), 35, 36
Special Agricultural Safeguard (SSG), 235
Special Economic Zones (SEZs), 102
special import license (SIL), 19–20
Special 301 Report, 2014, 147, 151
Special Safeguard Mechanism (SSM), 234, 236, 237
Srinivasan, T.N., 21
steel and aluminium exports, 6, 8
steel industry, 4, 46, 52, 128
sterling balances, 123–24, 125
Stiglitz, Joseph, 62
Subsidies and Countervailing Measures Code, 1995, 317
subsidies and protection, agriculture, 222–25
Super-301 actions
    additional 'culprits, 135–36
    EEC policies, 136–37
    priority watch list, 134, 151
    unfair traders, 134–35
'swadeshi' tax, 35, 36

tariff hikes, 2018-19 Budget, 51, 55
tariff rate
    chemicals and automobiles, 86
    final products, 85, 86
    on non-agricultural goods, 85
    single, 87–88
    two-part, 86
Tax Reforms Committee, 38, 39
Tendulkar, Sachin, 32
textiles and clothing industry, 93–96

INDEX

AD duties on imports, 94–96
   India, 249–50
   MMF segment, 93–94, 96
   polyester fibre, 94
   underperformance, 93
   workforce, 93
theory of optimal taxation, 87
Third World Intellectuals and NGOs: Statement Against Linkage (TWIN-SAL), 298
Thomas, Naveen J., 93
Times of India, The, 140
Tokyo Round, 216
Tong, Yeo Cheow, 296
trade
   barriers, 28, 32, 177, 201, 231, 233, 235, 254, 258, 267, 271, 284–85
   diversion, 205, 246, 247, 248, 259
   and labour standards, 251
   preferences, 204–5
   reform process, 35–39
   sanctions, India-China, 160–63
   war, 150–54, 162, 261, 303
trade liberalization, 49, 78, 175, 176, 189
   Doha agenda, 192–95
   Mexico, 250–51
   and privatization, 61, 62, 64, 65
Trade Policy Review (TPR), 40, 86, 87, 298
Trade Promotion Authority (TPA), 232
Trade-Related Intellectual Property Rights (TRIPS), 181, 183, 185, 189, 194, 197, 277, 282–83
   impasse, 286–89
   India, 147–48
   IPR standards, 282–84
Trade-Related Investment Measures (TRIMs), 181
Trans-Pacific Partnership (TPP), 167, 267
Trump, Donald, 150–52

Ulam, Stanislaw, 9, 57
unemployment, 10, 307
unfair traders, Super-301 actions, 134–35
United Nations Conference on Trade and Development (UNCTAD), 177, 204
United Nations Framework Convention on Climate Change (UNFCCC), 312, 314
United Progressive Alliance (UPA), 74
United States, 6–8, 46, 55, 91, 123, 125, 138, 158, 162, 167, 169, 184, 201, 203, 205, 207, 211, 215, 236, 239, 240, 248, 255, 268, 286, 290, 295, 297, 299, 301, 303, 306–8, 317. *see also* India-US trade relations
   anti-dumping, 43
   'cap and trade' programme, 311, 312
   and dollar dominance, 109–12
   labour-intensive imports, 11
United States trade representative (USTR), 134–36, 146, 147, 149
UR Agreement on Textiles and Clothing (ATC), 189

Uruguay Round (UR) Agreement, 43, 46, 143, 147, 188, 215, 216, 231, 277
    average tariff rates, 177
    built-in agenda, 180–81
    Cairns Group, 219
    DSU negotiations, 193
    GATT tariff bindings, 176
    liberalization, 220–21
    single undertaking approach, 182, 183
    SSG, 235
    trade liberalization, 175, 176
US-China trade conflict, 240

Vajpayee, Atal Bihari, 52, 67, 68, 301
Vietnam, 29–32, 78–79, 167
Volcker interest-rate shock, 63, 65
Voluntary Disclosure Scheme, 38

Wade, Robert, 22, 23
wage inequality, 11
Waxman-Markey Bill, 315
Westphal, Larry, 22
Wilcoxen, Peter, 316
within-agriculture reciprocity, 225
Wolfowitz, Paul, 223
worker rights, 303–6
world merchandise trade, 219
world trade, 198, 215, 216, 219, 258, 282

World Trade Organization (WTO), 5, 40, 45, 49, 147
    AB, 239
    agreements, 215
    developing countries, 175–79
    DSB, 239, 240
    functions, 215
    GATT, 215–16
    India, 192–95
    Information Technology Agreement, 67
    labour standards, 295–98
    marginalization, 208–9
    members, 214
    membership, 31–32
    operating principle of, 235
    Qatar Round, trade negotiations, 188–91
    research, trade negotiations, 184–87
    'safeguard' measures, 235
    Seattle Round Agenda, 180–83
    social clause, 290
    TRIPS Agreement, 286–89
    US, dissatisfaction with, 238–41

yin-yang, India-China trade relations, 168–71

zero custom duty, information technology products, 67
zero-tariff, 204, 224

ABOUT THE AUTHOR

Arvind Panagariya is a professor of economics and the Jagdish Bhagwati Professor of Indian political economy at Columbia University, US. He is also the director of the Raj Center on Indian economic policies at Columbia University. He served as the first vice-chairman of the NITI Aayog from January 2015 to August 2017. Most recently, he has been appointed as the chairman of the 16th Finance Commission of India. He is the author of more than fifteen books, among them *India's Tryst with Destiny*, co-authored with Jagdish Bhagwati, which has been called 'a manifesto for policymakers and analysts'. The Government of India honoured him with the Padma Bhushan in 2012.

HarperCollins *Publishers* India

At HarperCollins India, we believe in telling the best stories and finding the widest readership for our books in every format possible. We started publishing in 1992; a great deal has changed since then, but what has remained constant is the passion with which our authors write their books, the love with which readers receive them, and the sheer joy and excitement that we as publishers feel in being a part of the publishing process.

Over the years, we've had the pleasure of publishing some of the finest writing from the subcontinent and around the world, including several award-winning titles and some of the biggest bestsellers in India's publishing history. But nothing has meant more to us than the fact that millions of people have read the books we published, and that somewhere, a book of ours might have made a difference.

As we look to the future, we go back to that one word— a word which has been a driving force for us all these years.

Read.